Richard Frederick Littledale

Plain Reasons against joining the Church of Rome

Richard Frederick Littledale

Plain Reasons against joining the Church of Rome

ISBN/EAN: 9783743329843

Manufactured in Europe, USA, Canada, Australia, Japa

Cover: Foto ©Lupo / pixelio.de

Manufactured and distributed by brebook publishing software (www.brebook.com)

Richard Frederick Littledale

Plain Reasons against joining the Church of Rome

PLAIN REASONS

AGAINST

JOINING THE CHURCH OF ROME.

BY

RICHARD FREDERICK LITTLEDALE,

LL.D. D.C.L.

"Can they teach that the judgment of the Bishop of Rome is superior to God's judgment? . . . I steadfastly affirm that if the Bishop of Rome sin against his brethren, and, though often admonished, do not hear the Church, he, the Bishop of Rome, I say, is by God's command to be held as a heathen man and a publican. For the higher is the rank the graver is the fall. But if he think us unworthy of his communion for this reason, that none of us will consent to believe contrary to the Gospel, he cannot on that ground separate us from the communion of Christ."—GERBERT (Pope Sylvester II. † A.D. 1003). to Segwin, Archbishop of Sens.

THIRTIETH THOUSAND, FURTHER REVISED.

PUBLISHED UNDER THE DIRECTION OF THE TRACT COMMITTEE

LONDON:
SOCIETY FOR PROMOTING CHRISTIAN KNOWLEDGE,
NORTHUMBERLAND AVENUE, CHARING CROSS;
43, QUEEN VICTORIA STREET ; 48, PICCADILLY;
AND 135, NORTH STREET, BRIGHTON.

NEW YORK: E. & J. B. YOUNG & CO.
1881.

ADDITIONS AND CORRECTIONS.

NOTE.

SINCE the issue of the current edition of "PLAIN REASONS," a formal reply from the Roman Catholic side has been published, entitled "Catholic Controversy," bearing the name of the Rev. H. I. D. Ryder, of the Oratory, Birmingham, as responsible editor, and circulated with the express approval of Cardinal Newman. All the points and criticisms of that work have been carefully examined, and the present addenda contain, besides much other matter, the chief results of the inquiry, being issued in this provisional form to avoid the delay involved in printing a new edition.

P. 21, line 10, after "writings," add "(not in the sense that he is *infallible* in all details, but that he is unimpeachably *orthodox.*)"
P. 21, lines 22, 23, omit "unless he be a worthy person."
P. 21, line 23, for "(iv. 587)," read "(iv. 586, 636.)"
P. 22, line 6, after "(iv. 151—6)," add "(7) that it is lawful to procure the giving of perjured evidence, 'if you have a great interest in employing perjury to expose the fraud of another person, in order to obtain your own rights'" (III. iii. 77) (8).
P. 24, line 11 of footnote, after "another man," add "The force of this example lies in the fact that the more approved Roman doctrine as to the Sacrament of matrimony (that of St. Thomas

ADDITIONS AND CORRECTIONS.

P. 15, line 9, after "Christians," add "and though the old glosses fill up carefully all the important matters in belief and practice, which, while not stated in the brief creeds, are yet practically contained in them, and have been constantly received; such as the nature and use of the Holy Eucharist, the inspiration of the Bible, the transmission of Holy Orders, and so forth."

P. 17, add footnote to "morals," line 15, "It follows, if these propositions be true, that St. Athanasius, when he had the *living voice* of the Church against him, not only the majority of the Bishops of his day, but the Pope also, must have been a heretic and rebel for refusing to accept Arianism. It is only on the ground that the 'living voice' is bound by the original belief and the historical witness of the primitive Church, and must be tested and judged thereby, that St. Athanasius can be defended."

P. 18, footnote, after line 3, insert "The flesh of the Virgin was conceived in original sin, and therefore contracted these defects. But the flesh of Christ took its nature, pure of fault, from the Virgin."—St. Thomas Aquinas, Summa, III., xiv., 3.

Page 18, line 18, after "future time," add "nor even what it has been at any time in the past; since the Vatican decrees are retrospective, and declare the infallibility of all the Popes who have ever spoken *ex cathedrâ*, however they may have contradicted one another."

P. 18, one line from bottom, after "published," add "by F. Croiset."

P. 21, line 10, for "no error," read "no theological error."

P. 21, line 10, after "writings," add "(not in the sense that he is *infallible* in all details, but that he is unimpeachably *orthodox*.)"

P. 21, lines 22, 23, omit "unless he be a worthy person."

P. 21, line 23, for "(iv. 587)," read "(iv. 586, 636.)"

P. 22, line 6, after "(iv. 151—6)," add "(7) that it is lawful to procure the giving of perjured evidence, 'if you have a great interest in employing perjury to expose the fraud of another person, in order to obtain your own rights'" (III. iii. 77) (8).

P. 24, line 11 of footnote, after "another man," add "The force of this example lies in the fact that the more approved Roman doctrine as to the Sacrament of matrimony (that of St. Thomas

Aquinas and the Council of Florence, and seemingly also that of the Council of Trent, Sanchez, and Bellarmine), is that the *bridal pair* are the real *ministers* of that Sacrament, while the priest does but attest and bless the union. Accordingly, Lady Mary occupied in the ceremony almost the same place as the Priest or Bishop does in administering other sacraments·; and by living with the Prince, and bearing him a child, gave far better evidence of the genuineness of her 'intention' than can be had in the case of any priest's ministration. Nevertheless, she repudiated the contract as null and void from the first; and so there is plainly no way in which any security of proof can be obtained as to intention and validity in other cases."

P. 25, line 6, after "this peril," add "nor was the doctrine of Intention ever more than a mere opinion of the schools, till it was made into a dogma by the Tridentine decree of March 3, 1547, after the breach between England and Rome, though it appears in a Bull of Eugenius IV., addressed to the Armenians, in 1439."

P. 25, line 26, after "that St. Peter was ever at Rome at all," add "for there is no first-hand or contemporaneous testimony to the fact, whether in Scripture or elsewhere, whence it is clear that God has not considered it important enough to be certified for us, as being a matter of faith."

P. 25, line 3 of footnote, after "heretical forgery," add "The next in value is a phrase in St. Cyprian, 'When the place of Fabian, that is, the place of Peter, and the rank of the sacerdotal chair, was vacant' (Epist. lii.), which, however, is not only somewhat vague, but is regarded by Rigaltius and Fell as a mere gloss which has crept into the text."

P. 26, line 15, for "is contrary to," read " is not supported by."

P. 26, line 18, add as footnote to "foundation of the Church":—"Archbishop Kenrick of St. Louis, in his speech prepared for, but not delivered in, the Vatican Council, and published at Naples in 1870, declares that Roman Catholics cannot establish the Petrine privilege from Scripture, because of the clause in the Creed of Pius IV., binding them to interpret Scripture only according to the *unanimous consent* of the Fathers. And he adds that there are five different patristic interpretations of St. Matt. xvi. 18: (1) That *St. Peter* is the Rock, taught by *seventeen* Fathers; (2) that the whole *Apostolic College* is the Rock, represented by Peter as its chief, taught by *eight;* (3) that St. Peter's *faith* is the Rock, taught by *forty-four;* (4) that *Christ* is the Rock, taught by *sixteen*; (5) that the Rock is the *whole body of the faithful.* Several who teach (1) and (2) also teach (3) and (4), and so the Archbishop sums up thus : ' If we are bound to follow the greater number of Fathers in this matter, then we must hold for certain that the word *Petra* means not Peter professing the Faith, but the Faith professed by Peter.'"

P. 27, last line, add to footnote, "who derived the suggestion from a Curialist gloss, first discoverable in Pope Agatho (A.D. 680), but adopted by subsequent Popes and their literary staff; failing, however, on this very ground, as an *ex parte* claim."

P. 28, line 5, after "that it," insert the words "is startlingly unlike, both in belief and practice, to the Christianity taught by our Lord and His Apostles, as recorded in the New Testament, and that it."

P. 28, footnote to sect. XI. :—" On any hypothesis of the fundamental dogmatic importance of the three great Petrine texts in the Gospels, it is hard to explain their entire absence from the writings of the Apostolic Fathers, who make in all 412 quotations from the New Testament. St. Luke xxii. 32, does occur once, but only in the interpolated text of St. Ignatius *Ad Smyrn.* 7, while even there it is referred to all the Apostles."

P. 29, after line 3, insert this paragraph :—" There are certain Divine manifestations in the Old Testament, technically known as '*Theophanies*,' *i.e.*, 'appearances of God,' which have been cited in defence of Saint and angel worship, because of the acts of homage done by those to whom they were granted. Such are : Abraham's vision of the Three Men (Gen. xviii. 1) ; Jacob's wrestling at Peniel (Gen. xxxii. 26) ; Moses at the burning bush (Exod. iii. 2) ; and Joshua with the Captain of the Lord's host (Josh v. 13, 14). Two opinions are held as to these : either that they are indirect revelations of God through the medium of created angels, which is, naturally enough, the Jewish view ; the other, and more Christian one, is that they are veiled manifestations of the Second Person of the Holy Trinity, which is strengthened in two of the cases (Gen. xviii. 1, and Exod. iii. 2) by the use of the incommunicable name of *Jehovah*, never imparted to any created being—a fact which St. Augustine, our chief authority for the first opinion, was not likely to have noticed, as being ignorant of Hebrew. But whichever view be taken, it will not help Saint or angel worship now, because the *only* Theophany under the Gospel is the *Incarnation* of our Lord Jesus Christ. No Saint or angel can henceforward represent Him, or be clothed with His attributes, nor can such a thing be even imagined."

P. 34, line 3, for (" Cont. Cels." vii), read (" Cont. Cels." v. c. 4).

P. 34, at end of page, add this paragraph, with the accompanying footnote : —" It is not till the *eighth* century that Roman controversialists can find any clear precedents for the modern practice, for all earlier examples cited will prove on examination either to attest only the belief that the Saints do in fact *pray for and with us*, not that we should *pray to them*; or, if going beyond this, to be either admittedly doubtful or notoriously spurious.¹ How far the usage even near the close of the thirteenth century was from reaching modern excesses may be seen in Joinville's account of the dying prayers of St. Louis of France, for mentioning that the king invoked St. James and St. Denis, he tells us that he recited the collects for their festivals. But these collects are addressed directly to God through Christ, merely commemorating the names of the Saints in question." ¹ Footnote: "It would seem, from the date at which Invocation of Saints first begins to crop up, as though it were simply a result of the common tendency of men to attribute their own views and motives to God. When the Empire became Christian, and so was regarded as a friend, it did not become less despotic, while the enormous powers wielded by the Crown trained its subjects to regard God chiefly as an infinitely magnified Emperor. But as the Emperors seldom administered justice, granted reasonable petitions, or did right, merely because it was right, but had to be approached and conciliated by the indirect road of confidential ministers and palace favourites, who needed to be won over first, it became readily believed that God could be best propitiated in the same way. And the fact that the same practice of invocation prevails amongst Mohammedans, always used to live under arbitrary and capricious despotisms, strengthens this view."

P. 44, line 3, for "vii. 14." read "vii. 18."

P. 48, three lines from bottom, after "extravagant worship," add "And George Cassander, a Flemish divine (1515–1566), who strove to pacify the religious disputes of the sixteenth century (and of whom the Dominicans Richard and Giraud say that he possessed, besides unusual learning, also great candour, sincere humility, absolute disinterestedness, a spirit of moderation and peace, and an ardent zeal for terminating polemical difficulties, as also that he died a good Catholic), wrote thus in a 'Consultation' drawn up by order of, and addressed to, the Emperors Ferdinand and Maximilian, after expressing regret that the decrees of Frankfort were not still upheld in France and Germany, as they had long been: 'It is too manifest to need many words of explanation, that the cultus of statues and images has been too prevalent, and that overmuch indulgence has been allowed to the popular taste, or rather superstition; to such an extent, that nothing seems left undone on the part of our people to attain to the supremest adoration which was wont to be paid to their images by the Pagans, and to the extremest folly which the Gentiles practised in fashioning and adorning their images and statues.'"—"Opera," pp. 978–9. Paris, 1616. Of course this book was speedily put on the Index.

P. 51, line 1, after "twenty other places," add "Again, that one

ADDITIONS AND CORRECTIONS.

handkerchief with which St. Veronica is said to have wiped the face of our Lord, thereby imprinting His likeness upon it, is shown in *seven* different places. They are Rome, Turin, Milan, Cadouin, Besançon, Compiègne, and Aix-la-Chapelle. Four Papal Briefs attest that at Turin, fourteen the one at Cadouin."²—¹Burton," Description of the Antiquities of Rome," p. 441.

P. 51, line 5, after "remove the doubt," add "and what is even worse, their moral guilt in giving the most solemn and public authorisation, in hundreds of places, to what they either do not know, and have no reason to think, to be true; or else do know to be certainly false; being so committed to fiction that they dare not tell the truth, lest all popular belief in religion should disappear when so much of it was once known to be baseless."

P. 53, add footnote to line 10, "put together." ¹ "In the porch of one of these churches, S. Maria delle Grazie, close to the Vatican, the text Hebrews iv. 16, is set up in large permanent letters, with this important change: 'Let us come to the throne of the *Virgin Mary*,' instead of 'throne of grace,' as it stands in the Bible."

P. 60, line 7, for "twenty-two," read "twenty-three."

P. 62, after line 7, insert: "EPISTLE TO THE GALATIANS,— 'God sent forth His Son, made of a woman, made under the Law,' iv. 4."

P. 66, line 25, delete "St. Cyprian."

P. 67, line 21, after "brethren," insert "St. Cyprian casually names her once, as Mother of Christ" (Epist. lxxii., *al.* lxxiii).

P. 67, footnote, line 2, for "glossed *consolari* in the Benedictine edition," read "explained as *consolari* in the Latin glossary at the end of the Benedictine edition."

P. 69, line 25, after "argue that," insert " as no mere *man* can be made an object of worship, much less can the Blessed Virgin, as a *woman*, and so belonging to the inferior sex, be so treated,¹ and that" and subjoin footnote: "¹ This line of argument shows that the Collyridian error was not that of holding the Blessed Virgin to be of superhuman nature."

P. 71, line 24, at end of paragraph, add "And it is a very remarkable fact that the first great step taken towards the cultus of the Blessed Virgin came, not from any Saint, but from one of the most notorious heretics and evil-doers in Church history, Peter the Fuller, intruded Patriarch of Antioch in the fifth century; who united in his teaching the errors of the Sabellians, Valentinians, Apollinarians, and Eutychians, was condemned and anathematized by more than one Pope and Council, and was infamous for his crimes as simoniac, tyrant, and murderer. He it was who first enjoined that mention should be made of the Blessed Virgin in all prayers."²—² Tillemont, "Mém." xvi., 375.

P. 72, subjoin footnote to "enjoys them all," line 8, ¹ "A

subordinate form of this argument is that as all reverence paid to the Blessed Virgin is due to her relation to her Divine Son, it is in fact honour paid to Him, and passes on to Him, through her as its medium. This plea is shut out by the fact that the proposition 'Praise offered to Mary, as Mary, is vain,' was condemned by Alexander VIII., on Dec. 7, 1690."

P. 73, for the second footnote, substitute the following: "[2] The Articles of Faith and the Liturgy compiled for the Chinese by F. Ricci, omitted the doctrines of the Incarnation, Crucifixion, Atonement, and Mediation of Christ, but inserted permission for the worship of Confucius, as vicegerent of God in Heaven and on earth (his image being placed on the altar, from which the crucifix was rigidly excluded); for adoration of the visible and material heavens; and for paying divine honours to the spirits of deceased ancestors. These usages were condemned as heretical and idolatrous by Cardinal Tournon in his Legatine Decree of Nov. 20, 1704, which was confirmed by a Brief of Clement XI. on Sept. 25, 1710. The Jesuits, with the aid of Cazale, Bishop of Macao, their own nominee and instrument, did to death, in the Inquisition of Macao, Cardinal Tournon, the Papal Legate sent by Clement XI. to stop their paganization of Christianity." Cartwright, "The Jesuits," chap. xii., citing the report lodged at Rome by Marcello Angelita, the Legate's secretary.

P. 78, at end of paragraph *c*, add this paragraph and footnote: "And the most probable origin and meaning of the ceremony of 'commixture' in the Roman Missal itself, when the priest, just before his own communion, puts a particle of the Host into the chalice, is that it is a survival of the very same custom in the West."[2]
[2] "So the learned Jesuit Maldonatus, who says: 'Because the priest could not steep the Eucharist at a more convenient time than at the fraction and communion, he therefore put that particle of the Host into the chalice, and afterwards separated it with a spoon, and *reserved* it.'"—"De Cærem. Disp." II., xxii. 3.

P. 79, line 18, after "(1 Cor., x. 16)," insert "Further, the Holy Eucharist is, firstly and chiefly, the Sacrament of Christ's *death* (1 Cor., xi. 26), but in His death His Body and Blood were not *united*, as in life, but *separated*."

P. 80, line 17, after "drink," insert "whereby He prescribes the *manner*, and not merely the *fact*, of receiving His Blood."

P. 84, after line 9, insert, "Thus it is clear that what so shocked St. Gelasius was exactly what is seen in every Roman church now, the priest alone receiving the chalice, and the laity abstaining from it. The case was not as if the priest had attempted to *consecrate* in one kind only."

Pope Paschal II. wrote thus to Pontius, Abbot of Cluny, in A.D. 1118:—"Therefore, according to the same Cyprian, in receiving the Lord's Body and Blood, let the Lord's tradition be observed; nor let any departure be made, through a human and novel institution, from what Christ the Master ordained and did. For we know that the Bread was given separately, and the Wine given separately, by the Lord Himself; *which custom we therefore teach and command to be always observed in Holy Church*, save in the case of infants, and of very infirm people, *who cannot swallow bread*." (Ep. 535, t. 163, p. 442., ed. Migne.)

P. 84, line 15, for "three Popes," read "four Popes," and for "last occasion," read "third occasion."

P. 85, add to footnote, "And the proposition that it is desirable to enable the unlearned to unite their voice to that of the Church, by employing the vulgar tongue in the Mass, is condemned as false and mischievous by Pius VI. in the Bull " Auctorem Fidei," of 1794, against the Synod of Pistoja."

P. 90, line 2, after "obligatory," insert "while, even when it is nominally provided, the preacher's text is probably the only Biblical element in the discourse, which is all but certain not to be a real comment or exposition."

P. 90, line 21, for "is at this moment," read "was, till quite lately."

P. 90, line 23, after "obvious reasons," add "A German version by Dr. Aḧioli in 1830–37, and a French one by the Abbé Glaire in 1861, have received Papal sanction."[1]

P. 90, line 28, add " In fact, no vernacular translation of the Bible ever appeared at Rome up to the overthrow of the Temporal Power in 1870."

P. 90, add as footnote to new paragraph, at " Papal sanction " ([1]) "In a petition to Pius IX., dated July 5th, 1870, signed by fifty-five French bishops, they solicited the necessary authorisation for the publication of a French version of the Old Testament by the Abbé Glaire. They urged as the motive of their request, not the good in itself of circulating the Holy Scriptures amongst the laity, but the necessity of counteracting the diffusion of Protestant Bibles in Catholic families, of which they complained, saying : ' It is unquestionable that nothing can nowadays prevent the reading of the whole Bible in the world '; a remark whence it is reasonable to infer that the licence to publish the French translation was requested on the ground of extern necessity, not as a thing in itself desirable."

P. 91, line 6, for "some twenty," read "a hundred and twelve."

P. 90, subjoin footnote to Sect. XXXVI., "Biblical Study," F. Curci, in the preface to his recent (1879) translation of the Gospels and Acts, states thus :—' The New Testament is of all books that which is least studied and read amongst us, insomuch that the greater part of the laity, even such as are instructed and practising believers, *do not so much as know that such a book exists in the world, and the majority of the clergy themselves scarcely know more of it than they are obliged to read in the Missal and Breviary.*' Curci, Avvert. Prelim. in N. T. § xi."

P. 96, line 18, strike out quotation *h*, "When impious heresy—save by the Scriptures," and substitute the two following: "(*h*.) Let us not utter those cold and unprofitable words, and say: 'I am a layman, I have a wife, and have children to take care of,' as many are wont to say when we urge them to active work on behalf of goodness, and to display much zeal in reading the Scriptures. He says: 'This is not my business. Have I given up the world? am I a monk?' What are you saying, man? Are monks the only persons whose duty is to please God, Who wills all men to be saved, and to come to the knowledge of the truth? . . . . Let us not deceive ourselves, but, in proportion as we are occupied with cares of the kind mentioned, let us all the more procure remedies for them from the study of the Holy Scriptures." St. Chrysostom, Hom. xxi., on Genesis v. and vi.

"(*i*.) Hearken, I pray you, all ye seculars, and procure books as medicines of your souls. If you get no other, at any rate get the New Testament, the Acts of the Apostles, the Gospels, as your continual teachers. If sorrow befall, look therein as into a medicine-chest; thence derive consolation for suffering, if privation, if death, if loss of friends shall happen to you: and do not merely look into it, but take everything from it, and keep it on your mind. This is the cause of all evil, not to know the Scriptures. We go to war without arms, and how can we be saved?" St. Chrysostom, Hom. ix. on Coloss. iii.

P. 97, after line 5, insert the three following quotations: "(*j*.) Let us then not despise the hearing of the Holy Scriptures. *For that is a Satanic notion which forbids us to behold the treasure*, lest we should acquire the wealth." (St. Chrysostom, Hom. ii. on St. Matt.)

"(*k*.) As the Apostles wrote, so did the Lord Himself; that is, He spoke through His Gospels, not so that a few might understand, but all men. Plato was a writer of books, yet he did not write for the people, but for the few, and scarcely three persons understand him. But they, the princes of the Church and princes of Christ, did not write for the few, but for the whole body of the people." St. Jerome, Comm. in Psalm. lxxxvi.

"(*m*.) What is Holy Writ, save a sort of letter from Almighty God to His creatures? . . . . . And if you had a letter from your earthly sovereign, you would not pause, rest, or sleep, till you had learnt what he had written. The Emperor of Heaven, the Lord of men and angels, has sent you His letters for your own life's sake, and yet you neglect to read those letters eagerly. Study, therefore,

I beseech you, and daily ponder your Creator's words, learn God's heart in God's words." St. Gregory the Great (" Epist." iv., Indict. xii. 31, to the physician Theodore).

P. 98, end of sect. xi., add :—"And we have an explicit condemnation of this doctrine from the mouth of a Pope in council, Gelasius I., in the Synod at Rome in 495 : 'They request us to grant pardon to the dead also ; a thing plainly not possible for us, since in that it is said, 'Whatsoever ye shall bind *on earth*,' He reserved those who are obviously no longer on earth, not to human judgment, but to His own judgment. Further, the Church dares not arrogate to herself what she sees was not granted even to the blessed Apostles, seeing that the case of the living is of one sort, and that of the dead of another'" (Mansi. "Concil.").

P. 102, after " 56,000 years," strike out "Modern indulgences," and substitute this paragraph with its footnote : "Several local indulgences at Rome are for 28,000 years ; and the Archbishop of Naples, in 1846, published indulgences of 3,800, 70,000, and 200,000 years, the qualification for the last being the recitation of three Paters, Aves, and Glorias, in honour of the Passion.[3] But for the most part, they."

[3] "Carové, 'Römischer Katholicismus,' Leipzig, 1861, p. 40, ff. There is a significant warning in a book containing a list of the privileges of the Redemptorist Fathers ("Elenchus Facultatum et Gratiarum Spiritualium, quibus potitur Congregatio SS. Redemptoris," Munich, 1860, p. 276), that it is not expedient in these days to issue, or even to mention publicly, indulgences of thousands of years outside Italy, as harm rather than edification would be likely to ensue. Pope Benedict XIV., by the bye, declares that indulgences of a thousand years and upwards are not genuine. 'De Synod. Diœces.' XIII., xviii. 9."

P. 108, add to footnote, " This is the special mark given us by St. Peter, whereby to recognise heretical teachers in the Church : 'Through covetousness shall they with feigned words make merchandise of you.'" 2 St. Pet. ii. 3.

P. 110, add to footnote : "And the plea, that since the commemoration of the departed in the Canon of the Mass is worded so as to include *all* at rest in Christ, no advantage can be shown to one more than another by the saying of any Mass, since all must profit alike thereby, is barred by the fact that this identical proposition, denying further that special payment for a Mass secures any special and distinct advantage, is condemned as 'false, rash, pernicious, and hurtful to the Church,' by Pius VI. in the Bull 'Auctorem Fidei,' of 1794, levelled at the Council of Pistoja. One argument urged at the Assembly of Florence in 1787, by one of the divines present, is noteworthy. He alleged that the number of privileged altars and masses in the diocese of Florence, empowered to release one soul from purgatory at each celebration, was so large (even apart from the vast numbers of plenary indulgences) as to exceed the ratio of deaths each day, while the same proportion held good everywhere else in the Roman Catholic world. Accordingly, purgatory must not only be empty, but the indulgences must be a long way in advance of any possible demands on its space, so that money could not honestly be taken for the purpose of saying masses to release any particular soul. 'Istor. dell' Assemblea di Firenze,' pp. 193-4, Florence, 1788."

P. 112, add to footnote : "And before the Council of Trent, the line publicly taken by the Roman Curia was, that the Pope *can dispense in every degree forbidden by Divine law;* and more specially : 'The Pope can dispense without assigning any reason in cases forbidden by Canon Law, and with sufficient reason in cases forbidden by Divine Law.' 'Practica,' fol. 88,—a manual for the use of the officers of the Curia.—Rome, 1514."

P. 113, line 1, after "expedited for them," insert "an abuse which the Belgian bishops, in a representation they made to the Vatican Council, asked to have at least modified, if not abolished, in view of the odium it excites, in that costly dispensations are granted speedily, while cheap or gratuitous ones are long delayed."

P. 114, last line, add new paragraph : "And this broad fact, emphasized by the nature of the now accredited Moral Theology of Rome, and by the very low standard of veracity amongst Roman Catholic populations, is the complete refutation of a claim, often loudly made, that the Church of Rome is the one divinely appointed channel through which the Holy Ghost exercises His functions of Ruler and Teacher. For, since He is revealed to us first and chiefly as the Spirit of *Truth* (St. John xiv. 17 ; xv. 26 ; xvi. 13), it is incredible that He should choose a medium so inconsistent with His own attributes."

P. 115, line 5, after "Carthage," add : "to try the case of one Apiarius, a priest of bad character, who had appealed to the Pope in bar of his deposition, and that contrary to the synodical laws of Africa, forbidding any such appeal.[1]"

[1] Tillemont. Mém. xiii. 775.

P. 115, line 6, for "the Pope," read "Pope Boniface I."

P. 115, line 18, for "on his part," read on the part of the Papal envoys [*executores*], that is to say, in fact, since they were only discharging his commission, on his part."

P. 115, line 21, after "the same use was made of them," insert "a second time in 424 by Celestine, successor of Boniface, in this same affair of Apiarius, in despite of the disproof furnished only five years previously, a fact the African Council forces on him in its synodical letter ('Cod. Eccl. Afric.' cxxxviii.), emphatically repudiating his claim of jurisdiction ; a third time."

Same page and line, for "thirty years," read "twenty-five years." Line 23, for "third," read "fourth." Line 24, add footnote to "Constantinople."[4]

[4] Not only were these Sardican Canons (which are the *sole basis* of the whole appellate jurisdiction of Rome) not Nicene, but there is grave reason to doubt if they ever existed at all, and were not simply a forgery at Rome. For (1) they are never heard of till as above in 419, and are then falsely alleged as Nicene. (2) After the African bishops had vainly searched for them, they tell the Pope, in 424, that they "could find no Synod which empowered him to send legates." (3) They are not referred to in the Acts of Constantinople in 381, or of Chalcedon in 451, though both dealing with the question of appeals. (4) They are unknown to SS. Athanasius, Basil, and Epiphanius ; (5) and also to the three great Church historians of the time, Socrates, Sozomen, and Theodoret. (6) They are never once cited or acted on in the West, *e.g.*, not being alleged by Leo the Great in his quarrel with St. Hilary of Arles, but are used by Rome only in dealing with Churches which, not having been represented at Sardica, were not so likely to have the genuine Acts in their archives. (7) No Greek text is known to have existed earlier than the sixth century; and that which does exist is only a translation of the Latin text, not an independent document, although the other Acts of Sardica were issued both in Greek and in Latin. As a rule, the three oldest Latin editions of the Canons, the *Prisca*, Dionysius Exiguus, and the true Isidore, differ verbally in their translation from the Greek, and thus check it and one another ; but they are the same word for word in the so-called Sardican Canons, thus showing that there was most probably never any Greek text at all, and that the Latin is the original. Against all this, the only plea of any weight is, that they are *perhaps* referred to as Nicene by the Synod of Constantinople in 382, in its Letter to Pope Damasus ("Theod. H. E." v. 9). But Canon IV. of Nicæa suits this reference (which is not a verbal quotation of any extant canon) as well as Canon VI. of Sardica ; while one fact makes it impossible that any Synod or Pope of the fourth or fifth century could have mistaken the Sardican Canons (even if genuine at all) for Nicene, to wit, that they *expressly name Pope Julius*, who did not begin to sit till 337, *twelve years later than the Council of Nicæa*. The spuriousness of these Sardican Canons has been lately confessed by a Roman theologian, Aloysus Vincenzi, in his "De Hebræorum et Christianorum Sacrâ Monarchiâ," pp. 221-230. Romæ, Typis Vaticanis, 1875.

P. 116, line 4, after "invented," add "at Rome."

P. 116, line 7, strike out the words "in gratitude—Donation of Constantine)."

P. 116, line 13, add these paragraphs : "And this fable was

gradually amplified, and followed up soon after the sixth century began, by the forged Acts of the Synod of Sinuessa, the forged 'Constitution of Silvester,' the forged 'Annals of Liberius and of Xystus,' the pretended history of Polychromius, and three more forged documents relating to Pope Silvester, namely, the letter to him from the Council of Nice, his reply thereto, and the Acts of a Council held by him."

"*d.* Soon after the middle of the eighth century, the Silvester fable was further enlarged by the pretended 'Donation of Constantine,' whereby, in gratitude for his cure, he bestowed on the Pope the sovereignty of Italy and the Western Provinces, a forgery which was successfully palmed off on King Pippin of France."

P. 117, lines 20 and 21, for "believed much earlier," read "believed and acted on much earlier," and subjoin footnote. "(¹) F. De Reynon, S.J., has been franker on this last head, saying, 'Yes, the impostor has attained his end. He has changed, as he wished, the discipline of the Church, but he has not arrested the general decay. God never blesses imposture. The False Decretals have never produced anything but mischief. 'Études Religieuses,' Nov., 1865."

P. 118, line 19, add "The synodical Letter of the Council of Sardica in 347, to Pope Julius I., seems to have been interpolated about the same time with this clause : 'For this will seem best and highly suitable, if the priests of the Lord from each and all of the provinces report to the Head, that is, to the See of Peter.'" The bad Latin in which this is couched, and its inconsistency with the context, have betrayed it.—(Hefele, "Conciliengesch." iv. 66).

f. "And all that part of the Canon Law which is known as the 'Decretum of Gratian' swarms with falsifications, deliberately introduced, and since worked up into the whole practical system of Roman jurisprudence."

P. 118, line 21, for "by inventing statements," read "by repeating or inventing statements."

"P. 118, add to footnote carried over from p. 117 :—" And other proofs of his bad faith exist, *e.g.*, his letter to the Emperor Michael III., in which he alleges that the chief reason for the deposition of Dioscorus by the Council of Chalcedon was not his heresy, but his having excommunicated Pope Leo the Great ; whereas the Council explicitly refused to take account of that charge, though pressed by the Roman legates."

P. 119, add to footnote :—"A defence has been set up for Zosimus, that he did but give too easy belief to a pretended retractation of error, made by Cælestius and Pelagius. But his own words, in a letter to the African Churches, which had complained of the heresy, are express and clear, that these two heretics had no need to retract, and though persevering firmly in their opinions, were nevertheless men of unblemished orthodoxy, falsely accused and unjustly condemned. One quotation must here suffice : ' Rejoice in learning that these men, whom *false judges* have accused, have *never* been separated from our body and *from Catholic truth.*' "—Baron. Ann. 417, xxv–xxx.

P. 120, lines 6 and following, for "Pope Urban IV.—witnesses," read "Pope Urban IV. seems to have known something about it, for, at once using it in a letter to the Greek Emperor, he kept back carefully the names of the witnesses."

P. 121, first line of footnote, after "decrees," add "(or, rather, of the second of them, since the former is certainly authentic)."

P. 123, line 2, after "falsifications," add "and he was far too learned a man to escape under the plea of ignorance or lack of critical judgment."

P. 123, footnote, add "For the like charges against Perrone, Guéranger, Weninger, &c., see Gratry's 'Letters to Dechamps.'"

P. 125, line 2, add "Again, Dr. Di Bruno quotes St. Cyprian as a witness in the third century to the doctrine of the Immaculate Conception. The passage cited is from a treatise ascribed to Arnald of Bonneval, an author of the *twelfth* century, whose writings, though bound up in the same volume as St. Cyprian's works in the editions of Bishop Fell and the Benedictines, are placed at the end, with a separate title, head-lines, and pagination, so that no mistake is possible."

P. 126, line 21, for "there is not one solitary mention, direct or indirect, of the Blessed Virgin," read "there is only this one solitary, casual, and unemphatic mention."

Same page, line 23, after "copious pen," add "Christ, born of the Virgin Mary." Epist. lxxii. (*al.* lxxiii.). A yet graver doubt of Cardinal Newman's good faith has since been justified by his preface to Mr. Hutton's work, 'The Anglican Ministry' (1879), wherein he strangely misrepresents the history and current of Anglican teaching on Eucharistic doctrine, though necessarily well acquainted with the long catena on that subject in No. 81 of 'Tracts for the Times,' a pamphlet of 424 pages, which flatly contradicts his assertions.

P. 127, insert before present first line, "F. Ryder's work, 'Catholic Controversy,' is full of misleading citations, many of them, indeed, admittedly derived from an exceptionally untrustworthy source, Mr. C. F. Allnatt's 'Cathedra Petri,' so that the guilt is not first-hand, but the practical result is of course identical, as no pains have been taken to verify and state the real facts. A few leading examples must suffice in illustration :—"

a. At p. 3, St. Chrysostom, Hom. 54 in Matt. v. 2, is given as a reference in a footnote, without actual citation of the passage, but ostensibly as *confirming* the citation in the text above, wherein the same Saint names St. Peter as a rock and foundation. On being tested, it proves to be this: "'On this Rock I will build My Church,' that is, *on the faith of his confession;*" thereby *disproving* the gloss put on the quotation which is given in full.

b. At p. 59, it is remarked that it is "somewhat anomalous that a Council [*i.e.*, Constantinople in 381], which told the Pope in its synodal letter, 'You have summoned us as your own members,' and was addressed in the answer as 'most honoured sons' (*See* Theodoret, H.E., lib. v., c. 9, 10), should have been under the presidency of an excommunicate." Of course, the reader assumes that the Council which wrote to the Pope is the *same* as that which was presided over by the excommunicated Meletius; that this synodal letter was addressed to the Pope *singly*, and was couched in terms of dutiful *obedience.* In fact, it was not the General Council of 381 which wrote, but a *second and minor synod* held in the next year (Hefele, Concilienges. viii. 102), which had of course never been presided over by Meletius, who was then dead; while, on verifying the letter in Theodoret, it is found to begin thus: 'To our most honoured lords and most pious brethren and *fellow-ministers* (συλλειτουργοῖς), Damasus, *Ambrose, Britto, Valerian, Ascholius, Basil, and other holy bishops assembled in the great city of Rome.*' That is, the letter is from one council to another council, wherein the Pope is only the bishop of highest rank present, and, even so, merely the 'brother and colleague' of those who address him inclusively. Next, the full text of the cited passage is this: 'Since *ye* [plural], exhibiting your brotherly affection towards us, assembling a synod by God's will at Rome, have invited us, as your own members, *by the letters of the most God-beloved Emperor,*—we [the Fathers say at some length] are sorry that *we are unable to attend.*' Nor does it appear that the letter of Pope Damasus, in the next chapter of Theodoret, was in reply to this synodal missive. The historian does not say so, nor is there a word to imply it in the letter itself, which is addressed to the bishops 'ruling in the East,' not 'assembled in Constantinople'; while Baronius and Valesius date it about 373 or 375, several years *before* the letter from the East,—a fact which can hardly have been overlooked.

c. At p. 62 we read, " St. Augustine could not with any show of consistency have contested the principle of appeals to Rome and Roman interference. In his 43rd letter (A.D. 398) he had suggested an appeal to Rome as a course that had been open to the Donatists when their schism first began."

What St. Augustine does say in this letter is that the Donatists had themselves appealed to the *Emperor Constantine* to appoint episcopal judges to try their case, and that he did so, "Melchiades, then *Bishop of Rome,* deciding with his colleagues, *whom the Emperor had sent* at the prayer of the Donatists." And a little later he adds, "Then do you say that Melchiades, Bishop of Rome, with his colleagues, the transmarine bishops, ought not to have usurped jurisdiction to themselves in a matter which had been already decided by seventy African bishops? . . . But what if he did *not* usurp it? *For the Emperor, being asked, sent bishops as judges to sit with him*, and to decide what was just upon the whole matter." And stating the objection, "Let us suppose that the bishops who judged at Rome were not good judges," he does not meet it by saying that as one of those judges was the Pope himself, the sentence must be final and infallible, but by saying that another appeal was possible : "There yet remained a *plenary council of the whole Church*, where the cause could be tried, and *even those very judges along with it*, that if they were convicted of having judged badly, *their sentence might be quashed.*" So, instead of St. Augustine suggesting an appeal *to* Rome, what he does suggest is that an appeal *from* Rome plus the Emperor, to a General Council, might have been made, but was not. And the implication that the Pope had no jurisdiction in the case, save what the State gave him, is precise.

d. P. 79, "Venerable Bede (A.D. 735) says of Pope Gregory : 'And whereas he bore the Pontifical power over all the world, and was placed over the Churches already reduced to the faith of truth, he made our nation, till then given up to idols, the Church of Christ' (Hist. Eccl., tib. ii. c. 1)." What Beda does say is this : 'Because, since he held *the premier Bishopric* in all the world (*Quia quum primum in toto orbe pontificatum gereret*) and had been set over (*prælatus*) the Churches this long while (*jamdudum*), converted to the true faith,[1] he made our nation, till then the slave of idols, a Church of Christ, so that we may use of him those words of the Apostle : 'That though *he is not an Apostle to others*, yet he is to us, for the seal of his Apostleship are we in the Lord.'"

[1] This, doubtless, refers to the Western Churches formed by the conversion of the barbarian conquerors of the Empire, and so excludes all more ancient Churches, whether in East or West, which lay outside the original patriarchal jurisdiction of the Popes, and had not derived their missionaries from Latin Christendom.

P. 127, after line 27, insert "I speak as to wise men; judge ye what I say." 1 Cor. x. 15. "Brethren, be not children in understanding; howbeit in malice be ye children, but in understanding be men." 1 Cor. xiv. 20.

P. 130, add to footnote, "; wherein this remarkable conclusion is reached : that while implicit obedience should be rendered to the Pope in ordinary matters, when no particular demands are made on the conscience, and when, in fact, infallibility is silent, it is precisely in grave crises, when the Pope has spoken out and specially called for obedience, that his command is to be 'decided on its own merits,' is to be submitted to the opinions of theologians, bishops, confessors, and friends, 'and if, *after all*, I could not take their view of the matter, *then I must rule myself by my own judgment and my own conscience.*' This is the exact reversal of the ordinary notion of a Final Court of Appeal, such as the Papacy claims to be."

P. 131, strike out in second footnote all from "The Medulla Theologiæ Moralis" down to "condemned," and substitute "Nor is this to be wondered at, for Suarez, one of the most famous and authoritative Jesuit theologians, has laid down that an heretical king may first be deposed, and then, if continuing to reign, may lawfully be murdered as a tyrant."—"Defensio Fidei," 721. This book was burnt by order of the Parliament of Paris, as well as Busembaum's "Medulla Theologiæ Moralis," as contrary to the laws of God and man. The latter work, however, has been constantly reprinted, and has appeared in at least fifty editions down to 1848."

P. 132, after line 7, insert "Leo X. has put the following proposition of Luther's under anathema by the Bull *Exurges:* 'It is contrary to the will of the Spirit that heretics should be burnt.'"

Line 27, after "blasphemous heresies," add "and subsequently urged the Emperor Maximilian to deal with his heretic subjects as the king of France had done."

P. 132, add to footnote [1]:—Full proof of the Pope's complicity will be found in Gachard, "Correspondance de Philippe II.," vol. ii., pp. 185-199.

P. 133, line 28, after "but by," insert "the direction in the Bull *Unigenitus* (A.D. 1713) to all Archbishops and Bishops to call in the aid of the secular arm to coerce and punish heretics as rebels, by"

P. 133, line 29, after "liberty of conscience," add "(as 'an absurd and erroneous opinion, or rather madness')."

P. 134, add to footnote:—"And Cardinal Hergenröther has made this pregnant remark in his work on Church and State; 'The Church does not, in principle, renounce any rights which she has once exercised.' 'Katholische Kirche und Christlicher Staat,' Vol. I., p. 804, note 1, 1872."

P. 137, footnote, line 3, after "(London, Simpkin & Marshall), 1873)," add "; and 'The Devotion of the Sacred Heart,' by Robert C. Jenkins (London : Religious Tract Society)." One line from bottom, for "Saints," read "Sinners."

P. 142, at the end of line 8, add "It is to be noticed also that the temper now fostered in the Roman Church, and regarded as one mark of a true Catholic, that of looking for miracles, and expecting them to occur almost as a matter of course, is severely condemned by Christ Himself, as a token of a hard and unbelieving disposition : 'A wicked and adulterous generation seeketh after a sign' (St. Matt. xvi. 4); 'Except ye see signs and wonders, ye will not believe' (St. John iv. 48). It is the temper of unbelief and doubt, which cannot or will not trust God, nor accept spiritual truths without, so to speak, a ready-money payment in visible wonders. And so St. Paul contrasts the two tempers: 'The *Jews* require a sign . . . . but *we* preach Christ crucified' (1 Cor. i., 22, 23.)"

P. 146, append as footnote to line 3, "teachers of conduct," "¹ For proofs see F. Curci, 'La Nuova Italia ed i Vecchi Zelanti,' Florence, 1881."

P. 149, line 14, insert as footnote to "may have sat in them," "² The simplest proof of this fact lies in the rejection of the 'Robber-Synod' of Ephesus in 449, which, in point of mere legal form, was as regularly a General Council as any which preceded or followed it, and has been so styled and regarded by the Monophysites from the time of its session to the present day. Contrariwise, the Council of Constantinople in 381, which was exclusively Eastern in composition, and thus lacked one visible mark of œcumenicity, has been fully recognised as a true General Council, in virtue of its universal acceptance by Christendom.

P. 150, fifth line from bottom, after "of the Church," add "and subject to its laws, even heretics by birth being as it were rebels and deserters, who may be justly compelled to submit" ("Conc. Trid." sess. VII. can. iv. viii.; Benedict. XIV. in the Brief "Singulari nobis;" Pius VII., Brief of Oct. 8, 1803; Perrone, "De Matrimonio Christiano.")

P. 151, line 4, for "Pius VI." read "Pius IV."

P. 151, line 4, for "certainly known to have planted," read "so much as thought probably to have planted."

P. 152, line 26, insert footnote to "551 ff.:" "¹ Hence, the proposition of Peter of Osma, that 'the Church of the City of Rome can err,' was condemned as 'scandalous and heretical' by Sixtus IV. in 1479."

P. 153, line 2, insert footnote.
¹ See note at end of volume.

P. 154, line 21, after "Church doctrine and order," add "and as having been therefore opposed and refuted by St. Paul." Same page and line, append footnote to "(Gal. ii. 11)."
¹ "It is on this passage that St. Cyprian makes the remarkable gloss: 'Nor did Peter . . . . . when Paul had a dispute with him, make any haughty claim, or take on himself arrogantly, as by saying that he held the Primacy.'"—("Epist." lv. sec. 14.)

P. 154, line 28, after "in the Church," add "asserts his own absolute equality with 'the very chiefest Apostles'" (2 Cor. xi. 5, xii. 11), and subjoin footnote.²

b

² " For having so done, and still more for his resistance to St. Peter personally, St. Paul, it would seem, has incurred the guilt of heresy, in virtue of the terms of the decree of Innocent X. and the Roman Inquisition in 1674, condemning as heretical the proposition that SS. Peter and Paul were equal in rank and dignity, and that St. Paul was not subject and subordinate to St. Peter in virtue of the supreme authority over the Church vested in the latter. And the sentence also strikes the following saints and doctors of the Church, who assert the equality of the two great Apostles : St. Hilary of Poitiers, St. Gregory Nyssen, St. Cyril of Alexandria, and St. Chrysostom. A citation from the last must suffice in evidence :" " He (St. Paul) shows himself to be *equal* with the other Apostles, but he compares himself, not with the rest, but with the *first* of them, pointing out that each had the *same dignity*."—Ad. Galat. ii. 3.

P. 155, add to footnote, " The guess that Babylon in 1 St. Peter v. 13, means Rome, rests on one passage in Eusebius (Hist. Eccl. ii. 15), constantly quoted as though it stated that such was the belief of St. Papias of Hierapolis, all but contemporary with the Apostles, and of St. Clement of Alexandria. Closer inspection of the text shows that these two Fathers are cited only in evidence of a tradition as to the origin of St. Mark's Gospel, while the opinion as to Babylon is merely given in another sentence as a general ' they say,' with no authority named. St. Peter's own opening words contain a very cogent argument the other way : ' Pontus, Galatia, Cappadocia, Asia, and Bithynia ' (1 St. Peter i. 1) are named in their order from *east to west*, natural enough in a writer at Babylon in Mesopotamia addressing people in Asia Minor, but the exact reverse of the order which a writer at Rome would be likely to adopt, if sending a letter to the East."

P. 156, line 22, after "most of the Fathers," insert " notably Origen, St. Cyprian, St. Ambrose, St. Hilary, St. Gaudentius, St. Augustine, St. Jerome, and St. Leo the Great."³ And subjoin footnote :

³ "Similarly Pope Innocent III. (1198-1216), in a passage which bears also on another Roman difficulty : 'Although the most blessed Virgin Mary was higher and more glorious than all the Apostles, yet it was not to her, but to them, that the Lord committed the keys of the kingdom of heaven.' "—(" Epist. ad Episcop. Valent. et Burgens.")

P. 156, line 23, for the sentence " being merely—Apostles," read "being, not the act of gift itself, but only the promise of it, whose fulfilment was the power of binding and loosing sins, bestowed in common on all the Apostles."

P. 156, add to footnote ² : " The whole debate on the Papal claims in virtue of the 'Privilege of Peter,' really turns upon this evidence, for the New Testament contains all that we *know* about St. Peter's authority and teaching; but F. Ryder, in his 'Catholic Controversy,' has not so much as ventured to touch it, and has thus yielded the key of the position, implicitly confessing thereby that there is *no case.*"

P. 157, line 3, after "the most ancient," add "(and indeed for some centuries the only)."

P. 157, line 22, after "provided for," insert "(Gen. xv. 4; xvii. 7, 8, 19; Exod. xxviii. 1; Numb. xviii. 1–9; 2 Sam. vii. 12–16)."

P. 157, add to footnote, "It is no answer to say that as the New Testament is *older* than the Canon Law, the provisions of that law cannot be applied as tests of validity to any charter in the Gospels. For the assertion that the Gospels bestow a certain 'privilege' on St. Peter, giving him and his heirs sovereign jurisdiction over the Church, is not in the New Testament itself, but is a gloss invented and read in thither by Roman authorities, and embodied in their Canon Law. It is therefore quite fair to ascertain how that law tests and judges all other privileges, and to show that its invariable rules of interpretation necessarily set aside the ' Privilege of Peter' itself, because failing to meet their requirements for validity. As the Canon Law is the formal voice of the Roman Church, and largely made up of what are now treated as the infallible utterances of Popes, it cannot be appealed from by Roman Catholics."

P. 158, line 17, after "pagan creed," add: "It is very remarkable that in the letter to the Church of Corinth, ascribed to St. Clement, and most probably his composition, the address is that of the collective *Church* of Rome to its sister Church, not that of the *Bishop*, even writing in the name of the Church, a fact preserved to us independently by St. Irenæus (Adv. Hær. iii. 3), while St. Ignatius mentions no Bishop, past or present, in his Epistle to the Romans, and similarly St. Cyprian praises the orthodoxy of the *Romans*, when he disputes that of the Pope. Clearly, then, it was the City which gave importance to the Pontiff, not conversely."

P. 158, insert footnote to "his primacy," nine lines from bottom:
[1] "Benedict XIV. himself admits the human origin of the Papacy, though he tries to qualify the admission. His words are : 'Though it may thus be said, in a certain sense, that the supreme monarchy over the Church is annexed to the Roman See only by human right (*jure*) . . . yet it does not appear that the opinion of those can be maintained who have asserted that the aforesaid annexation is of human right in such wise that it could be parted from that Church.' ' De Synod. Diœc.'" II., i. He probably refers to the view of the famous Cardinal D'Ailly, which is that Rome might be destroyed for its sins, like Sodom, or abandon the faith, like Jerusalem, so that the chief Pontiff could and would

transfer the seat of the Primacy in either event. (Richer, "Vindic. Doctr. Major. Schol. Paris," III. p. 14).

P. 159, line 10 of footnote, add "Yet that even he had to treat the question as a purely disciplinary one, not touching dogma, appears from the fact that so far from anathematizing the authors of the Canon as heretics, he repeatedly extols their orthodoxy."

P. 159, five lines from bottom, after "did accept," insert "The Council in Trullo in 692 re-enacted this Chalcedonian canon in its own thirty-sixth one, and Pope John VII., to whom the Trullan canons were sent for confirmation by Justinian II., accepted them without alteration in 705." Fleury, H.E., ix. 136, 137.

P. 160, line 14, add; "The phrase 'convenire *ad*' can mean only one thing in Latin, namely 'assemble at'; and if 'agree with' were the sense, as Roman controversialists allege, the phrase would then run 'convenire *cum*.' The real force of the passage, consequently, is that the reason for going to Rome for doctrinal information was because it was such a mart, that representatives from all Churches could be met there, and all their various local traditions be thus collected and compared easily, of course checking and testing the Roman tradition itself."

P. 160, in footnote, five lines from bottom, after "hundreds of hands," add "; and those who confer it raise the candidates only to *equality* with themselves."

One line from bottom, after "successor," add "; so that the new Pope can *receive* only what the Cardinals (themselves of merely mediæval and human institution) have to *give*. And they cannot give powers which exceed their own; which, however, include the government of the Roman Church *sede vacante*, though they are certainly not heirs of St. Peter."

P. 161, line 4, for "in Pontifical Letters," read "in dogmatic Pontifical Letters, in reply to a formal application from three Eastern Patriarchs to him as Pope to declare his opinion."

Line 6, for "Gregory II.," read "Leo II."

Lines 7 and 8, for "Honorius was certainly damned," read "Honorius and his accomplices in heresy were certainly damned.¹ The Seventh and Eighth so-called General Councils repeat the sentence." Subjoin footnote¹: "Æterna condemnatione mulctati sunt;" words which cannot be honestly softened down to denote only the human anathema.

P. 161, add to footnote carried over from p. 160, "St. Peter Damiani, in the eleventh century, speaks of Liberius as not only a heretic, but an apostate."—"Liber *Gratissimus*," cap. xvi.

Add to footnote, two lines from bottom, after "New Roman Dogma," "In the 'Somme des Conciles,' by the Abbé Guyot, Vol. I. p. 315 (Paris, 1868), the condemnation of Honorius is simply cut out from the judgment pronounced in Session XIII. of the

Council; just as it has been cut out of the Roman Breviary, where, till the reform of Clement VIII., it stood in the office of Leo II. on June 28."

P. 162, add to footnote, "It is important to add that the offer of this title during the Council of Chalcedon was not made by that Synod itself, nor with its authority, though often cited as if such were the case. It was the private and unofficial act of certain Alexandrian petitioners (one priest and two deacons) against Dioscorus, who endeavoured thus to conciliate the favour of the Roman Legates."—See Baron. "Ann." 451, lxxxi. A homily, ascribed to St. Cyril of Alexandria, in which the title of 'Archbishop of the Universe' is applied to the Pope, is spurious. Even if genuine, it would prove but little, for St. Gregory Nazianzen speaks of the appointment of St. Athanasius to the See of Alexandria as giving him 'superintendence over the whole world' ($\tau\tilde{\eta}\varsigma$ οἰκουμένης πάσης ἐπιστασίαν)."—Orat. xxi., Opp. i., 377, Paris, 1609.

P. 165, add at end of sect. LXXVIII., "c. Further, the very fact that since the Reformation, the creed of the Roman Church has been three times altered by accretions, in 1564, 1854, and 1870 (while the Church of England has held to the old belief), is in itself a powerful argument against the fact or the good of Papal infallibility, *even on the assumption that these alterations are doctrinally sound.* For if they be true now, they must always have been true, and hence the long delay in defining them can be accounted for in only one of two ways: Either the Popes did not themselves know what is truth on these subjects; or, if knowing it, kept back the truth, and failed to teach it, thereby suffering millions of Roman Catholics to continue in error, which a timely word would have removed."

P. 166, footnote, line 5, after "1786," add "in rebuke for his having defended certain Jansenist catechisms, which had been condemned by the Congregation of the Index, but not otherwise."

At end of footnote, add, "In 1822, Pius VII. ratified a decree of the Inquisition, licensing all Copernican treatises on astronomy; while in 1835, the works of Copernicus, Kepler, and Galileo were taken off the Index: which amounts to a Papal admission that Paul V. and Urban VIII. erred in their definition of heresy, and so were fallible teachers."

P. 167, lines 2-5, for the sentence "declaring — excommunication," read "declaring, as a *perpetual* decree, 'by the fulness of Apostolic power,' an edition of the Vulgate, then just issued, the sole authentic and standard text for ever, since having been corrected by his own hand, 'relying on the authority of the Prince of the Apostles,' and that any departure from it, even in *private* readings, discussions, or explanations, should incur the greater excommunication."

P. 167, add to first footnote, after "Bellum Papale," " Cardinal

Bellarmine wrote as follows on this subject to Clement VIII.:
'Your Blessedness knows to what peril Sixtus V. exposed the Church and himself, when he attempted the correction of the Holy Bible according to the tenor of his personal opinion (*juxta propriæ doctrinæ sensus*); nor do I know if a greater danger ever occurred.' In his 'Autobiography' (ed. 1591, p. 291), Bellarmine mentions that he advised Gregory XIV., instead of publicly prohibiting this faulty edition, as several eminent persons recommended, to save the credit of Sixtus V. by quickly reprinting it, after correction, under that Pope's name, with a preface, saying that some errors had crept into the first issue through haste in its publication, by reason of the carelessness of the printers and of other persons; though a little before he lays the blame on Sixtus himself, as having deliberately altered the passages in question for the worse (*permulta perperam mutata* is his exact phrase)."

P. 170, append as footnote to line 2, "Canon Law."

[1] "A letter by Bishop Strossmayer, bearing date Nov. 27, 1870, and reprinted in the *Kölnische Zeitung* of July 13, 1881, puts this fact very clearly, thus : 'The Vatican Council was wanting in that freedom which was necessary to make it a real Council, and to justify it in making decrees calculated to bind the consciences of the whole Catholic world. . . . Everything which could resemble a guarantee for the liberty of discussion was carefully excluded. . . . And as though all this did not suffice, there was added a public violation of the ancient Catholic principle, *Quod semper, quod ubique, quod ab omnibus.* In a word, the most hideous and naked exercise of Papal infallibility was necessary before that infallibility could be elevated into a dogma. If to all this be added that the Council was not regularly constituted, that the Italian Bishops, Prelates, and officials were in a monstrously predominating majority, that the Apostolic Vicars were dominated by the Propaganda in the most scandalous manner, that the whole apparatus of that political power which the Pope then exercised in Rome contributed to intimidate and repress all free utterance, you can easily conceive what sort of *liberty*—that essential attribute of all Councils—was displayed at Rome.' This indictment makes it useless to allege the validity of the dogma as the *concurrent* act of both Pope and Council."

P. 172, insert at end of sect. LXXXIII. :

"What is more, the consideration of dates alone will refute the plea of development. For the growth of any dogma or pious opinion must keep pace, if that plea be true, with the gradual evolution and accurate definition of the theological verity out of which it springs. It cannot advance by leaps and bounds, nor be separated by any long interval of time from the full recognition and formulation of its parent-dogma. But the cultus of the Blessed Virgin and of

ADDITIONS AND CORRECTIONS. xxiii

St. Joseph depends entirely on their personal relation to our Lord, and so upon the doctrine of the Incarnation. Yet, whereas the last word on that doctrine was practically spoken when the Monothelite heresy was condemned in the Sixth General Council, A.D. 680, and no further expansion of statement respecting it has since been made, the cultus of the Blessed Virgin, as now understood (that is, addressing her in prayer as the direct bestower of graces and favours), is hardly seen even in germ until the eleventh century, five hundred years later ; nor that of St. Joseph till past the middle of the eighteenth century, eleven hundred years later. No ingenuity can bridge these gaps."

P. 175, append footnote to last line, "longer purse."
¹ "This point, involving the sin of simony, too frequent in the annals of the Papacy, is of much importance, because in Roman teaching simony is not only mortal sin and sacrilege, but also *heresy* of the worst sort (see Pope Paschal II., cited by Ferraris, 'Prompta Bibliotheca,' s. v. *Simonia*, and André, 'Droit Canon'), and voids all offices and benefices procured through its means, directly or mediately, nor can any prescription be ever acquired for their enjoyment, no matter what be the efflux of time, as they are null from the very first ; and *Non firmatur tractu temporis quod ab initio non subsistit*. For the effect of this on the existing Papal succession, see sect. CIII."

P. 176, add to footnote, "And even if the genuineness of this passage be disputed, the same testimony is borne by St. Jerome."—("Chronicon," A.D. 352, and "De Script. Eccl.," 97.)

P. 177, line 8, for "all Rome on his side," read "the clergy and the people of Rome on his side ; that is to say, two-thirds of the new legal constituency, and the whole of the original constituency (which did not lose its right of voting till fifty years later, at the election of Pope Lucius III. in 1181), were in his favour."

Page 177, line 18, after "others," insert "(*e.g.*, Boniface I., Boniface II., Vigilius, Sergius I., Stephen VII., John IX., Christopher, and Sergius III., whose elections were either highly doubtful or certainly invalid.)"

P. 177, line 26, after "final recognition," insert, "except in the schism of 1046, when three rival Popes were all set aside, and a new one, Clement II., appointed."

P. 179, add to footnote, "In order to distract the attention of the faithful ever more and more from the adorable person of Jesus Christ, from His teachings and His example, new cults and practices arise unceasingly on all sides. . . . and with the most imminent risk of degenerating into strange exaggerations and ridiculous superstitions."—(Curci, "Avvert. Prelim. in N.T.," § 10.)

P. 185, after line 10, insert "Even as early as the beginning of the third century, we have contemporaneous evidence (that of the great St. Hippolytus) against the characters of two of these canonized popes, Zephyrinus and Callistus. The former is described as covetous and venal, as well as illiterate and ignorant of Church definitions; the latter as swindler, embezzler, and heretic, while we are told that his sole claim to the title of 'Martyr' arose from a flogging and imprisonment he received for wanton brawling in a Jewish synagogue. 'Refutation of all Heresies,' ix. 6. Of St. Hippolytus himself, Anastasius the Librarian says that he is 'a most sacred and mighty doctor, and a faithful witness to the truth.'"

P. 186, footnote, four lines from bottom, after "all others together," add "the ratio of Roman Catholics in Liverpool, where they are denser than anywhere else in England, being 27·1 per cent. in 1881."

At end of footnote add, "In Prussia, where Roman Catholics are one-third (33·3 per cent.) of the whole population, and not so relatively poor as in England, they produced, in 1870, 52·6 per cent. of the criminals brought to trial; in 1871, 56·7 per cent; in 1872, 56·3 per cent. ; in 1873, 58·2 per cent ; in 1874, 57 per cent.; in 1875, 63·5 per cent. ; in 1876, 67·5 per cent. ; in 1877, 60·7 per cent.; in 1878, 63·7 per cent. What is more, a heavier proportion holds for the graver crimes. In 1878 the Roman Catholic murderers charged were 18·7 per cent. more than the Protestant ones ; homicides were 53·5 per cent., assaults, with fatal results, 38·6 per cent., poisoning 100 per cent., serious and repeated cases of theft, 30 per cent., robbery and extortion, 36 per cent., common larceny, 49·8 per cent., in excess of the Protestant criminals."

P. 187, line 14, after "beatified in 1861," add "and canonized December 8, 1881";[1] and subjoin footnote.

[1] He was an indescribably squalid tramp (1748-1783), who spent his life in wandering from one place of pilgrimage to another, making Rome his headquarters, and never seems to have fulfilled any one duty of life, nor to have ever tried to do good to any human being, by so much as intercessory prayer; being simply a European specimen of the lowest type of Indian fakir.

P. 188, line 7, after "in 1765," add "a work republished with the approval of many French prelates in 1822-27."

At the close of sect. XCV. add new paragraph : "A defence is sometimes set up for the system of Casuistry, that it deals only with the *legal* side of moral offences, and must not be construed as though it weakened *moral* obligations. But when it is remembered that the only tribunal involved is simply that of the *confessional*, and that the practical result of the acquittal of any person on merely casuistical grounds is to entitle him to absolution as a matter of right, and to access to the sacraments, so that he is justified in regarding himself as fully approved by the Church as the guardian of morals, this defence breaks down. And the more ingenious is the special pleading in defence of casuistical maxims, he more clearly are they shown to blur and confuse those distinctions between right and wrong which God has made broad and clear for all unwarped minds and consciences; while as to the plea, that in practice no such startling inferiority in moral qualities is exhibited by practising Roman Catholics, when compared with their neighbours, as must needs follow if these charges against the moral theology of their teachers be true; the reply is obvious, that it is just in proportion as the laity do *not* follow their teachers in these respects, but accept the ordinary secular standard of truth and falsehood, and so forth, that they rise to the level of natural morality."

P. 191, line 7, after "Sixtus IV.," add "(whom Machiavelli records as the chief accomplice in the Pazzi conspiracy to murder the Medici at Florence)."

P. 191, add to sect. XCVII. at end :—"Cardinal Bellarmine sums up the facts thus : ' A few years before the heresies of Luther and Calvin, there was, according to the testimony of contemporary writers, neither justice in the ecclesiastical courts, nor discipline in the morals of the clergy, nor knowledge of sacred things, nor respect for holy things,—in short, there was scarcely any religion left.'"—Concio xxviii. Opp. tom. vi.

P. 192, nine lines from bottom, for "squired by Cardinals," read "squired by the household retainers of Cardinals."

Footnote, four lines from bottom, for "xviii," read "xvii."

P. 193, seven lines from bottom, after "France," insert "while Belgium has been the theatre of many grave scandals, of which the State and the Courts had to take cognisance."

P. 194, add to footnote, "The reason why it is necessary to insist on the wickedness of the local Roman Church is this : The four Notes of the Church are not separable, but must be always united, for it is not enough that one, two, or even three of them should be present together. But if the Roman See be the very head and heart of Christendom, if it be, in truth, the *whole* Church in concentration, it must always have exhibited all the four Notes plainly at least, if not in a higher degree than they could be seen anywhere else. And thus these complete proofs that Rome has not been the centre of Holiness, dispose of its claim to be the one and only centre of Unity. In fact, instead of Christianity in Europe having depended on union with and submission to Rome, the truth is that Christianity in Rome was saved from ruin only because of its survival elsewhere, as in France and Germany, which enabled Rome to profit by her being in communion with them, so as to recover herself."

P. 195, lines 19 and 20, for "are estimated," &c., read "amounted, by the census of 1880, to no more than 6,143,122, out of a total population of more than 50,000,000."

P. 201, one line from bottom, after "historic title," add "As to the many gaps occasioned by simony, it will suffice to adduce the case of Alexander VI., elected Pope in 1492, through the bribery of twenty-two out of twenty-seven Cardinals, effected in the conclave by Cardinal Ascanio Sforza, as recorded by Von Eggs, the Roman Catholic historian of the Cardinals, in his 'Pontificium, sive Purpura Docta,' III. 54. Alexander then sold the Cardinalate itself to the highest bidders (Guicciardini, Ist. d'Italia, V.), and thus his own Popedom and their Cardinalates were all void. But Julius II. was elected in 1503 in a conclave of thirty-seven cardinals, of whom twenty-six were of Alexander VI.'s creation (Palatii, 'Fasti Cardinalium'); and Leo X. was elected by Cardinals all of whom had been created by Alexander and Julius. There has thus been no possibility of a legitimate election and transmission in the Papacy since 1492, when the electoral body was vitiated at its very source."[1]

And append footnote:[1] "It is to be steadily remembered that the claims made by the Papacy on the obedience of all Christians are not merely of a purely *spiritual* kind. They are still more largely matter of a *legal* system, of which the Pope is the *ex-officio* head, and involve the exercise of a strictly legal authority and jurisdiction. Therefore, the question whether he be in rightful possession of his office, without any legal flaw or break in its transmission to him, is of the first importance. Mere tenure of the office itself is no more than a presumption in his favour; since it is not enough to be Pope *de facto* without being also *de jure;* and he is bound to prove the legitimacy of his succession before he can claim anything in virtue of it. But the Roman See is exactly the single diocese in Christendom whose succession, from the very first, is a maze of doubt, confusion, and irregularity, and where such proof is consequently unproducible. And, even if it were granted that retrospective action might have cured the several defects of title as they occurred, no such legalising process was resorted to in time, and it is centuries too late now. The case, in fact, is analogous to that of a Jew under the Old Testament, claiming to be High Priest, as senior lineal representative of Aaron, whereas his own pedigree established that he was sprung from a series of illicit connexions and adulteries on the part of his ancestors and ancestresses, vitiating his legitimacy twenty times over."

P. 203, add to footnote: A remarkable saying of Pope Pius II., recorded by Platina in his "Vitæ Pontificum," but erased from several editions, merits citation here: "Marriage has been taken away from the priests for good reasons; but it ought, for much better reasons, to be restored to them."

P. 204, six lines from bottom, append footnote to "New Testament": [1] "Dupin points out the remarkable fact that 'during the eight first centuries of the Church, whenever mention was made of Church authority, these terms, Jurisdiction, Sovereignty (*majestas*), or Tribunal, were not employed, but only that of Ministry of the Chair.'"—"Antiq. Eccl. Discip.," i. 3.

ADDITIONS AND CORRECTIONS.

P. 206, line 7, after "Rome," append footnote: [1] "See Tillemont, Mém. iv. 312, 631, and also Firmil. Epist. § 6, 25.; which leaves no doubt that Pope Stephen issued what is now known as the 'Greater Excommunication' against the two Saints."

P. 206, line 14, after "by the Pope," add: and "another Bishop, Paulinus, acknowledged as lawful Patriarch of Antioch."

Same page, add to footnote carried over from p. 205, "Perhaps even more startling is the conduct of the Jesuit missionaries in China, in 1706, during the episode of the 'Chinese Rites' (sect. XXV. note). The Pope had issued a Brief declaring these rites to be superstitious and idolatrous, and forbidding them to all the Roman Catholic clergy and laity in China. The Jesuits at once circulated a rival edict, procured from the heathen Emperor, to the effect that no Christian priest should be suffered to minister in China without an Imperial licence, not to be granted till he undertook to accept the Chinese Rites, and that, too, in the sense put on them by the Emperor; binding him at the same time never to leave China again, so that he could not rid himself of complicity by withdrawal from the country."—Cartwright, "The Jesuits," pp. 105, 106.

[3] See note at end of volume.

P. 209, first footnote, first line, for "was planted from Rome," read "was probably, though not certainly, planted from Rome."

And at end of same note, add "And the Churches of Asia Minor never laid any claim to jurisdiction over the Churches of Gaul, which they planted."

Third footnote, third line, after "Felix," add "; that is to say, besides the twelve Welsh counties, about six-and-twenty shires, out of the forty into which England is divided, were not evangelised from Rome."

P. 216, lines 17, 18, for the sentence "Save the one—African Churches," read "Save the one closely restricted right to order the hearing of certain appeals, alleged to have been granted by the Council of Sardica in 347, but of extremely doubtful authenticity (See above, note 4 to p. 115), and rejected by the Eastern and African Churches," &c.

P. 216, line 23, add footnote to "appear": "Even the Formulary of Pope Hormisdas (519), forced on the Eastern Bishops by the Emperor Justin for political reasons, does not assert any claim of jurisdiction, but only that Rome is the centre of unity, and norm of doctrine. This Formulary dropped into abeyance the moment that it ceased to be upheld by the State."

P. 217, footnote to line 9, after "Constantinople":—"So it is plain, notwithstanding these decrees, Nestorius was always regarded and treated as Bishop of Constantinople till he was deposed at Ephesus. And he was deposed there, not in virtue of the Pope's judgment, which was read there, but of proofs adduced of his false doctrine."—Tillemont, "Mém.," xiv. 364.

Add to note ² :—" The orthodoxy of the Pope's Tome was questioned at the Council, and a delay of five days was granted for its examination. That over, one hundred and sixty Bishops publicly declared that they accepted it only because it agreed with St. Cyril's teaching, and with the Creeds of Nicæa and Constantinople. And even the Roman Legate Paschasinus, for himself and his colleagues, said thus : ' It is clear that the faith of Pope Leo is the same as that of the Fathers of Nicæa and Constantinople, and that there is no difference. *That is the reason why the Pope's letter, which has restated this faith because of the heresy of Eutyches, has been received.*"
—Fleury, " Hist. Eccl." vi. 400.

Append as note to line 17, after " Church," ³ " Fleury, " H.E." vii. 487. It is noticeable that this act was accompanied by a declaration that no breach of communion with the Roman *Church* was intended, but only with the *Pope* individually. Cardinal St. Peter Damiani describes him as a criminal of the worst kind.—"Liber *Gratissimus*," cap. xvi.

P. 219, line 30, for " Second General . . . 382," read "Council of Constantinople in 382, in their Synodical Epistle," &c.

P. 220, line 3, after "altered their views," insert " The broad rule, governing all such cases of strong patristic language concerning the authority of the Papal chair, being that whenever the belief of these Fathers about doctrinal truth and their belief about Roman authority happened to clash, it was always the latter, and not the former, which had to give way; the exact converse of modern usage within the Roman obedience."

P. 221, after line 16, insert new paragraph :—" 9. Again, in testing any catena of authorities alleged in favour of Papal supremacy and jurisdiction, all the following have to be struck out at once, even when the quotations are authentic : (*a*) claims and assertions made by Popes themselves or by their Legates for them, since it is not the *fact* of such claims having been made that is in dispute, but their *rightfulness ;* and *ex parte* statements are not evidence ; (*b*) all expressions of respect and deference for the Roman Chair which fall short of specifying and admitting the precise kind of authority claimed for it by Ultramontanes ; (*c*) all passages whose alleged force is disproved by the context or by the acts of the person or persons concerned ; (*d*) examples of acts of authority which are not exclusively Papal, but are common to other Patriarchs or Bishops, such as the deposition of criminous prelates, and that form of diplomatic recognition known as ' restoration of sees ' ; (*e*) language used by Western writers in Gaul after the date of Valentinian III.'s edict, and elsewhere after the reception of the False Decretals as genuine. When these are cleared away, the most imposing chain of authorities is reduced to a couple of doubtful and broken links, incapable of sustaining anything. This caution applies especially to a catena of the sort in F. Ryder's 'Catholic Controversy.'"

Line 23, append footnote after "null and void."

[1] "The wording of the Bull leaves it doubtful whether this clause refers only to persons who, having been born and reared in Roman Catholicism, have at any time departed therefrom, or whether it be also intended to bar the promotion of all such as, having been at any time outside the Roman communion, have conformed thereto. But that this latter is the more probable interpretation appears from these maxims laid down by Ferraris ('Prompta Bibliotheca Canonica,' s. v. *Hæreticus*): 'All public and notorious heretics are, *ipso facto*, irregular [*i.e.* incapable of ecclesiastical office], and remain so *even after conversion and absolution*.' 'Even secret heretics are more probably irregular, for since excommunication is incurred by secret heresy, so is irregularity also.' 'All heretics in belief, their harbourers, defenders and abettors, are incapable of holding benefices and ecclesiastical offices, and all bestowal of such upon them is legally null and void . . . and such incapacity for benefices and ecclesiastical offices abides in them *even if they be converted and abjure their heresy, especially if they have been publicly or notoriously heretics*.' 'The sons, and also the grandsons, of a heretic father, and the sons, but not the grandsons, of a heretic mother, are by law incapable of holding ecclesiastical offices and benefices, and are irregular. They become capable, however, if their parents be converted and return to the Catholic Church, whether they be born before or after such conversion.' On these grounds, therefore, all those of the Anglo-Roman clergy who are converts (including the two Cardinals) are irregular, and their promotion void, unless they were not in heresy while members of the Church of England."

P. 225, insert Note on Section CIX. :—" The still extant answer of Dinoth, Abbot of Bangor-Iscoed, at the Synod of St. Augustine's Oak, in 603, to the claims put forward by the Roman missionaries to the obedience of the British Churches in virtue of the Papal appointment of St. Augustine as Metropolitan, deserves citation: 'Be it known to you without any ambiguity, that we all and singly are obedient to the Pope of Rome and to every true and devout Christian, to love each in his own order with perfect charity, and to aid each one of them to become sons of God in word and deed. And I know not of any other obedience than this due to him whom ye style Pope, nor that he has a claim and right to be Father of fathers. And the aforesaid obedience we are ready to yield at once to him and to every Christian. Further, we are under the jurisdiction of the Bishop of Caerleon-upon-Usk, who is, under God, appointed to oversee us, and to make us keep the spiritual path.'"
—Haddan and Stubbs, "Councils and Ecclesiastical Documents," vol. i. p. 122.

PREFATORY NOTE.

I. THIS book makes no attempt to cover the whole area of the controversy to which it relates. Indeed, as Roman disputants are perpetually shifting their ground, instead of always appealing, as Anglicans do, to the Word of God and the historical witness of the Church Catholic, it would be practically impossible to do that. It is confined strictly to a few practical questions which affect all members of the Church, laity and clergy alike, and omits not only all purely speculative discussions, interesting to theologians alone, but also all matters of which it can fairly be said that Rome and England have any common ground of agreement, however they may differ in details, or in mode of expression.

II. It is defensive, and not aggressive in design, and is therefore not addressed to born Roman Catholics, nor does it undertake to measure their responsibility, or to point out their duty. To their own Master they stand or fall. But it is addressed to those who have seceded, or are tempted to secession, from the Church of England to the Roman communion; that they may see what is the true nature of the accountability with which they are charging themselves in following their own private judgment, rather than the providential order of God; and to remind them of that saying of the Master: " No man, also, having drunk old wine, straightway desireth new; for he saith, The old is better." (St. Luke v. 39.)

R. F. L.

LONDON, ALL SAINTS, 1879.

CONTENTS.

	PAGE		PAGE
Books on the Roman Controversy	9	A Modern Novelty	75
On Change of Religion in General	11	Four Arguments of the Council of Trent for Half-Communion	76
Only Valid Grounds for a Change	12	Refutation of the Plea of Honouring the Sacrament	77
Strong Presumption against Rome at the outset	13	Refutation of the Plea from Ancient Usage	78
Less Likelihood in Rome of knowing God's Will	13	Uncertainty of the Doctrine of Concomitance	79
No Romanism in the Old Creeds	14	Custom cannot supersede Law	81
The Roman Church Uncertain and Unscriptural	15	Half-Communion declared Heretical by Popes	83
Twofold Witness of the Bible and Church History	15	Divine Service in a Dead Language	84
The Roman Church uncertain in Faith	17	Discouragement of the Bible	87
The Roman Church uncertain in Morals	20	Lack of Aids to Biblical Study amongst the Clergy	91
The Roman Church uncertain in Sacraments	22	What the Old Testament says about Itself	91
Uncertainty as to St. Peter	25	What the New Testament says	93
Roman Creature-Worship	28	The Fathers on Bible-reading	94
Roman Inconsistency in the Invocation of Saints	35	Indulgences	97
Roman Image-Worship	36	What Indulgences used to be	98
Proof that Roman Image-Worship is Idolatrous	39	The Roman Doctrine of Indulgences	101
The Fathers on Image-Worship	42	Novelty of this Doctrine	102
Relics	49	Indulgences destroy Devotion	103
The Blessed Virgin more Worshipped than the Father or Christ	51	Their Inconsistency with Scripture	103
Quotations from Liguori's "Glories of Mary"	55	Their Mischievousness, even if Valid	104
The Mass converted into Worship of the Blessed Virgin	56	Roman View of Purgatory contradicts Scripture	105
What this Innovation amounts to	59	And Contradicts other Roman Doctrine	106
What Scripture tells us of the Blessed Virgin	60	The Mass Traffic	108
Examination of the Texts	62	Uncertainty of the Mass Traffic	110
The Evidence of the Fathers as to the Blessed Virgin	66	Necessary Result of the System	111
Roman Arguments for Mariolatry	71	Marriage Dispensations	112
Denial of the Chalice to the Laity	74	Roman Untrustworthiness	113
		Proofs of the Charge	115
		Falsification of the Fathers	118
		Forged Greek Catena	120
		Faith not to be kept with Heretics	120

CONTENTS.

	PAGE
Roman Divines and Controversialists	122
Stifling Intellect and Conscience	127
Private Judgment	129
Cruelty and Intolerance	130
Superstition	135
Cultus of the Sacred Heart	136
Amulets and Charms	138
Roman Penances	142
Contradictions of Ancient Theory and Practice	144
Moral Failure of Roman Catholicism	145
Roman Arguments in Defence	147
Replies: The Church subordinate to Christ's written Word	148
No Promise of Ecclesiastical Infallibility	148
Disproof from the Jewish Church	150
The Roman Church not the whole Church	150
Present Weakness of the Eastern Church no Disproof	153
The "Privilege of Peter" in the New Testament	153
What the "Privilege of Peter" really was	156
Civil Origin of Roman Primacy	157
Disproofs of Papal Infallibility	160
Papal Infallibility Useless in the Past	163
Breaks-down of Infallibility	165
Papal Infallibility no help in the Future	168
Questions raised by the Infallibility Dogma itself	169
Dilemma of the Dogma	171
Development	171
The Notes of the Church: Is the Roman Church One?	172
The Great Schism	177
Further Disunion in the Roman Church	178
Two Distinct Religions in the Roman Church	179
No Identity of Belief in Rome	180

	PAGE
Maximizers and Minimizers	182
Other Points of Disagreement	183
Is the Roman Church Holy?	184
Nature of Proofs tendered	184
The Catalogue of Canonized Popes	185
The Roman Theory of Holiness	186
Liguorianism fatal to Holiness of Teaching	187
Wickedness of the Local Church of Rome	188
Close of the Fifteenth Century	191
Documents of the Reformation Era	191
Present Condition of the Roman Clergy	193
Is the Church of Rome Catholic?	194
Uncatholicity of the Roman Spirit	196
Is the Church of Rome now Apostolic?	198
The Succession in the Roman See Long Broken	199
The Plea of Ignorance not adducible	202
Jurisdiction and Mission	204
Bishops Excommunicated by Rome presided over Great Councils	206
Claim as Heir to St. Peter	207
Claim as Patriarch of the West	207
Claim from Conversion	208
St. Gregory the Great's own Action	210
Claim from Subsequent Voluntary Cession	210
The Anglo-Roman Hierarchy Schismatic	211
Further Proof of Uncanonical Character	215
The Historical Truth as to Papal Jurisdiction	215
The Argument as to the "Safer Way"	222
Conclusion	223

BOOKS ON THE ROMAN CONTROVERSY.

BOSSUET	"Defensio Declarationis Cler Gallicani."
PALMER	"Letters in Controversy with Wiseman."
PALMER	"Episcopacy of British Churches Vindicated."
FULLWOOD	"Roma Ruit."
PUSEY	"Truth and Office of the English Church."
PUSEY	"Is Healthful Reunion Impossible?"
COURAYER	"Validity of English Ordinations."
LEE	"Validity of Holy Orders in Church of England."
BAILEY	"Defensio Ordinum Ecclesiæ Anglicanæ."
BAILEY	"Jurisdiction and Mission of the Anglican Episcopate."
CHURTON	"Defence of English Ordinal."
SCUDAMORE	"England and Rome."
SCUDAMORE	"Letters to a Seceder."
PHILLPOTTS	"Letters to Charles Butler."
ROBINS	"Whole Evidence against the Claims of the Roman Church."
GLADSTONE	"Rome and the Newest Fashions in Religion."
JANUS	"The Pope and the Council."
QUIRINUS	"Letters from Rome on the Council."
POMPONIO LETO	"Eight Months at Rome during Vatican Council."
JENKINS	"Privilege of Peter."
HUSSEY	"Rise of the Papal Power."
ROBERTSON	"Lectures on Growth of the Papal Power."
GRATRY	"Lettres à Mgr. Déchamps."
RENOUF	"Condemnation of Pope Honorius."

RENOUF	"Case of Pope Honorius Reconsidered."
WILLIS	"Pope Honorius and the New Roman Dogma."
LORD LINDSAY	"Œcumenicity in Relation to the Church of England."
MOZLEY	"Essay on Development."
WORDSWORTH	"Letters on the Church of Rome."
MEYRICK	"Liguori's Moral Theology Discussed."
NICHOLSON	"The Sacred Heart, Letters to Cardinal Manning."
EWER	"Catholicity in its Relationship to Protestantism and Romanism."
PAUL PARFAIT	"L'Arsenal de la Dévotion: Notes pour servir à l'Histoire des Superstitions."
PAUL PARFAIT	"Le Dossier des Pèlerinages."
PAUL PARFAIT	"La Foire aux Reliques."
BURGON	"Letters from Rome."
GIBBINGS	"Taxes of the Apostolic Penitentiary."
ENDELL TYLER	"Primitive Worship."
ENDELL TYLER	"Image Worship."
ENDELL TYLER	"Worship of the Virgin Mary."
CLAY	"The Virgin Mary and the Traditions of Painters."
CARTWRIGHT	"The Jesuits."
VÉRON	"Rule of the Catholic Faith." Translated by Waterworth.
MAHAN	"The Exercise of Faith."
Church Quarterly Review	Articles on: "Legal Evidence of Scripture on Petrine Claims," April, 1878; "Dogmatic Position of Church of England," July, 1878; "Further Evidence on Petrine Claims," October, 1878; "The Petrine Claims at the Bar of History," April, 1879; "Lack of Prescription for the Petrine Claims," January, 1880.
Contemporary Review	"Ultramontane Popular Literature." January, 1876.

PLAIN REASONS
AGAINST JOINING THE CHURCH OF ROME.

On Change of Religion in General.

I. To change one's religion, or even one's communion, is a very serious and solemn, nay, a very awful, step to take, whatever that religion may be. On the face of things, it at least looks like revolt against God's will, since we were born and reared in our first creed without any act or choice of our own, and just as He was pleased to ordain for us. Nothing, therefore, can really justify a change of religion except a reasonable belief, based on sufficient evidence, that we shall be certainly *obeying God's will better* than formerly, and that by *knowing more truth* about Him and His laws than we did before. If, for some reason or other, a man found that he could not make a living in England, because his trade had fallen off, or there were too many hands engaged in it, he would probably cast about to see if he could better himself by emigration. He would be a very foolish person, however, if he were to break up his old home, and put himself to all the great cost, inconvenience, and delay of a long voyage, and subsequent settling-down in an unknown country, on the mere *chance* that he might do better in Australia, or

Colorado, or Brazil. He would be bound to inquire about a great many things first, such as whether there were any demand there for his kind of work, whether the climate would suit his constitution, what the rate of wages, and the cost of provisions and other necessaries, might be, whether the laws of the government were such as could be trusted to protect his life and property. It has very often happened to unfortunate emigrants to be lured to ruin and death, by trusting, without examination, to the golden pictures of interested emigration agents; yet, on the whole, some pains to inquire into such important details are usually taken by intending voyagers. But the reverse is the case too often in the far more weighty concern of changing one's religion, which is far too rarely the result of careful thought, devout prayer, and serious inquiry.

Only Valid Grounds for a Change.

II. Whenever any one, therefore, is solicited by others, or inclined for himself, to leave the Church of England for the Church of Rome, he is bound first, as his plain duty towards Almighty God, Who placed him where he now is, and to his own conscience, to ask these questions before deciding to make the change:—

1. Shall I know more about God's will and Word than I now do?
2. Shall I be more likely to obey that will as He has been pleased to declare it?
3. Shall I have a surer warrant than now that I shall have access to those means of grace which God has ordained for the spiritual profit of His people?

These are the really cardinal points in the inquiry; for the question is not one of *liking*, but of *duty*. All appeal to any matters besides, however they may strike our taste, our imagination, or our fancy, is out of court. For example, it is of no use to employ the greatly *superior numbers* of Roman Catholics as an argument, for Buddhists are twice as numerous, and some centuries older. And we have to remember that our responsibility for evils in a communion which we choose for ourselves differs both in kind and degree from that for evils in one where God has placed us.

Strong Presumption against Rome at the Outset.

III. We are met, at the very outset of the inquiry, by a very remarkable fact. It is not disputed by the Roman Catholic Church—nay, it is affirmed as plainly as by the Church of England—that the chief source of all our knowledge, as Christians, of the nature and will of Almighty God, is His written revelation in the Holy Scriptures of the Old and New Testament, which, as the Vatican Council decrees, are " held as sacred and canonical, not because they have been approved by the Church's authority, but because, having been written by the inspiration of the Holy Ghost, they have God for their author, and have been delivered as such to the Church herself." (Sess. iii. cap. 2.) Nevertheless, the fixed policy of the Roman Church, for some centuries, has been to *forbid* the study of the Scriptures in the vulgar tongue by the *laity* wherever such forbidding could be fully enforced, and to restrict it seriously in all other places (see below, sect. XXXV.); while there has been little or no *encouragement* to the *clergy* to study them in any language, so that Roman Catholic books of Biblical literature, for a century and a half past, have been scanty, meagre, and unimportant, nor are there a dozen at this moment in English deserving of attention.

Less Likelihood in Rome of knowing God's Will.

IV. At once, then, it is plain that a Roman Catholic is *less* likely than an English Churchman to know God's will and word, so far as they are set down in the Bible.

A Roman Catholic layman by birth has for the most part not read the Bible at all; if he be an Italian, a Spaniard, a Belgian, a Portuguese, or a Frenchman, all but certainly he knows nothing whatever about it; and a Roman Catholic clergyman, out of Germany, has few helps to Biblical study put into his hands, because relatively little of the sort of late is by Roman Catholic pens, so that he is not able to make amends to his flock for their lack of familiarity with the Divine records. And the necessary presumption from these facts is that the Roman Church is *afraid of being brought to the test of the Bible;* for if there were such a clear general agreement between her system and its teachings as to make it plainly confirm her special tenets and practices, it would be her interest to promote its study everywhere, as the most indisputable testimony in her favour. A man who refuses to bring his title-deeds into court, damages his own claims thereby more than his opponent can do.

No Romanism in the Old Creeds.

V. So far as the chief facts and doctrines of the Christian religion have been collected and condensed into brief and popular forms for the benefit of the Christian flock, as being what must be held in order to salvation, they are embodied in the Three Creeds, the Apostles', the Nicene, and the Athanasian. As all these are held, taught, and publicly used by the Church of England, with the advantage of being in the vulgar tongue, and not in a dead language, there is nothing to be got by way of additional religious knowledge on these heads—the only ones necessary to salvation—by joining the Roman Church; for the fourth creed (that of Pius IV.) which she has added, gives no further information on these main truths, but merely on certain comparatively minor points, as is proved by the fact that all Christendom was able to do quite well without it till so recent a date as 1564, nor is it, even now, propounded to ordinary lay Roman Catholics for reception. And it is very noticeable that not one of the special doctrines which distinguish the Church of Rome from the Church of England (and in particular, no hint, however faint, of Papal authority, though a *fundamental* tenet in Roman teaching)[1] can be found in these three old creeds, or in any ancient gloss upon them, though they were intended to contain all that is necessary to be held and believed by ordinary Christians.

The Roman Church Uncertain and Unscriptural.

VI. The two great indictments against the Church of Rome are (1) that she has only *uncertainty* to offer her followers, instead of certain truth, in faith, morals, and sacraments; and (2) that many important parts of her system are in *direct contradiction to the revealed will of God.*

That she has nevertheless held steadily in the main to the great saving truths of the Gospel is a most comforting and hopeful fact; but in the Church of England all truth which the Roman Church holds is held and taught, while the errors which too often deform and disguise that truth are absent.

As the favourite boast of Roman controversialists is that they alone have religious *certainty* to offer, it is necessary to show first of all why this is conspicuously not the case; why, in fact, there is actually *less* religious certainty in Rome than in any other Christian Church.

Twofold Witness of the Bible and Church History.

VII. The Christian religion, as a Divine revelation, came perfect from God's hands, and (as the Vatican decrees themselves declare, Sess. iii. cap. 4) is not like a human science, such as medicine or mechanics, which can be improved on and altered by man's skill. It was, as the

---

[1] "Moreover, we declare, affirm, and define that every human creature is subject to the Roman Pontiff, and we pronounce this to be altogether necessary for salvation." Boniface VIII., Bull, "Unam Sanctam."

Apostle says: "*once for all* (Greek, ἅπαξ) delivered to the saints" (St. Jude 3), and it may not be changed even by an angel from heaven (Galatians i. 8). There are two trustworthy witnesses which tell us what *is* the Christian religion: the Bible, and Church history. The Bible gives us the first inspired statement of the facts; Church history tells us how those facts were understood by the earliest Christians, who were taught by the Apostles and by men who knew the Apostles. And because the Church is Christ's body, having an unbroken supernatural life, the teaching of great Christian writers fifteen hundred years ago is as much part of the *living voice* of that Church as anything spoken in our own day; just as with us in civil affairs, all unrepealed statutes and unreversed judicial decisions in leading cases, however old, are as much part of the living voice of English law as any recent Act or judgment of the Courts. Whenever, then, we hold any doctrine which is found alike in the Bible and in the teaching of the Christian Church ever since, we can be quite *certain* that here is an integral piece of the true original Christian religion.[1] But if we cannot find it in the Bible at all, nor in Church history for a very long time, then the evidence is all against it, and there is very great unlikelihood of its being part of the Gospel revelation.

For the broad rule is that, while the *antiquity* of a doctrine does not prove its *truth*, since it may be a mere survival from one of the early heretical sects; yet its *novelty* proves its *falsehood*, as not being part of the original and unchangeable revelation of God. When we can lay our finger on any particular tenet or practice, and say, "Up to such and such a date this was unknown to Christians, and did not come in till afterwards," we have disproved its claim to be part of the primitive Faith, just as we should disprove the genuineness of a panel

---

[1] Véron, "Rule of the Catholic Faith." See below, Sect. CI.

picture declared to be three or four hundred years old, if we showed it to be painted on mahogany, a wood which did not come into practical use till about 1720.

The Roman Church uncertain in Faith.

VIII. But in the modern Roman Church these two corroborating witnesses, the Bible and history, have both been set aside, and it is not only practically taught that the "living voice of the Church"—meaning thereby merely the ecclesiastical authorities *for the time being*—may at any time modify or alter the old belief, just as a Parliament of Queen Victoria may repeal any statute of an earlier reign, but that the Pope alone, *without the consent of the Church*, as the Vatican decrees lay down (Sess. iv. cap. 4), can decide infallibly on all matters of faith or morals. So the *faith* of Roman Catholics depends now on the weakness or caprice of a single man, who may be himself unsound in the faith, wicked, or mad, as several Popes have been. Pius IX., on his own responsibility and authority, did add, in 1854, a new article to the Roman Catholic creed, that of the Immaculate Conception of the Blessed Virgin, a doctrine not only undiscoverable in the Bible or in any ancient Christian writer, but implicitly contradicted by St. Augustine, explicitly denied by St. Bernard (commonly called "the last of the Fathers"), and by the greatest of all Roman Catholic divines, St. Thomas Aquinas, and openly disputed as false by orthodox Roman Catholics for many centuries[1]; so, therefore,

[1] "Mary, sprung from Adam, died because of sin; Adam died because of sin; and the Flesh of the Lord, sprung from Mary, died to blot out sin."—St. Augustine, Enarr. in Psalm xxxiv. 3.

"Where will be the peculiar privilege of the Lord's Mother, who is held to be the only one rejoicing in the gift of progeny and in virginity of person, if you grant the same to her own mother? This is not to honour the Virgin, but to detract from her honour. . . . How can that conception be alleged as holy which is not of the Holy Ghost,—that I may not have to say, which *is* of sin—or be accounted as a festival when it is not holy? The glorious Virgin will gladly go without this distinction, whereby either sin will seem

not lawful for any Roman Catholic to hold or teach, unless he reject this clause of the creed of Pope Pius IV. published by the Council of Trent: " Neither will I ever take or interpret the Scriptures otherwise than according to the *unanimous consent* of the Fathers." Another Pope may invent some other new tenet, and declare it part of the Gospel; or may deny, and order others to deny, some ancient and universally received Christian doctrine. In fact, so perfect and entire is the Christian creed, that it is scarcely possible to *add* anything to it in one direction without *taking from* it in another, as this very doctrine of the Immaculate Conception shows; for it takes away from the Lord Jesus Christ that peculiar attribute assigned to Him by Holy Writ, of being *alone* without sin (2 Cor. v. 21; Heb. iv. 15, vii. 26; 1 St. Peter ii. 22; 1 St. John iii. 5). And thus no Roman Catholic can any longer tell what his religion may be at any future time.[1] They try to escape from this terrible difficulty by saying that it is only when the Pope speaks in a certain formal way, called *ex cathedrâ*, that he is infallible, and that a miracle then prevents him from going wrong, but that at all other

to be honoured, or a false holiness alleged."—(St. Bernard, "Letter clxxiv. to the Canons of Lyons on the New Feast of the Conception of the B.V.M.")

" The Blessed Virgin was not sanctified till she had been born from the womb. . . . and she could not be cleansed from original sin while she was yet in the act of her origin, and still in her mother's womb. . . . She was sanctified in the womb from original sin, so far as personal defilement, but not set free from the guilt to which all nature is liable."—("St. Thomas Aquinas, Summa," III. xxvii. 1.) And see below, sec. LXXIX.

[1] Here is a case in point. In 1687, Pope Innocent XI. condemned as heretical and otherwise erroneous sixty-eight propositions in the writings of Michael de Molinos, teaching the doctrine known as Quietism. But Pius IX. beatified, in 1864, Margaret Mary Alacoque, who had imbibed Quietist opinions, and reproduced the teaching of Molinos, not merely in substance, but well-nigh verbally, as regards propositions 1, 2, 4, 5, 20, 21, 25, 43, 61, and 62, in her " La Dévotion au Cœur de Jésus," published in 1698. There is thus a direct conflict of infallibility as to Quietist doctrines.

times he is liable to err. Yet as no way is provided for knowing when he *does* speak *ex cathedrâ* (unless, perhaps, his saying so himself), all Roman Catholics are reduced to *guess-work*, as to what is or is not to be held or believed; and besides, the enormous powers now lodged in the Pope's hands, and the vast number of those who are pledged to obey him, whatever he does, enable him to force almost any teaching he pleases, right or wrong, on all Roman Catholic bishops, under pain of being deposed for refusal. And they in turn can put pressure in the same way on all their clergy, so that any false doctrine put out by some bad or ignorant Pope might be thrust into every Roman Catholic pulpit in the world, and be given a monopoly there. So there is no longer any security or certainty for *faith* in the Roman Church, especially as any attempt to remonstrate, or to resist any Papal utterance (even if afterwards proved to have been heterodox), would be summarily put down as rebellion, if not as blasphemy.

Nor is this the mere extravagant cavil of an opponent. It is a case substantially contemplated and admitted by the Roman Canon Law itself, in one of its most arrogant claims for the Papacy; thus: "If the Pope, neglectful of his own and his brethren's salvation, be found useless and remiss in his duty, and, furthermore, keeping silence from good (a thing which is very hurtful to himself and others), and, nevertheless, leads countless people in troops to hell along with himself—hell's chief bond-slave —to be beaten with him for ever with many stripes: let no mortal presume to judge him, since he who is to judge all men is himself to be judged by none, *unless he be found deviating from the faith*."—(" Decret." I. xl. 6.)

The Roman Church uncertain in Morals.

IX. Again, one great use of religion—in one sense the very greatest use—is to guide and govern man's *conduct* and *morals*. It is of the utmost importance, seeing how man's own standard of right and wrong shifts and wavers, according to the fashion of the day,—as, for example, in the last century, drunkenness was popularly thought no disgrace,—that the Church should have a fixed and certain rule of morals, and that rule as pure and lofty as in God's own Word. Yet the Roman Church not only has got no such standard now, but has actually set up one which is lower and baser, and more uncertain by far, than the popular one of ordinary folk who make no pretence to be religious. It has come about in this way. Partly in order to make religion a very easy thing, so as to prevent men from shaking it off altogether; but partly also to provide excuses for many evil things constantly said and done to promote the interests of Romanism itself, a system has been steadily built up, called *Casuistry*, for dealing with separate *cases* of sins which, at any rate, seem to be condemned by broad, general laws of God. And this casuistry is now governed by a principle called *Probabilism;* the simple meaning of which is this: that if something be plainly forbidden by God's law of morals, and you have a mind to do it, you *may* do it in the teeth, not only of the Bible, but of most of the chief writers on morals, provided you can get an opinion of one casuistical writer in your favour, even though it be plainly weaker and *less probable* than that of those who bid you obey God's law. It is just as if a man could claim acquittal of any crime he had committed, though forbidden by the laws of Great Britain, and punished scores of times over by the courts of justice, if he could plead that he had got an opinion from some tenth-rate barrister that there was no wrong in doing it.[1] If, as a

---

[1] This rather understates the matter. A *learned* person may be *his own* guide, provided he have thought the question out diligently; one of the *general public* is at liberty to follow a single author of exceptional superiority, even though contradicting what is usually held; but a person *unversed in letters* may adopt the opinion of *anyone* whom *he* thinks possessed of learning and insight. So the rule is laid down by F. Gury, "Compend. Theol. Moral.," vol. i. p. 39. concl. 8. A *precisely similar* casuistry amongst the Jews is condemned by Our Lord (St. Matt. xii. 1-15; xv. 1-12; xxiii. 16-24; St. Luke xiii. 14-18).

matter of fact, a high line were taken by Roman casuists on moral questions, perhaps no great practical harm would be done by this theory, but there is hardly any sin, however heinous, for which they do not find excuses. And the chief authority on morals now in the Roman Church is Saint Alfonso Liguori, whose teaching all Roman Catholic confessors are now encouraged to follow in the confessional, since he has been raised to the rank of a "Doctor of the Church." As a Saint, according to Roman doctrine, there can be no error in his writings; but as a Doctor, not only is there no error, but his teaching is to guide Bishops and clergy in forming their judgments on difficult cases, and to be a standard whereby they are themselves to be judged (Leo IV., cited by Benedict XIV., "De Canonizatione," IV. xi. 16). Now, he says, for example, (1) that the actual assassins of a man are not equally guilty with their instigator, whom he admits to incur excommunication ("Theol. Moral." iv. 364); (2) that if A murder B, in order that C may be suspected of the murder, and thereby suffer loss of any kind, A is not bound to make C any compensation, unless he be a "worthy" person (iv. 587); (3) that if a clerical adulterer be attacked by the husband, he may lawfully kill the husband, and does not incur "irregularity"[1] thereby, provided his visit was secret, so that he had a reasonable expectation of escaping detection, though, if he have openly braved the danger, he does incur irregularity (iv. 398); (4) that an adulteress may deny her sin on oath, either by saying that she has not broken the marriage tie (since adultery does not void it); or, if she have gone to confession, that she is innocent of the sin, because it has been washed away in confession; or, again, that she has not committed it, *i.e.* so as to be bound to acknowledge it (iv. 162); (5) that a man

---

[1] Disability for clerical office. This is here, no doubt, a question of *fact*, not of morals. But *what* a fact! And Liguori has no words of blame for it.

may swear aloud to any false statement, provided he add some true circumstances in an undertone, unheard by the bystanders (v. 168); (6) that it is lawful to swear to a quibble or to perjure one's self before a judge, if any great loss or inconvenience would follow to a witness from speaking the truth (iv. 151–6); (7) that a nobleman, ashamed to beg or work, may steal to supply his needs if he be poor (iv. 520). Further, Liguori republished as a text-book, and dedicated to Pope Benedict XIV., the "Marrow of Moral Theology," by Busembaum the Jesuit, from which the following maxims are taken: (1) A man in great need may steal what is necessary for the relief of his own want; and what a man may steal for himself, he may also steal for any other very destitute person; (2) anyone trying to prevent such a theft may be lawfully killed by the thief (Tom. iii., lib. iii., par. 1, tract 5, c. 1). Escobar, another famous casuist, lays down that a member of a religious order who lays aside his habit for a *short time*, in order to commit some sin undetected, does not sin heinously, nor incur excommunication ("Theol. Mor." I. xliv. 213). These are only a very few examples out of many, affecting all the moral Commandments. So there is now no *moral* certainty in the Church of Rome.[1]

The Roman Church uncertain in Sacraments.

X. Thirdly, there is the greatest possible doubt as to the validity of every sacramental office or act performed in the Roman Church. Roman controversialists attack the Church of England as having only doubtful Orders and sacraments, but the only plausible reason they offer for this accusation is, that just one document out of a long series which attests the episcopal character of William Barlow, a bishop of Henry VIII.'s time, who had a fourth

---

[1] See below, sec. XCV. Scavini and Gury, the two other chief text-books in use, are just as immoral. And those who wish to see what the practical results are should consult the "Practicæ Resolutiones Lectissimorum Casuum" (Antverpiæ, 1660), of Antoninus Diana, Examiner of Bishops under Urban VIII., Innocent X., and Alexander VII.

share in consecrating Archbishop Parker, is missing;[1] and, therefore, *may* perhaps have never existed. So far as that is concerned, *all* the documents necessary to prove the consecrations of *all* the Bishops of Christendom for the first four hundred years are hopelessly lost, many Roman ones were destroyed in the sack of 1527, and many of the later French ones disappeared in the Revolution; yet no one treats these losses as disproofs. But the uncertainty which hangs over every rite and ceremony in the Roman Church is not one which could be cleared up by finding any papers; it is of the very essence of the whole system, and cannot be set right anyhow. It is due to the doctrine of Intention, peculiar to the Church of Rome, and decreed, under anathema for rejecting it, by the Council of Trent (Sess. vii., Can. xi.), according to which it is necessary that the Bishop or priest who performs any religious ceremony should inwardly mean to do what the Church intends to be done in and by that ceremony. If the minister withhold this inward assent, either from personal unbelief, from ill-will, or any other cause, the act is null and void, and conveys no grace whatever. And so Cardinal Bellarmine, one of the most learned, able, and famous of Roman Catholic divines, says:—" No one can be certain, with the certainty of faith, that he receives a true sacrament, because the sacrament cannot be valid without the intention of the minister, *and no man can see another's intention*" ("Disput. Controv., De Justific." III. viii. 5). What this practically means is

---

[1] So is Bishop Gardiner's record, but *his* rank is never disputed; while out of Cardinal Pole's seven consecrators, four have no records, the consecrators of two more have no records, and there remains only Thirlby to make the succession perfect, who, as being consecrated by Hodgskin, *one of Parker's consecrators*, is the only one of the seven whose papers are all extant. By 25 Henry VIII. c. 20, s. 5 & 6, Cranmer would have incurred the penalties of præmunire had he failed to consecrate Barlow. And had the king wished to prove that his mandate was as good as consecration, he would have taken pains to make it publicly manifest that Barlow had not been given any authority save that of the Crown, instead of leaving it doubtful.

that no Roman Catholic can be sure that he himself has ever been baptized, confirmed, absolved, or given Holy Communion; for even if he be morally certain of the honesty and piety of the bishops and priests who have professed to do these things for him, he has no warrant at all that they have been validly ordained, since the bishop who professed to ordain them may have withheld his intention, or have himself in turn been invalidly consecrated.[1] And indeed, the frequent Roman practice of having but one consecrator of a bishop imports another uncertainty into Roman orders, for Liguori lays down that priests ordained by a bishop who has had but one consecrator are *doubtfully* ordained ("Theol. Mor." VI. ii. 755). Yet again, Romans teach that unless the ordinee also give his *active* assent to the rite, not merely submitting to it passively, far less being reluctant, his ordination is invalid (Togni, "Instruct. pro Sac. Eccl. Minist."). Who is to warrant such assent? And, as in Italy at the Renascence and till after the Reformation, the higher clergy were very widely infidel (see below, note on sec. CII.), as also in France just before the Revolution (Jervis's "Hist. Ch. of France," chap. viii.), while in Spain they were often secretly Jews in religion, only conforming outwardly,[2] there is the most serious possibility, if the doc-

---

[1] It is, however, a tenable opinion in the Roman Church (though less approved than Bellarmine's) that *external* intention to comply with the rubrics of a rite is sufficient without *internal* intention as to the effect of the rite (Drouven, "De Re Sacramentali."). But this does not remove the doubt, since there can be no sufficient proof of even so much. For in 1880 a committee of Cardinals pronounced the marriage of the Prince of Monaco and Lady Mary Hamilton, contracted in 1869, and with issue, null and void, on the ground of lack of inward consent on her part, though her external compliance with the rite was not questioned; and she was re-married to another man. All that Perrone gives in aid, is to say that doubts may arise as to matter and form as well as in respect of Intention (De Sacram. iii.).

[2] Mocatta, "The Jews and the Inquisition"; Graetz, "Geschichte der Juden," x. 100; Kayserling, "Geschichte der Juden in Portugal," p. 291; Llorente, "Hist. Inquis." ii. 8.

trine of Intention be true, that Holy Orders have failed
in all these countries, and therefore that the orders of the
Anglo-Roman bishops and clergy, all derived from these
sources, have failed too; whereas in England there has
never been, even in the laxest times, any such clerical
unbelief prevalent as to import this peril. Thus there is
the greatest uncertainty attaching to all Roman *sacraments*, on the showing of Romans themselves.

Uncertainty as to St. Peter.

XI. This is not all the doubt and uncertainty which
surrounds Roman Catholicism. Its most salient, distinctive, and peculiar doctrine is, that the prime and
essential condition for salvation is to be in communion
with the Pope of Rome, as heir and successor of St.
Peter, first Pope of Rome, and therefore supreme Vicar
of Christ, and Head of the Church on earth. Now this
doctrine is in itself a sufficiently startling variation from
what the New Testament lays down as the one chief
requisite for salvation, namely, belief in the Lord Jesus
Christ, and union with Him (St. John iii. 16, 36; xi. 25;
Acts vi. 31; 1 John v. 12, &c.), not saying one word about
St. Peter in any such connexion. But when we come to
look into the matter more closely, it becomes the merest
heap of guesses. It is little more than a *guess*—though no
doubt one with much in its favour—that St. Peter was ever
at Rome at all; it is only a *guess* that he was ever Bishop
of Rome, and for this there is very little evidence of any
kind;[1] it is only a *guess* that he had the power to appoint
any heir to his special privilege, whatever that was; it
is only a *guess* that he did so appoint the Bishops of
Rome—and for these two guesses not the smallest scrap

---

[1] The *only* ante-Nicene testimony which expressly assigns the See
of Rome to St. Peter is the apocryphal "Clementine Homilies,"
rejected by the Roman Church as a heretical forgery. The first
post-Nicene witness who is quite clear on the subject is Optatus of
Milevi (A.D. 386), and he is contradicted by St. Epiphanius and
Rufinus. See the whole evidence in "The Petrine Claims at the
Bar of History." (*Church Quarterly Review*, April, 1879.)

or tittle of evidence ever has been produced, or can be so much as reasonably supposed ever to have existed; yet, if all these points be not clearly proved by plain and convincing Scriptural and historical evidence, there is no basis whatever for the huge fabric of Papal claims, which is, in truth, the most vague and uncertain of structures. And it is to be added, that the Ultramontane interpretation put on the three great texts in the Gospels which are relied on to support the "Privilege of Peter,"—namely, St. Matt. xvi. 18, that St. Peter is the rock and foundation of the Church; St. Luke xxii. 31, 32, that St. Peter was infallible, and charged with guiding the faith of the other Apostles; and St. John xxi. 15-17, that he was given jurisdiction over the Apostles and the whole Church—is contrary to the "unanimous consent of the Fathers," who agree by a great majority that either Christ Himself, or St. Peter's confession of Christ, is the rock and foundation of the Church (the Council of Trent decrees that the *Nicene Creed* is this foundation);[1] that the words at the Last Supper were spoken in view of St. Peter's coming apostasy, in warning that he would fall below the other Apostles; and that the words spoken at the Sea of Tiberias after the Resurrection were no more than the reinstatement of St. Peter in that Apostolic office from which he had been degraded by his denial of Christ. So, it is not lawful for any Roman Catholic, in the face of the creed of Pope Pius IV., to maintain the Ultramontane view of these three texts. Thus, the following Fathers explain the *rock* to be Christ, or faith in Christ, and not St. Peter: Origen; St. Hilary, Doctor; St. Chrysostom, Doctor; St. Isidore of Pelusium; St. Augustine, Doctor; St. Cyril of Alexandria, Doctor; St. Leo the Great, Pope and Doctor; St. Gregory the Great, Pope and Doctor; Venerable Bede,

---

[1] "The symbol of the Faith . . . the one and firm foundation, against which the gates of hell shall not prevail."—Sess. iii.

Doctor; St. Gregory VII., Pope; while St. Epiphanius, Doctor; St. Basil the Great, St. Ambrose, and St. Jerome, Doctors, take it both ways, leaning, however, more to the view that Christ is the rock. One or two citations will serve as examples : "'And I say unto thee, that thou art Peter, and upon this rock I will build my Church;' that is, upon the rock of his confession" (St. Chrysostom, Hom. 54 in Matt. xxvi. 4). "The Son of God is the rock from which Peter derived his name, and on which He said that He would build His Church" (St. Gregory the Great, "Comm. in Ps. ci. 27"). And the Collect for the Vigil of SS. Peter and Paul in the Roman Missal settles the point for all Roman Catholics : "Grant, we beseech Thee, Almighty God, that Thou wouldst not suffer us, whom Thou hast established *on the rock of the Apostolic Confession*, to be shaken by any disturbances."[1] As to St. Luke xxii. 31, 32, *no Father whatever* explains it in the modern Ultramontane fashion, which is not even found till Cardinal Bellarmine invented it about A.D. 1621.[2] And St. John xxi. 15–17, is explained as the mere restoration of St. Peter to his forfeited rank by St. Gregory Nazianzen, Doctor, St. Ambrose, Doctor, St. Augustine, Doctor, St. Cyril of Alexandria, Doctor. Here is a specimen : "By this triple confession of blessed Peter, his sin, consisting of a triple denial, was done away, and by the words of our Lord, 'Feed my sheep,' a renewal, as it were, of the apostleship already bestowed on him is understood to take place, removing the shame of his

---

[1] Here are some famous Roman Catholic divines who deny expressly or indirectly that St. Peter is the Rock: St. Peter Damiani, B. Albert the Great, Cardinal Hugo of St. Cher, Tostatus, and St. Thomas of Villanova. See them and several more, with full citations, in Denton's "Commentary on the Gospels" for St. Peter's Day. It is only since the Council of Trent that the other view has prevailed.

[2] The germ, however, is in St. Thomas Aquinas (Summa, Sec. Secund. I. 10).

after fall, and taking from him the cowardice of human frailty."—(St. Cyril Alex., "Comm. in St. Johan. xxi.")

Roman Creature-Worship.

XII. There is one thing, however, which *is* certain about the Roman Church, that it directly and plainly contradicts the revealed will of God in several important particulars. Here are some of them.

Throughout the entire *Old* Testament, God Almighty continually reveals and declares Himself as a *jealous* God, one Who will not share a tittle of His rights and glory with another. "I, the Lord thy God, am a jealous God" (Exod. xx. 5). "I am the Lord; that is My name, and My glory will I not give to another, neither My praise to graven images" (Isa. xlii. 8), &c. Throughout the entire *New* Testament, the Lord Jesus Christ declares Himself, and is declared by His Apostles, to be the one, single, and only way to the Father; to be perfect and entire in His human love for man, His intercession, and His answer to prayer: "No man cometh unto the Father, but by Me" (St. John xiv. 6). "If ye shall ask anything in My name, I will do it" (St. John xiv. 14). "Come unto Me, all ye that labour and are heavy laden, and I will give you rest" (St. Matt. xi. 28). "Love one another, as I have loved you." "I am the Good Shepherd, and know My sheep . . . and I lay down my life for the sheep" (St. John x. 14, 15). "Neither is there salvation in any other; for there is none other name under heaven given among men whereby we must be saved" (Acts iv. 12). "There is one mediator between God and man, the Man Christ Jesus, Who gave Himself a ransom for all" (1 Tim. ii. 5, 6). "The love of Christ passeth knowledge" (Eph. iii. 19). "It behoved Him to be made like unto His brethren, that He might be a merciful and faithful High Priest in things pertaining to God, to make reconciliation for the sins of the people" (Heb. ii. 17). "Wherefore He is able also to save them to the uttermost that come unto God by Him, seeing He ever liveth to make intercession for them" (Heb. vii. 25), &c.

We have only four examples in the New Testament of acts of reverence being done to Saints, and in all these cases *they were promptly rejected and forbidden*, showing that they were offensive to the Saints, as savouring of disloyalty to that God Whom they love and serve.

"And as Peter was coming in, Cornelius met him, and fell down at his feet, and worshipped him. But Peter took him up, saying, Stand up, I myself also am a man" (Acts x. 25, 26).

"Then the priest of Jupiter .... would have done sacrifice with the people; which when the Apostles, Barnabas and Paul, heard of, they rent their clothes, and ran in among the people, crying out, and saying, Sirs, why do ye these things? We also are men of like passions with you, and preach unto you that ye should turn from these vanities to serve the living God" (Acts xiv. 13-15).

"And I [John] fell at his feet [the angel's] to worship him. And he said unto me, See thou do it not. I am thy fellow-servant, and of thy brethren that have the testimony of Jesus: worship God" (Rev. xix. 10).

"I fell down to worship before the feet of the angel which showed me these things. Then saith he unto me, See thou do it not, for I am thy fellow-servant ... worship God" (Rev. xxii. 8, 9).[1]

Contrariwise, our Lord Jesus Christ never refused nor blamed an act of worship offered to Himself, thereby showing that there is a fundamental principle involved. (St. Matt. ii. 11; viii. 2; ix. 18; xiv. 33; xv. 25; xvii. 14; xx. 20; xxviii. 9, 17; St. Mark v. 6; St. John ix. 38; Heb. i. 6; Rev. v. 8).[2]

---

[1] It cannot be supposed that Cornelius meant to do *divine* homage to St. Peter, or St. John to the angel, so that the rebukes in these two cases clearly forbid *secondary* worship.

[2] It is also to be added that wherever the phrase "invoke" or

Nevertheless, in direct rebellion against the plain letter and spirit of both the Old and New Testaments, the Roman Church practically compels her children to offer far more prayers to deceased human beings than they address to the Father or to Christ. It is not true, as is often alleged in defence, that the prayers of the departed Saints are asked only in the same sense as those of living ones, with the added thought that they are now more able to pray effectually for us. The petitions are not at all limited to a mere "Pray for us;" but are constantly of exactly the same kind and wording as those addressed to Almighty God, and are offered kneeling, and in the course of Divine Service, which is not how we ever ask the prayers of living friends. A few specimens are here set down from the "Raccolta" (Eng. Transl., Burns & Oates, 1873), a collection of prayers specially indulgenced by the Popes, and therefore of indisputable authority in the Roman Church.[1]

1. "Hail, Queen, Mother of Mercy, our Life, Sweetness, and Hope, all hail! To thee we cry, banished sons of Eve, to thee we sigh, groaning and weeping in this vale of tears. Turn then, O our Advocate, thy merciful eyes to us, and after this our exile, show us Jesus, the blessed fruit of thy womb, O merciful, O loving, O sweet Virgin Mary.

"V. Make me worthy to praise thee, O sacred Virgin.

R. Give me strength against thine enemies."

2. "We fly beneath thy shelter, O holy Mother of God, despise not our petitions in our necessities, and deliver us always from all perils, O glorious and blessed Virgin."

"call upon" in prayer is used in the New Testament, it is *always* of God and Christ, never of any other. These are the texts where it occurs: Acts ii. 21, vii. 59, ix. 14, 21, xxii. 16; Rom. x. 12, 13, 14; 1 Cor. i. 2; 2 Cor. i. 23; 2 Tim. ii. 22; 1 Pet. i. 17. In its secular use it is applied to St. Paul's appeal to Cæsar.

[1] It does not, however, contain nearly all the indulgences. None of the local ones, attached to churches, altars, pilgrimages, &c., of which there are thousands, appear in it.

3. "Heart of Mary, Mother of God . . . worthy of all the veneration of angels and men . . . Heart full of goodness, ever-compassionate towards our sufferings, vouchsafe to thaw our icy hearts . . . In thee let the holy Church find safe shelter; protect it, and be its sweet asylum, its tower of strength . . . Be thou our help in need, our comfort in trouble, our strength in temptation, our refuge in persecution, our aid in all dangers . . ."

4. "Sweet Heart of Mary, be my salvation."

5. "Leave me not, my Mother, in my own hands, or I am lost. Let me but cling to thee. Save me, my Hope; save me from hell."

6. "Michael, glorious prince, chief and champion of the heavenly host . . . vouchsafe to free us all from every evil, who with full confidence have recourse to thee."

7. "Benign Joseph, our guide, protect us and the holy Church."

8. "Guardian of virgins, and holy father Joseph, to whose faithful keeping Christ Jesus, innocence itself, and Mary, Virgin of virgins, were committed, I pray and beseech thee by these two dear pledges, Jesus and Mary, that being preserved from all uncleanness, I may with spotless mind, pure heart, and chaste body, ever most chastely serve Jesus and Mary. Amen."

These are only a few specimens culled out of many, and it is easy to test their true nature by substituting the names of the Father and Christ for those which occur in them; so nothing less can be said than that they encroach sorely on the incommunicable attributes of God. Even if they did not, the whole practice of the Invocation of Saints is founded on pure *guesswork*. Not one syllable can be discovered in the Old or New Testament which gives the least ground or suggestion of it; God has never been pleased to reveal it, nor can the smallest evidence or trace of it be found for nearly four hundred years after Christ. It is at best a mere conjecture that the Saints do know what passes on earth, and can hear and join in the prayers of the faithful.[1] It *may* be so, but God has not chosen to make it known to us, and it is a very perilous thing to fly in the face of His holy Word on the mere chance that a guess of ours may be correct; a guess, too, which, as put in practice, casts a doubt on the perfect sympathy of Christ.

It may, perhaps, be argued that expressions of devotion, even if somewhat unguarded, are not to be rigidly weighed and judged. Some extracts from a formal theological work, Liguori's "Glories of Mary," are therefore added here:—

"Queen, Mother, and Spouse of the King, to her belong dominion and power over all creatures."

"She is Queen of Mercy, as Jesus is King of Justice."

"In the Franciscan chronicles it is narrated that Brother Leo once saw a red ladder, on the top of which was Jesus Christ; and a white one, on the top of which was His most holy Mother, and he saw some who tried to ascend the red ladder, and they mounted a few steps and *fell;* they tried again, and again *fell*. They were then advised to go and try the white ladder, and by that one they *easily ascended*, for our Blessed Lady stretched out her hands and helped them, and so they got safely to heaven."

If this (which Liguori *twice* uses in proof of the tenet it involves) be not blasphemy against the Lord Jesus Christ, and a formal denial of His power to save and His being the way to heaven, there are no such sins possible.

Yet, even before Pius IX. made Liguori a "Doctor of

---

[1] And this is all that Peter Lombard (A.D. 1150) ventures to assert when treating of the doctrine of Invocation. He says: "It is *not incredible* that the souls of the Saints . . . understand what is passing in the outer world." "Sentt." iv. dist. 45. It was thus but a *guess* to the leading Roman theologian only seven centuries ago. And Véron ("Rule of Catholic Faith") denies it to be an article of the Faith, though a probable opinion.

the Church," the Congregation of Rites decreed in 1803 that, "in all the writings of Alfonso de' Liguori there is not one word that can be justly found fault with."

It may be just remarked here, as showing how modern this sort of thing is, that the most popular of all devotions to the Blessed Virgin, the Angelus, does not appear to have been used at all till Pope John XXII. instituted it in 1316; while its latter clause, "Holy Mary, Mother of God, pray for us sinners now and in the hour of our death," cannot be found earlier than 1507,[1] and was first sanctioned for general use by a bull of Pius V., July 7, 1568, while the use of the Ave Maria before sermons is due to St. Vincent Ferrer (1419).

This is quite in accordance with what we should expect, seeing how clear is the evidence of the early Christian Fathers against any practice of invocation of the kind now popular. Here are a few samples :—St. Irenæus (A.D. 180): "As the Church has freely received from the Lord, so does she freely minister, nor does she do anything by *invocation of angels* ... but by directing her prayers clearly, purely, and openly to the Lord, Who made all things, and calling on the name of our Lord Jesus Christ."—("Cont. Hær." ii. 32.)

St. Clement of Alexandria (A.D. 200): "Since there is only one good God, both we ourselves and the angels *supplicate from Him alone.*"—("Stromat." vii. 7.)

Origen (A.D. 230): "Every prayer and supplication, and intercession and thanksgiving, is to be sent up to God, Who is above all, through the High Priest, Who is above all angels, He being Word and God. For it is not reasonable that they who do not understand the knowledge of angels, which is above man's, *should invoke them.* If their knowledge ... *were* understood, this very knowledge

---

[1] Cardinal Baronius alleges that the first part of this addition was made by the Council of Ephesus.—"Ann. Eccl." 431. The devotional use of St. Luke i. 28 and 42 in the West cannot be traced higher than Odo, Bishop of Paris, in 1198, nor in England till 1247.

would not suffer us to dare to pray to any other but to God, the Lord over all, Who is sufficient for all, through our Saviour, the Son of God."—("Cont. Cels." vii.)

"To those who *place their confidence in the Saints*, we fitly produce as an example, 'Cursed is the man which hopeth in man;' and again, 'Do not put your trust in man;' and another, 'It is better to trust in the Lord than in princes.' If it be necessary to put our trust in anyone, let us leave all others, and trust in the Lord."—("Hom. i. in Ezek." xvii.)

St. Athanasius (A.D. 370): "It is written, 'Be my protecting God, my house of refuge and saviour,' and 'The Lord is the refuge of the poor;' and whatever things of the same sort are found in Scripture. But if they say that these things are spoken of the Son, which would perhaps be true, let him confess that *the Saints did not think of calling on a created being to be their helper* and house of refuge."—("Orat. cont. Arianos," i. 62.)

Council of Laodicea (circa A.D. 360)—the same which settled the canon of Scripture—"Christians ought not to forsake the Church of God, and depart and *invoke angels*, and hold meetings, which are forbidden. If anyone, therefore, be found giving himself to this hidden *idolatry*, let him be anathema, because he hath left our Lord Jesus Christ, the Son of God, and hath betaken himself to idolatry."—(Canon xxxv.)

It is true that just after this time we find the first germs of the practice at the close of the fourth century in St. Gregory Nazianzen (A.D. 390) and St. Gregory Nyssen (A.D. 396); but their slight apostrophes are very unlike the newer ones, even if their example could set aside a Divine principle: and yet later, St. Chrysostom (A.D. 407), commenting on Coloss. ii. 18, says that the "voluntary humility and worshipping of angels" there condemned by St. Paul, refers to "such as say that we must not approach God through Christ's mediation, that being too great a thing for us, but through the angels,"—exactly the popular Roman plea.

Roman Inconsistency in the Invocation of Saints.

XIII. Even apart from the theological heresy and rebellion of the practice, as just exemplified, and the absence of any *certainty* of its utility, however modified and purged from these sins; there is another fact which shows the further inconsistency and uncertainty about it. If there be any truth in the doctrine at all, one thing must necessarily follow, that the fittest persons to invoke are the *most eminent* Saints, those of whose holiness and acceptance with God there can be no doubt whatever. But in actual practice this is not the case at all, except as regards the Blessed Virgin and St. Joseph. For example, take the "Raccolta." There is not one indulgenced prayer to the Archangel St. Gabriel, or to any Apostle, except SS. Peter and Paul, not even to St. John, the Beloved Disciple; none to St. Stephen the Protomartyr, nor to St. Mary of Bethany. But there are such prayers to purely minor and wholly insignificant persons, like St. Aloysius Gonzaga, St. Stanislas Kostka, St. Michael de' Santi, and St. Nicholas of Bari, who cannot, on any estimate of their merits, be ranked with the great New Testament worthies, nor even with saints like St. Athanasius or St. Augustine, who are never popularly invoked at all. Often, too, prayers are addressed to persons whose life and acts make it fair to say that if they be so much as just barely saved, it can only be by God's prerogative of mercy, as in the case of Pope Pius V., the ruthless inquisitor, the stirrer-up of war and rebellion, the encourager of Philip II. in his many crimes, including the slaughter of his own son Carlos, the instigator of the Emperor in breaking his treaty with the Turks, on the ground that no faith or oath need be kept with an infidel, the plotter against the life of Queen Elizabeth.[1]

[1] For these acts of Pius V., see his own Bulls, Young's "Life of Aonio Paleario;" Prescott's "Reign of Philip II.," iv. 7, and Lord Acton's letter to the *Times*, Nov. 27, 1874.

And sometimes, at least, they are addressed to persons who there is no reason to suppose ever existed at all; such as St. Filumena, a virgin martyr, never heard of till 1802, and invented them on the faith of a fragmentary inscription which was declared on the faith of somebody's dream, to prove her existence.[1] There is thus a further uncertainty as to whether many of the personages invoked are real Saints,[2] and the practice is shown to be a mere restless love of novelty and fashion, not a matter of true and fixed religious principle.[3]

Roman Image-Worship.

XIV. Next, let us take the worship of images and pictures. Here it must first be said (*a*) that the Roman Church in terms denies that any such act as can be strictly called *worship* is done to pictures and images, even by the most ignorant, since no one believes that these representations can see, hear, or help of themselves; (*b*) that there is no question as to the lawfulness of making some such images and representations, if not intended to receive homage, as even the Jews had the brazen serpent,[4] and the figures of the cherubim in the Holy

---

[1] The value of this dream is easily tested. It was revealed therein that "Filumena" is "filia luminis," Latin for "daughter of light" (an impossible formation), whereas it is a very common Greek name (Φιλουμίνη), meaning "Beloved."

[2] Véron ("Rule of Catholic Faith") says that it is not matter of Faith that *any* person, not named as a Saint in the Bible, is a Saint at all, or capable of being invoked. A curious instance has been adduced by Professor Max Müller ("Chips from a German Workshop," iv. 174-187), that the legend of Saints Barlaam and Josaphat ("Mart. Rom.," Nov. 27), is the story of Buddha in a Christian dress.

[3] The writer remembers seeing, a few years ago, in the churches of several Belgian towns the older saints and images practically deserted in favour of some brand-new statues of John Berchmans, a young Jesuit then recently beatified, round which the worshippers crowded, as the last new thing out.

[4] But Hezekiah broke the serpent *because* incense was burnt before it, 2 Kings xviii. 4. The Abbé Glaire, in his "Dict. Eccles.," *s.v.* *Nehostan*, omits to mention this inconvenient fact.

of Holies, where, however, only one man ever saw them, and that only once a year; and the early Christians set up pictures of our Lord in the catacombs, still to be seen there. But, on the other hand, there is a very suspicious fact which meets us at the outset of the inquiry as to the actual Roman practice, as distinguished from any finespun theories in books, namely, that many Roman Catechisms omit the Second Commandment, while *no* Roman catechism teaches that there is either danger or sin in any making or using of images for religious honour, short of actual paganism. The point is not, as Roman controversialists are apt to put it, whether their way of dividing the Decalogue, which makes the First and Second Commandment (as the English Prayer-book and Catechism have them) one precept, and then restores the number ten by making the Tenth Commandment into two (a plan which seems only to repeat the Seventh Commandment, to make St. Matt. v. 28 superfluous, and is not followed by the Vulgate or Douai in Deut. v. 21, where the word "covet" is not repeated in the Tenth Commandment as there given), be a better or a worse way than the Anglican; nor whether the whole text of the commandment against image-worship be not found unmutilated in Roman Catholic Bibles; but whether in practice one Roman Catholic in a million ever knows that image worship can be abused or sinful without virtual apostasy from Christianity.[1] The Shorter Lutheran

---

[1] Even in Schneider's "Manuale Clericorum," a popular Jesuit book in Latin, for the use of students for the *priesthood* (Ratisbon, Pustet, 1868), where there is a very full set of questions for examination of conscience on the Decalogue, extending over pp. 403-411, there is no hint whatever at the Second Commandment, which is entirely suppressed; but the first question under the First Commandment is, "Has he believed everything which the Holy Roman Church believes, or held an opinion contrary to the Roman faith in any matter?" Bellarmine's Catechism, the most authoritative of all, as approved by two Papal Briefs, cuts out the Second Commandment entirely. See M'Caul, "Why does the Church of

Catechism cuts down the First and Second Commandments just in the same way as many Roman ones do; but, then, on the one hand, Lutherans have free access to the Bible in their own language, and, on the other, nothing of the nature of image-worship has ever been practised amongst them.[1]

Intelligent and shrewd heathens, when arguing in favour of idols, say exactly what Roman Catholic controversialists do in defence of their practice, namely, that they do not believe in any sentient power as residing in the mere stone, wood, or metal, of which their idols are made, but regard them as representing visibly certain attributes of Deity, to bring them home to the minds of worshippers; and that homage addressed to these idols on that ground is acceptable to the unseen spiritual Powers, who will listen to and answer prayers so made indirectly to themselves; and, in fact, Athenagoras, a Christian apologist, who lived in the second century (A.D. 177), tells us that such was the defence set up by the Roman pagans of that time on behalf of idolatry, and adds that they appealed to the miracles and cures wrought by such images as proofs of their truth ("Apol." xviii. xxvi.).

Rome hide the Second Commandment from the People?" wherein he cites twenty-nine Catechisms, large and small, used in Italy, France, Belgium, Austria, Bavaria, Silesia, Poland, Spain, Portugal, England, and Ireland, in twenty-seven of which the Second Commandment is entirely omitted, and mutilated in the other two.

[1] It is worth remarking that Roman Catholics, who translate the passage in Exod xx. 5, "Thou shalt not *adore* them," sometimes complain that the Authorized Version, "Thou shalt not *bow down to them*," is a misleading rendering, and goes too far. As a fact, the Hebrew verb *shachah*, here found, strictly means to *bow* or prostrate one's self, and only secondarily comes to mean worship or adoration, and is translated *bowed down* in the Douai Version of Genesis xlii. 6, speaking of Joseph's brethren's obeisance towards him.

Proof that Roman Image-Worship is Idolatrous.

XV. If it be true, as Roman controversialists often allege in this country, that no more is intended by their use of images than the Church of England intends by allowing the erection of religious pictures, windows, and sculptures, commemorating events of the Gospel, in churches, or even than the loving use of the portraits of dear friends and kindred; then the practice, however dangerously misleading it may sometimes have been, is clear from any just charge of idolatry. But it is not true. And the proofs to the contrary are to be found, not in some remote and barbarous heathen country, amongst an ignorant flock of newly-converted pagans, who have not yet quite shaken off their early habits, but in Rome itself, the very centre of Latin Christendom.

Thus (*a*), at the Church of Sta. Maria del Divino Amore, near the Piazza Borghese, there is a yearly festival, not of the saint, nor yet of the church, but of the *sacred image* there preserved; (*b*) in the Church of St. Agostino there is an alleged miraculous image of the B. V. M. and Child, to which Pius VII. annexed an indulgence of 100 days for every one devoutly kissing its feet; (*c*) the Bambino, or image of the Infant Saviour, in the church of the Ara Cœli, is regarded as a wonder-worker of exceptional efficacy; and (*d*) there is another miraculous picture of B. V. M. in Sta. Maria in Cosmedin. Now, when a special picture or image is no longer regarded as a mere historical memorial, on an exact level of value for that purpose with every other one representing the same person or event, but as endued with supernatural powers, and to be reverenced accordingly, that is idolatry in the strictest sense; for, as explained above, no heathen, however brutishly degraded, supposes his idols to be in themselves sentient and divine, but merely attributes to them just the powers which the Roman authorities publicly and officially ascribe to these and many other so-called miraculous images.[1] And so we come to superstition like that of Louis XI., who prayed to images of the Virgin of Embrun and the Virgin of Clery as two distinct, and to some extent rival, persons; a kind of competition we have seen revived in our own day between the Virgins of Lourdes and of La Salette, where acute jealousy exists between the custodians of the rival springs. "It is all up with Our Lady of La Salette," complained a French partisan of that shrine not long ago, in language whose very coarseness is instructive, "Our Lady of Lourdes has cut her out."[2]

And it is further necessary to add in final disproof of the common Roman denial (as, for instance, in Cardinal Wiseman's "Lectures on the Catholic Church," xiii.), that any real worship is paid to images, and that they are merely regarded as edifying memorials, the following quotations from the greatest of all Roman theological works, the "Summa" of St. Thomas Aquinas, to which the present Pope Leo XIII., in a recent encyclical, has ordered the teaching of the schools of religious philosophy to be strictly conformed:—

"The same reverence should be displayed towards an image of Christ and towards Christ Himself, and seeing that Christ is adored with the adoration of *latria*, (*i.e.* supreme religious worship) it follows that His image

---

[1] It is not open to Roman Catholics to say that this is a mere "pious opinion," and not binding; for Pius VI. by the Bull "Auctorem Fidei" in 1794, condemned the proposition that particular devotion to a special image is blameworthy, as "rash, pernicious, injurious to the pious and wonted custom of the Church, and to the providential order of God" in such matters. And the public crowning of certain images by Papal authority is decisive.

[2] "C'en est fait de Notre Dame de La Salette; Notre Dame de Lourdes l'a flanquée." It may be added here that in Chartres Cathedral there are two rival Virgins, Our Lady of the Pillar, in the nave, Our Lady of the Crypt, underground, one black, the other white, having separate confraternities and clients.

is to be adored with the adoration of *latria*."¹—("Summa" II. xxv. 3.)

"The Cross is adored with the same adoration as Christ, that is, with the adoration of *latria*, and for that reason we address and supplicate the Cross *just as we do the Crucified Himself.*"—(III. xxv. 4.)²

"In that images of the Saints denote their excellence, they may be, and ought to be, adored with a certain inferior adoration or *dulia*,³ like the Saints themselves whom they represent, though not with that absolute kind which is offered to their prototypes, but relative only."— ("Summa, Sec. Secund." xciv. 2.)

Not only is St. Thomas Aquinas a Doctor of the Roman Church, and therefore an authority which may not be challenged, but the collect for his festival in the Breviary and Missal contains this petition,—" Grant to us, we beseech Thee, to embrace with our understanding what he taught, and to fulfil by our imitation what he did." The excuses and explanations offered by Roman Catholic controversialists to allay objections to the system are therefore presumably insincere, and against the

---

[1] It is necessary to bear clearly in mind that *latria* is the name for the very highest kind of worship, *due to God only*. So Bellarmine : " The first [species of excellence] is the Divine and Infinite excellence, to which corresponds the first species of worship, which is called by theologians *Latria.*"—" De Sanct. Beatitudine."

[2] "The Legate's Cross shall be on the right, because *latria* is due to it" (Pontificale Roman. " Ordo ad Recip. process. Imperatorem "). For the uncertainty of Roman doctrine on this head see Cardinal Newman, " Via Media," (Vol. II., pp. 118 and 419, ed. 1877).

[3] This distinction between *latria* and *dulia* (both of them Greek words) has no warrant from the Greek Testament, which has the verb *douleuo* (δουλεύω), " to serve," in the following texts, where *God's* service is meant : " Ye cannot *serve* God and mammon " (St. Matt. vi. 24 ; St. Luke xvi. 13) ; " *Serving* the Lord with all humility " (Acts xx. 19); " He that in these things *serveth* Christ " (Rom. xiv.); " Turned to God from idols to *serve* the living God " (1 Thess. i. 9), &c. The third passage above is not in all editions of St. Thomas.

received doctrine and practice of their Church. And even if they were true, they would still leave the modified image-worship perilously near being under the Prophet's ban: "What profiteth the graven image that the maker thereof hath graven it? the molten image, and a teacher of lies, that the maker of his work trusteth therein, to make dumb idols? *Woe unto him that saith to the wood, Awake; to the dumb stone, Arise, it shall teach!*" (Habakkuk ii. 19.) And as regards allowing the images of saints the inferior worship called *dulia* (which strictly means *slavery*, the service due from a slave to his owner),—while that of *hyper-dulia*, or *extra-slavery*, is to be paid to the Blessed Virgin and her images,—it is to be remarked that this too is expressly condemned in the Decalogue, which not merely says of images, "Thou shalt not *bow down* to them," but adds, "nor *serve* them," as even the Douai Bible reads.

The Fathers on Image-Worship.

XVI. And if we inquire into the "unanimous consent of the Fathers" as to images, we find them expressly condemned by the following, without mentioning those whose entire silence implies their ignorance of any such use. St. Irenæus (A.D. 120-190) mentions the use of images of Christ, with religious honour done to them, as a peculiarity of the Carpocratian heretics, distinguishing them from Catholic Christians.—("Cont. Hær." i. 25.)

Minucius Felix (A.D. 220): "*Crosses, moreover, we neither worship nor wish for.* You [heathens], who consecrate wooden gods, do worship wooden crosses, perhaps as parts of your gods; for your very standards, as well as your banners and ensigns of your camp, what are they but crosses gilt and decked?"—("Octavius," xxix.)

Origen (A.D. 230): "We say that those are the most untaught who are not ashamed to address lifeless objects ... and though some may say these objects are not their gods, but imitations and symbols of real ones, nevertheless they are untaught, and slavish, and ignorant, who imagine that the hands of low mechanics can fashion likenesses of Divinity; for we assert that the very lowest amongst us (Christians) have been set free from this ignorance and want of knowledge."—("Cont. Cels." vi. 14.) "The statues and gifts which are fit offerings to God are the work of no common mechanics, but are wrought and fashioned within us by the Word of God, to wit, the virtues whereby we imitate the Firstborn of all creation."—("Cont. Cels." viii. 17.)

"What sensible man can refrain from smiling when he sees that one who has learned from philosophy such profound and noble sentiments about God or the gods, turns straightway to images, and offers to them his prayers, or imagines that by gazing on these natural things he can ascend from the visible symbol to that which is spiritual and immaterial?"—("Cont. Cels." vii. 44.)

Lactantius (A.D. 300): "It is indisputable that wherever there is an image, there is *no religion*. For if religion consist of divine things, and there be nothing divine except in heavenly things; it follows that images are outside of religion, because there can be nothing heavenly in what is made from the earth ... thus there is no religion in images, but a mimicry of religion."—("Div. Inst." ii. 19.)

Fathers of the Council of Elvira (A.D. 306): "It has been decreed that there ought not to be pictures in churches, lest what is worshipped and adored be painted on the walls."—(Canon xxxvi.)

Eusebius (A.D. 338) speaking of the image of Christ traditionally said to have been erected by the Syrophenician woman, says: "It is no wonder that those of old amongst the Gentiles who were benefited by the Saviour, made these things. We have heard of likenesses of Paul and Peter, and of Christ Himself, preserved in pictures, the ancients being naturally wont to honour them in this way as saviours, *according to the heathen custom* prevailing amongst men."—(" Hist. Eccl." vii. 14.)

St. Epiphanius (A.D. 370) in a letter preserved in St. Jerome's translation, tells how he found a painting of Christ on a curtain in a church at Anablatha, and tore it up, as "contrary to the authority of the Scriptures and contrary to our religion."—(St. Hieron. Epistle 51.)

St. Ambrose (A.D. 370) writing of the alleged finding of the true Cross by St. Helen, says: "She therefore found the title; she adored the King—*truly not the wood, for this is a heathen error, and the vanity of the ungodly*, but she adored Him Who hung on the Wood."—(" De Obit. Theodos.") Compare this with the Good Friday office for the adoration of the Cross in the Roman Missal, with its rubrics: "The priest, taking off his shoes, advances to *adore the Cross*, genuflecting thrice before he kisses it. . . . Then the ministers of the altar and the other clerks and the layfolks, two and two, genuflecting thrice as aforesaid, *adore the Cross*. Later on an antiphon is sung, beginning, 'We *adore* Thy Cross, O Lord.'"[1]

The same St. Ambrose, in another place, uses words to express the impossibility of reconciling heathen language and practice, which precisely apply to modern Roman apologies for the usage now discussed. Speaking of an ably-drafted petition on behalf of the pagan religion, which had been presented to the Emperor Valentinian, he says, "But this gold, if you handle it carefully, is precious outside, while within it is common metal. Ponder, I pray you, and examine the Gentile sect: they utter beautiful and imposing sentiments, but defend what is devoid of truth. *They talk about God, they worship an image*."—(" Epist. xviii. ad Valentinianum.")

---

[1] Doubtless this is *intended* to be in honour of the Atonement, but it is at least unfortunate that such dangerously misleading terms should be used.

St. Augustine (A.D. 430) supplies very valuable testimony, because he lets us know that those heathen arguments in favour of idols which he refutes are identical in meaning, and almost in exact wording, with the defence now set up by Roman divines for the cultus of images. Here is subjoined a parallel between St. Augustine's heathen and the decrees of the Council of Trent.

St. Augustine.

"*Confounded be all they that serve graven images, that boast themselves of idols.* But some disputant, who thinks himself learned, comes forward and says, 'I do not worship a stone, nor that image which is without feeling; for it is not possible that your prophets should have known that they have eyes and see not, and I be ignorant that the image in question has no soul, and sees not with its eyes, nor hears with its ears. I do not worship *that;* but I bow before (*adoro*) what I see, and serve him whom I do not see.' Who is he? 'Some invisible power,' he replies, 'which presides over that image.' By giving this sort of explanation of their images, they think themselves very clever, as not worshippers of idols." ("Enarr. in Ps." xcvi. 11.)

Council of Trent.

"The images of Christ, of the Virgin Mother of God, and of the Saints, are to be had and retained, especially in churches, and due honour and veneration to be paid to them; not because there is believed to be any divinity or virtue in them, on account of which they are to be worshipped, or because from them anything is to be asked, or because trust is to be reposed in images, as the heathens of old put their trust in idols; but because the honour which is exhibited to them is referred to the prototypes which they represent; so that through the images which we kiss, and before which we uncover our heads and lie prostrate, we adore Christ and pay veneration to the saints, whose likeness the images bear." (Conc. Trid., sess. xxv.)

Thus it is plain that down to St. Augustine's death in A.D. 430 there was no devotional use of pictures and images lawful amongst Christians,[1] and even very little merely decorative use; of which latter it is just possible to find some slight traces in a few of the Fathers, such as St. Chrysostom, St. Cyril, and St. Gregory Nyssen. By degrees, as learning and civilization decayed in the West, through the inroads of the barbarians into the Empire, and in the East through the crumbling away of province after province under the advance of Mohammedanism, image worship amongst Christians arose, spread and developed, during the time known as the "Dark Ages," *i.e.*, from about A.D. 600 to 1,000. Just before the first-named of these dates, Serenus, Bishop of Marseilles, finding that the pictures and images in the churches of his diocese were superstitiously used, destroyed them and cast them out of the buildings. Pope Gregory the Great wrote him two letters, one in 595 and the other in 600, blaming him as too hasty, because pictures of religious subjects are useful for teaching the ignorant; but adding that, of course, no sort of worship of these pictures ought to be tolerated. His words are: "I give you warning that news reached us some time ago, that you, my brother, noticing some persons as adoring images, broke up and cast out these church images. *And we praise you for having been zealous lest anything made with hands should be adored*, but we are of opinion that you ought not to have broken those images. For the reason why a picture is used in churches is, that those who are unlettered may, at any rate, read by seeing on the walls what they cannot read in books. So, brother, you ought to have preserved them, and have prohibited the people from worshipping them." (Ep. VII.

---

[1] He does say in one place: "I know of many who are worshippers of tombs and pictures;" but adds, that "the Catholic Church condemns them, and daily strives to correct them, as evil children."—("De Mor. Eccl." I. xxxiv. 75, 76.)

ii. 3.) Serenus, being on the spot, and knowing better than the Pope hundreds of miles away, did not restore the images, and got a second letter in reply to his message of non-compliance. The Pope goes over the same ground, saying: " Fired with inconsiderate zeal, you broke the images of the saints under this excuse, because they should not be adored. *And in so far as you forbade their being worshipped, we entirely praised you,* but we blamed you for breaking them. . . . It is one thing to worship a picture, and another to learn by the story told in a picture what is to be worshipped. . . . So, if any one wish to make images, by no means forbid it, *but in every possible way avoid worshipping images . . . and let the people humbly prostrate themselves in honour of the Almighty and Holy Trinity alone."*—(Ep. IX. iv. 9.)

Now, though this shows a great declension from the earlier standard, yet it explicitly contradicts the teaching of modern Romanism, which encourages that kneeling and prostration before pictures which St. Gregory limits to the worship of God alone. It is not till the Eastern Church had entered on its decrepitude that the falsely-styled Seventh General Council was held at Nicæa in 787, which gave the first formal authorization to the worship of images, doubtless influenced by reaction against the Arianizing temper of the Iconoclasts. Regarding this, the following facts are important :—

1. It was attended by 375 bishops, and reversed the decrees of a previous council of 338 bishops, who had condemned image-worship at Constantinople in 754.

2. It was promptly rejected by Western Christendom in a council of more than 300 bishops at Frankfort in 794, including the prelates of Germany, Gaul, Spain, Italy, and England, with two papal legates.

3. It is styled over and over again a " pseudo-synod " by French, German, and English Catholic writers down to the middle of the fourteenth century, so that it never has had that acceptance by Christendom which is necessary

to make a council rank as General and binding, nor can it ever acquire it now. (See proofs in Palmer's "Treatise on the Church," IV. x. 4.)

4. Its Acts are extant, and prove that the Holy Scriptures, and the practice and teaching of the early Church, went for almost nothing in guiding its decisions, which are based chiefly on wild and puerile legends; such, for example, as that a workman employed in putting up hangings in a church happened to drive a nail into the head of a picture of St. Peter, and was at once seized with a racking headache, not curable till, at the Bishop's order, he drew out the nail, when the headache disappeared immediately!

5. Such as the Council is, however, it expressly denies and rejects the doctrine of St. Thomas Aquinas, cited above, in that it strictly confines the honour of *latria* to God alone. Image-worship, then, stands condemned by Holy Scripture and by all ancient Church authority, finding its warrant only in a late, corrupt, and ignorant age. Some more candid Roman Catholics, such as the great canonist Van Espen, have admitted that there is actual idolatry practised in the Roman Church,—his words are: "Notwithstanding the manifold decrees of synods, and notably of the wholesome injunctions of the last, the Council of Trent, so great, multiplied, superstitious, and almost *idolatrous* cultus of images and statues on the part of the vulgar and ignorant people is commonly seen, that the Gallican Bishops [at the time of the Council of Frankfort] do not seem to have groundlessly feared lest, if they permitted the worship of images, it would be very difficult to draw back the ignorant vulgar from superstitious cultus and extravagant worship."[1] But notwithstanding this, it is impossible to find any serious warning against this danger and sin, much less any frank prohibition and condemnation

---

[1] "Jus. Eccl." II. i. xxxvii.

of it, in any popular Roman catechism or manual of doctrine. Excuses and quasi-arguments sometimes do occur, indeed, against Protestant charges, but they seem half-hearted and insincere in their deprecation.

Relics.

XVII. As relics are not found offered for veneration in every Roman Catholic place of worship, it is possible that many persons never practically join in devotion to them, and it is thus not necessary to say much on this head. It will be enough to remark, in the first place, that the supreme worship of *latria* is accorded by the consent of leading Roman theologians to all alleged relics of the Passion, such as the nails of the Cross, the crown of thorns, the seamless coat, &c.; while *dulia* is similarly allowed to relics of the Saints (Dens, "Theol." v. p. 45). And next, that so great is the uncertainty of *all* relics alleged as ancient—there are, of course, genuine ones of modern saints—that in few cases is the evidence offered on behalf of their genuineness such as would induce the authorities of any public museum in Europe to purchase an alleged historical relic with no more to be said in favour of its authenticity;[1]

---

[1] Thus the Blessed Virgin's girdle, venerated at Quintin, is attested in this wise, that, after the archives of the church had been burnt in 1600, it was stated at an inquiry in 1611 that documents then lost had recorded the bringing of the relic from the East by a former seigneur at the date of the Crusades; and after the shrine had been carried off and destroyed in the French Revolution, some unknown person is said to have recovered this relic and brought it to the dean, who recognized it. There is no attempt whatever at proving the first or the last step here; and even the first step, being more than a thousand years later than the date of the relic itself, assuming its genuineness, is rather too far in advance of the real beginning of proof. One of the best-attested ancient relics extant is St. Peter's Chain, which is all but certainly that which the Empress Eudocia brought from Jerusalem to Rome in A.D. 438. But its history begins then, four centuries after the event, and at a

while, in many instances, there is direct proof of either error or fraud. It is usual with Roman controversialists to plead against objections to the *same* relic being shown in more than one place, that sometimes, as in the case of St. John the Baptist's head, each relic is only a portion, conventionally spoken of as entire; while in other cases the relics are of different Saints bearing the same name. But here is a crucial instance which cannot be evaded by either method. The body of the Apostle St. Bartholomew is declared in the Roman Breviary and Martyrology to have been translated from Benevento to Rome by the Emperor Otto III. (983-1002), and is alleged to be *entire*. It is attested by Bulls of Alexander III. and Sixtus V. But the Church of Benevento alleges that the *entire* body of St. Bartholomew is there still, and produces Bulls to that effect from Leo IX., Stephen IX., Benedict XII., Clement VI., Boniface IX., and Urban V., the earliest of which Popes reigned fifty years after the death of Otto III. Here, then, are *two entire bodies;* but Monte Cassino claims the possession of a *large part* of the body, and so does Reims. There are, besides, *three heads*, one at Naples, one formerly at Reichenau, and a third at Toulouse; *two crowns of the head*, at Frankfort and Prague; part of the *skull* at Maestricht; a *jaw* at Steinfeld, part of a *jaw* at Prague, *two jaws* in Cologne, and a lower *jaw* at Murbach; an *arm and hand* at Gersiac; a *second* arm, with the flesh, at Bethune; a *third* arm at Amalfi; a large part of a *fourth* arm at Foppens; a *fifth* arm and part of a *sixth* at Cologne; a *seventh* arm at Andechs; an *eighth* arm at Ebers; *three* large leg or *arm*-bones in Prague; part of an *arm* at Brussels; and other alleged portions of the body, not reckoning trifles

---

time when, as St. Augustine lets us know ("De Opere Monach." xxviii.), a thriving trade in forged relics had sprung up; of which Palestine was naturally the head-quarters.

like skin, teeth, and hair, in twenty other places.[1] This is, no doubt, an extreme instance; but there are many very similar, and it admirably illustrates the *uncertainty* of relic-worship, and the culpable remissness of the Roman authorities in taking no measures to remove the doubt.[2]

The Blessed Virgin more worshipped than the Father or Christ.

XVIII. The next particular in which the modern Church of Rome is in rebellion against the revealed will of God, is the manner in which she has made the worship of the Blessed Virgin not merely equal, but practically far exceed, that paid to her divine Son and His Almighty Father. This is committing the pagan sin, denounced by St. Paul, of those who "worshipped and served the creature more than the Creator, who is blessed for ever" (Rom. i. 25).

As there is great disingenuousness on this subject displayed in all books meant to allure proselytes or to answer objections, it is necessary to give precise details in proof of the charge. The little book by Dr. Di Bruno, "Catholic Belief" (Burns & Oates, 1878), is very cautious indeed on this head. Three chapters are devoted to the subject. The first of these explains and defends

---

[1] Baring-Gould, "Lives of the Saints," August 25.
[2] The Council of Trent, giving up the question of ancient relics as insoluble, decreed that no *new* relics should be received without the authentication of the Bishop (sess. xxv.). But in practice this is merely his testimony to the fact that a certain relic has been honoured as such for a long time. No attempt at a real inquiry into its genuineness is made. And Wetzer and Welte, in their "Kirchenlexicon," acknowledge that the Crusaders, notably after the sack of Constantinople, brought great quantities of spurious relics from the East. Sometimes there are open disputes. The seamless coat is claimed by Trèves and by Argenteuil, and each denies the genuineness of the rival relic.

the title "Mother of God" as applied to the B. V. M. With this English Churchmen have no quarrel, for the Church of England acknowledges and is bound by the decrees of the General Council of Ephesus, which affirmed her right to the title of *Theotokos*. The second argues that it is fit to honour and love one whom Our Lord so signally loved and honoured; that to dishonour her would be to dishonour Him; and that honour and love shown to her are for His sake. A little—very little—is said about having recourse to her intercession, and it is remarked that by asking for her *prayers*, Catholics at once admit that she is not the fountain or source of grace and merit, but must herself apply for them to her Son and Saviour. But here, again, for the most part, what is said is beside the question. The Church of England honours and loves the Blessed Virgin, employs her Song in its daily service, places the feasts of her Annunciation and Purification amongst the red letter days of the Calendar, and preserves a record of her Conception and Nativity there too; while, without counting ancient churches, or churches replacing ancient ones, there are no fewer than six-and-thirty modern churches in and round London alone dedicated in her honour. If the Roman Church were content with this sort of reverence and affection, there would be no fault to find, but the fact is very far indeed from being so. Di Bruno's third chapter is on the Immaculate Conception, and avoids the main issue.

1. In the "Année Liturgique à Rome," 5th edition, 1870, which gives a list of all the festivals observed in each and all of the churches of that city, there are set down *twenty-two* festivals of our Lord, including the Invention and Exaltation of the Cross, which are only colourably in His honour; while there are *forty-one* of the Blessed Virgin, two of which, however, are Candlemas and Lady Day, also included under our Lord's festivals. But taking away these indeterminate ones on both sides, there

remain *twenty* feasts of our Lord to *thirty-nine* of the Blessed Virgin, giving her all but *double* the amount of honour paid to Him.

2. Out of the 433 public churches and chapels of Rome, *five* are dedicated to the Holy Trinity, *fifteen* to our Lord, together with *four* of the Crucifix and *two* of the Sacrament, making *twenty-one;* there are *two* dedicated to the Holy Spirit, and *one hundred and twenty-one* to the Blessed Virgin, more than *four times* all those others put together. These ominous tokens at the heart of Romanism do but too faithfully denote the current teaching and practice, exaggerated and forced on within the last twenty years beyond all previous bounds.

3. It has been already shown from the "Raccolta" that language is used in prayer to the B. V. M. identical with that addressed to God, so that the assertion of apologists that she is merely asked to pray for us, and to obtain by her prayers those gifts which are not her own to confer, is obviously false. There are, of course, many such prayers to be found, but they are very far indeed from covering the whole facts. It now remains to be shown that in practice she receives not only the *same* in kind, but *more* in quantity.

First, then, the popular devotion of the Rosary, when it was first invented several centuries ago, consisted of the recitation of a certain number of *Psalms*, with prayers intercalated; in its second stage, it consisted of several repetitions of the *Lord's Prayer*, with the Creed added at intervals—whence the mediæval name of *Paternoster*, given to the string of beads,[1] a term still surviving in "Paternoster Row," where rosary-makers used to live; but now, and for a long time past, the rosary is made up of 166 beads, on which are recited *one* Creed, *fifteen* Our Fathers, and *a hundred and fifty* Hail Marys; thus entirely transforming the original devotion, and giving

---

[1] Siegel, "Christ-Kirch. Alterth." s.v. "Rosenkranz."

ten times as much to the B. V. M. as to Almighty God.

4. Next, one of the most general private devotions in Roman Catholic countries is the Angelus, recited thrice daily, with three Hail Marys in each recitation, so that she is addressed at least *nine* times a day in prayer; whereas no similar devotion to the Father or Christ is recommended.

5. Again, the month of May every year is now specially dedicated to the Blessed Virgin, and termed the "Month of Mary," every day of which is supposed to be chiefly occupied with devotions in her honour; a token of affection and reverence which is not paid even to our Lord, for the Lenten services are by no means so special in character, save in Holy Week alone. And already even May is found insufficient, so that September begins to be treated as a supplementary Month of Mary. It is no mere titular honour, for in Roman Catholic countries special altars are set up during May in honour of the Virgin Mother; huge images, decked with flowers and other adornments, block the view of the high altar itself; processions throng streets and roads; litanies and novenas take up most of the time spent in church; and all this with a fervour and eagerness never displayed on festivals of Christ. Frequent as are the offices and strong as are the expressions in honour of the Blessed Virgin in the Missal and Breviary, yet the main structure of these ancient formularies is so far unfavourable to Mariolatry, that it shows as a mere excrescence upon them; and, therefore, no one who seeks for proofs of the manner in which it has become the most powerful factor in the Roman Catholic religion can find it there. It is necessary to have recourse to the manuals of popular devotion; the private offices of the most widespread confraternities and guilds; the shrines of pilgrimages, of which the overwhelming majority, especially amongst the newer ones, are connected with Virgin-worship; to

attend the sermons of the ordinary Roman preachers; to examine the devotions in actual daily use amongst the people, before it is possible to realize the true extent of the practice, which is held in considerable check here in England, in deference to public opinion, and because it has not even yet, after thirty years' vigorous effort, been found possible entirely to Italianize Anglo-Romans, and to root out the traditions of a more orthodox teaching amongst them.

Quotations from Liguori's "Glories of Mary."

XIX. But a few illustrations will help to show what the accredited teaching on the subject now is. And Liguori's "Glories of Mary," as being a work at once highly popular and fully approved by the Roman Church herself, shall be cited again, especially as it has been formally recommended to Anglo-Romans by Cardinals Wiseman and Manning:—

"Mary is our only refuge, help, and asylum."

"In Judea, in ancient times, there were cities of refuge, wherein criminals who fled there for protection were exempt from the punishment they had deserved. Nowadays these cities are not so numerous; there is but *one*, and *that is Mary*.

"God, before the birth of Mary, complained by the mouth of the Prophet Ezekiel that there was no one to rise up and withhold Him from chastising sinners, but that He could find no one, *for this office was reserved for our Blessed Lady, who withholds His arm until He is pacified.*"

"Often we shall be heard more quickly, and be thus preserved, if we have recourse to Mary, and call upon *her* name, *than we should be if we called on the Name of Jesus our Saviour.*"

"Many things are asked from God, and are not granted; they are asked from Mary and are obtained."

"At the command of the Virgin all things obey, *even God.*"[1]

"The salvation of all depends on their being favoured and protected by Mary. He who is protected by Mary will be saved; he who is not, will be lost."

"Mary has only to speak, and her Son executes all."

These are only specimens from scores of similar expressions in this work, wherein Liguori, carrying into his own practice the maxims of truthfulness which he inculcated upon others, unblushingly ascribes them to great Saints and Fathers of the early Church, sometimes on the faith of notorious forgeries, but often without even such a pretext for calumniating their memory.

What wonder can it be, then, when such is the teaching, that the logical and practical conclusion should be that it saves time, trouble, and uncertainty to go to the Blessed Virgin with prayer, rather than to the Father or Christ?

What wonder that the *very last words* which the Roman Ritual puts into the mouth of the dying are, "Mary, Mother of grace, Mother of mercy, do thou protect me from the foe, and receive me in the hour of death." Our Lord's own last words upon the Cross, and His first martyr's dying ejaculation, are prefixed, indeed; but these highest examples of Scripture are not enough, the aid of the Father and Christ, so invoked, is not sufficient, and the last and surest appeal must be made to Mary, as the most powerful succour of all.

The Mass converted into Worship of the Blessed Virgin.

XX. It might seem, too, as if the Mass, whatever criticisms may be made on other aspects of it in the

---

[1] As this may be challenged, here is the Latin: "*Imperio Virginis omnia famulantur, etiam Deus.*"

Church of Rome, is at any rate so peculiarly a pleading the Passion of the Son to the Father, that no possibility exists of converting it into an instrument of Mariolatry. Yet Ultramontane ingenuity has been adequate to the task. The "Raccolta," already mentioned, has its indulgenced prayers classified according to the object or intention of each group; and the first such group in the volume consists of devotions to the Most Holy Trinity, followed in order by those to the Almighty Father, to the Holy Spirit, to Our Lord, and then to St. Mary. Naturally, an inexperienced reader does not look for Marian devotions till this fifth part is reached; but, in fact, the indulgenced Votive Mass of the Holy Trinity is entirely taken up with acts of praise and thanksgiving for the graces, gifts, and privileges bestowed on the Blessed Virgin, and almost every prayer in this section is of the same kind, while the most fervent petition of all by far is addressed to the Blessed Virgin herself, beginning thus :—

"I acknowledge thee, and I venerate thee, most Holy Virgin, Queen of Heaven, Lady and Mistress of the Universe, as Daughter of the Eternal Father, Mother of His well-beloved Son, and most loving Spouse of the Holy Spirit. Kneeling at the feet of thy great Majesty, with all humility I pray thee, through that divine charity wherewith thou wast so bounteously enriched on thine Assumption into heaven, to vouchsafe me favour and pity, placing me under thy most safe and faithful protection, and receiving me into the number of those happy and highly-favoured servants of thine whose names thou dost carry graven upon thy virgin breast."

As this Mass of the Holy Trinity is quite separate from the Votive Masses of the Blessed Virgin, which are of very frequent occurrence, it is easy to see how St. Mary is constantly made the principal idea and subject of thought and devotion brought before the minds of the people even at Mass itself, so that an opinion has even been advanced by some writers that she is bodily co-present with Christ in the Eucharist and is there fed upon by communicants.[1] And, accordingly this kind of devotion opens up another great Roman difficulty, which is this:—Whereas it is constantly alleged by modern Roman controversialists that the difference between the honour paid to Almighty God and to the Blessed Virgin, or to any other saint or image of a saint, is so great and manifest that no one can possibly go wrong on this head; contrariwise, the greatest of all Roman polemical divines, Cardinal Bellarmine, says: " As to external acts of adoration, *it is not easy to make distinction*, for, generally speaking, the external acts are common to every species of worship, and the *only exception*, the only peculiar rite, to be reserved for the worship of God Himself, is sacrifice, and what is connected with sacrifice, temples, altars, and priests." (" Disput. Controv., De Sanct. Beat.," i. 12.) But when special altars of Mary are erected, when hundreds of priests belong to orders, such as the Marist Fathers, peculiarly vowed to her service, when votive gifts and offerings, such as were of the nature of sacrifice in pagan times, as lights, incense, and flowers, are incessantly made to her, and when, finally, the Mass itself is celebrated again and again in her honour, and her Litany is usually sung before the Sacrament in the rite of Benediction,[2] what

[1] Oswald, "Dogmat. Mariologie," 177; Corn. à Lapide in Ecclus. xxiv. 29; Faber's " Precious Blood," 28, 29; Salazar in Prov. ix. 4, 5, n. 144, 145. All quoted by Dr. Pusey, "Eirenicon," part i. 168-172. Also see Canon Oakeley, "Letter to Manning," p. 23, Longmans, 1866. Oswald is indeed now on the Index, yet there seems to be no *explicit* condemnation of this tenet, but only of a certain mode of stating it, not the only mode which leads to dangerous consequences.

[2] "Afterwards, the Litany of B. V. M., or some motett proper to the day, is sung in honour of the Blessed Sacrament." Oakeley, " Ceremonial of the Mass," appendix, p. 141. Thus the road is now open to the belief that the B. V. M. is to be worshipped in the Blessed Sacrament also, and by degrees to the loss of all thought of Christ therein.

becomes of Bellarmine's safeguard, and how can an ordinary ignorant lay person distinguish that which is nearly invisible even to the eyes of a trained scientific theologian?[1]

What this Innovation amounts to.

XXI. Now, all this amounts to nothing less than a revolution in the Christian faith. It is not a gloss, a development, a modification, but a radical *change*. Taken from the extreme point of view, and as actually carried into practice in the most Ultramontane quarters, it is the dethronement of the Almighty Father and the Lord Jesus Christ, and the substitution of another sovereign ruler, another object of worship. Judged more gently, and according to its less extravagant forms, it is at least equivalent to that change in the political constitution of a kingdom or empire, when the personal government of an absolute monarch is suddenly limited, and altered into a system like that of Great Britain, where the sovereign retains indeed the prerogative of highest social rank, but where every actual exercise of substantial authority and bestowal of honours are lodged in the hands of those who are nominally subjects accountable to the sovereign, as the Prime Minister, the Judges, and so forth, but who are in real fact not only independent of the Crown, but dictate its policy in great and small things alike, from making war and peace down to nominating a tide-waiter. And just as it is to the Prime Minister of the day that politicians with us look for place, title, and measures, practically leaving the Queen

---

[1] Especially is this difficult when it is remembered that Bellarmine is really speaking of the Sacrifice of the Mass, and in strict theology this is not an act of homage to Christ Himself, but to the Father only; and, accordingly, Canon XXIII. of the Third Council of Carthage enjoins: " When assisting at the altar, prayer is always to be directed to the Father."

out of account, so it is with the modern clients of the Blessed Virgin in the Roman Church, who go to her, and not to God.

What Scripture tells us of the Blessed Virgin.

XXII. Where, then, is the warrant for so amazing a change to be found? Let us first try Holy Scripture. There are exactly twenty-two passages where the Blessed Virgin is named, directly, or indirectly, as follows, in the order of their occurrence in the New Testament:—

St. Matthew.

1. Her mere name in St. Matthew's genealogy of Christ.—i. 16.
2. The removal of St. Joseph's doubts of her purity, and the birth of Christ.—i. 18–25.
3. Her presence when the Wise Men came to adore her Son.—ii. 11.
4. The warning to St. Joseph to take the young Child and His Mother to Egypt.—ii. 13.
5. The notice to return with them from Egypt.—ii. 20–21.

(*) 6. Christ's answer when told that His Mother and brethren desired to speak with Him, declaring that all who do God's will, rank as His mother and brethren.—xii. 46–50.

7. St. Mary named as Christ's Mother by the unbelieving Jews.—xiii. 55.

St. Mark.

(*) 8. Same reply as that recorded in St. Matthew to the news that His Mother inquired for Him—iii. 31–35.

9. His Mother named by the Jews, as above (7).—vi. 3.

St. Luke.

(*) 10. The Annunciation, Visitation, and "Magnificat," containing the phrases, "Highly-favoured" (*marg.* "graciously accepted," or "much graced;" Vulgate, "full of grace"); "Blessed art thou among women"; "Whence is this to me, that the Mother of my Lord should come to me?" and "All generations shall call me blessed."—i. 26–57.

11. The arrival at Bethlehem, and the Nativity.—ii. 5–7.
12. The shepherds see her with the Child and St. Joseph in the manger.—ii. 16.
13. She is said to have kept and pondered all these things.—ii. 19.
14. She goes to Jerusalem for the Purification.
15. She marvels at the prophecy of Simeon, which includes the piercing of her own soul with a sword.—ii. 33–35.

(*) 16. She goes up to Jerusalem at the Passover, loses our Lord and finds Him again, being rebuked by Him for the search, and does not understand His meaning.—ii. 41–50.

(*) 17. He is "subject" to her and St. Joseph at Nazareth. —ii. 51.

(*) 18. He replies to the woman who extols the blessedness of His Mother, "Yea, rather, blessed are they that hear the Word of God, and keep it." —xi. 27, 28.

St. John.

(*) 19. Christ, at the marriage in Cana, refuses to permit even His Mother to suggest to Him what He should do.—ii. 1–5.

20. He goes with her and His disciples to Capernaum.—ii. 12.

(*) 21. His Mother stands beside the Cross, and He gives her and St. John to each other as mother and son.—xix. 25-27.

Acts of the Apostles.

22. St. Mary is named amongst the company of those who continued in prayer with the Apostles.—i. 14.[1]

Examination of the Texts.

XXIII. Only the texts marked (*) have any possible bearing on the question, for or against. If grouped, the result is as follows :—

In favour of the cultus it is possible to cite (*a*) the three titles of honour in St. Luke i. "Full of Grace," "Blessed," "Mother of the Lord;" (*b*) Christ's subjection to her at Nazareth; and (*c*) His giving her as mother to St. John.

Against it : (*a*) His rebuke to her for seeking Him in the Temple, and her failure to understand His meaning; (*b*) His refusal to let her dictate His action at Cana; (*c*) His declaring that all who hear God's Word and

---

[1] This analysis of texts is usefully illustrated by examining the Lessons, Epistles, and Gospels of the Breviary and Missal for such feasts of the Blessed Virgin Mary as are not really feasts of Our Lord, and by seeing the straits to which the compilers have been put to get anything that will even seem to fit. Thus, several Epistles are supplied from the Song of Songs, although it is not till about A.D. 1150 that any writer treats the Blessed Virgin Mary as the Bride, and from Ecclus. xxiv., which is entirely about the Eternal Wisdom; while the Gospel for the Conception and Nativity is simply the pedigree in St. Matthew i., and that for the Assumption is St. Luke x. 38-42, which is all about Martha and Mary of Bethany, the mere coincidence of the latter name having prompted the choice. The text Rev. xii. 1 is not cited above, because Roman Catholics are not agreed that it means the Blessed Virgin, by reason of the difficulty in explaining vv. 6, 13 and 14 of her.

keep it are His "brother, and sister, and mother."
(*d*) His declaring further that to keep God's Word is
even a greater thing than motherhood to Himself; (*e*)
the absolute silence preserved as regards the Blessed
Virgin, save for the one cited reference at the beginning
of the Acts, from the time of the Passion, not one word
about her being found in any of the Epistles.

Now, two out of the three laudatory epithets of the
Blessed Virgin are conferred on ordinary believers in
the New Testament. The word translated either "highly-
favoured" or "full of grace" ($κεχαριτωμένη$), in St. Luke,
i. 28, is from the very same verb which appears as "made
accepted" in A. V., and "graced" in the Douai version
of Ephesians i. 6, "wherein He hath made us accepted
($ἐχαρίτωσεν\ ἡμᾶς$) in the beloved," and is not, in mere
wording, so strong as the expression used of St. Stephen
and St. Barnabas, "full of faith and of the Holy Ghost"
(Acts vi. 5; xi. 24). We do get, by-the-by, the precise
phrase, "full of grace" A. V. and Douai ($πλήρης\ χάριτος$),
once in Scripture, but then it is applied to Our Lord
Himself, and Him alone (St. John i. 14). And the
title "Blessed" is represented by two words, one of
which is the same as that used by our Lord nine times
in the Beatitudes (St. Matt. v. 3), and the other that
which He uses in His account of the Last Judgment,
in the sentence, "Come, ye *blessed* of My Father," &c.
(St. Matt. xxv. 34). These, consequently, prove nothing
either way for the purpose in hand. There remains,
therefore, only the third title, "Mother of the Lord,"
and Christ Himself has been pleased, on two several
occasions (*6 and *18), either to *restrict* very seriously
the conclusions which we might otherwise draw from it,
or to *extend* to all true believers the privileges and favour
which it implies.

As to Our Lord's subjection to His blessed Mother,
it was, so to speak, a necessary part of His humiliation
in taking our nature upon Him. As the words of St.

Luke are, "was subject to *them*," this passage, if pressed, makes as much for St. Joseph's authority as for that of the Blessed Virgin, but extravagantly as his cultus, too, has been forced on of late years, from a bare commemoration in a feast of inferior rank—and that modern, and, as the Jesuit, Guyet, in his great work on Church festivals, "Heortologia," Venice, 1739, tells us (p. 140), kept hardly anywhere when he wrote[1]—to its present position, it is not yet claimed for him that he, too, rules our Lord in Heaven now. However, that dogma is already seen in germ in Faber's hymns, and elsewhere :—

> With her Babe in her arms, surely Mary will be,
> Sweet spouse of our Lady, *my pleader with thee* ;[2]

so that here Christ Himself, as well as the Blessed Virgin Mary, intercedes with St. Joseph, who is thus set positively above God Himself. This goes even beyond the new Trinity substituted for the old one :—

Jesus, Mary, Joseph, I give you my heart and soul;
Jesus, Mary, Joseph, assist me in my last agony;
Jesus, Mary, Joseph, may I breathe forth my soul in peace with you;

a prayer indulgenced with 300 days, and in the "Raccolta." St. Joseph has now been "granted the title of universal patron, guardian, and protector of the whole Church ;" albeit Guyet (p. 100) protests against calling him a patriarch, or ranking him with or before the Apostles, as a mere caprice of persons eager for novelties. One would like to know, too, how human beings have got authority to confer heavenly rank and office. It is much as if the inmates of a London workhouse were to undertake the creation

---

[1] It was first put in the Roman Kalendar by Sixtus IV. 1471-1484, and is absent, for example, from the Kalendars of the Sarum, York, and Hereford Missals, and from that in the Hours of the monks of St. Justina in 1541.

[2] So in the edition of 1871. Some editions read "my arms."

of dukes and prime ministers.[1] But we find the statement concerning our Lord's subjection immediately preceded by a warning given by Himself to show that the parental authority had already been mistakenly exercised (St. Luke ii. 49); as also that, at the very outset of His ministry, He gently sets aside His Mother's one attempt to influence Him, and that it is never repeated, though we are told of similar acts on the part of the Apostles. Nothing can be found which hints at any human authority over Him after His baptism.

Lastly, it has been argued that the words from the Cross, "Behold thy mother," "Behold thy son," were spoken not merely in respect of St. John, but to all the faithful of all time, and denote the grant of universal motherhood and authority to the Blessed Virgin. What they do prove is Christ's loving care for His Mother; and further, that the "brethren" of our Lord named in Scripture, were not, as some have thought, the Blessed Virgin's children by St. Joseph, since had that been so, the duty of tending her would have devolved on them by every law of nature and of man. But the theory of universal motherhood can be at once refuted by simply pointing out that this attribute is expressly ascribed to the mystical Church by Scripture: "Jerusalem above is free, *which is the mother of us all.*" (Galat. iv. 26.)[2]

---

[1] We have, in truth, a ruling by Christ Himself, which seems to assign a much lower rank to St. Joseph in the economy of grace. By placing St. John the Baptist on a level with the very greatest prophets and saints of the Old Testament, without making any exception in favour of St. Joseph, then probably dead, and yet adding that "the least in the kingdom of heaven"—that is, under the Gospel dispensation—"is greater than he" (St. Matt. xi. 11; St. Luke vii. 8), Our Lord has practically decided St. Joseph's position; and this new cult therefore undertakes to set aside His decision.

[2] This is curiously illustrated by the Epistle of the Churches of Vienne and Lyons (circ. A.D. 170), which uses the phrase "the Virgin Mother" to denote the Church, with no explanation, thus: "And great joy was caused to the Virgin Mother, receiving those

The entire silence of Scripture as to the Blessed Virgin, from just before the Day of Pentecost, at least implies that no special office, rank, or authority was bestowed on her in the Church founded on that day, and has a further bearing too. The authorized tradition of the Roman Church, established as such by the indulgenced "Chaplet of St. Bridget," is that the Blessed Virgin Mary lived sixty-three years on earth, and was immediately after her death assumed into heaven as its Queen, with many miraculous circumstances. Her death must thus have fallen considerably within the time covered by the Acts of the Apostles, which come down to A.D. 63; but no mention is made there—nor, indeed, anywhere for some centuries—of so great an event, with such far-reaching consequences.

The Evidence of the Fathers as to the Blessed Virgin.

XXIV. Since Holy Writ gives no ground nor colour to the cultus of Blessed Mary, can we find sufficient evidence in the writings of the Fathers?

1. In the Ante-Nicene period, the following extant writers never so much as name St. Mary at all; St. Barnabas, St. Hermas, St. Clement of Rome, St. Polycarp, Tatian, Athenagoras, Theophilus, St. Hippolytus, St. Gregory Thaumaturgus,[1] St. Cyprian, St. Firmilian, St. Dionysius, Arnobius, and St. Methodius.[2] 2. St. Justin

---

alive, of whom she had been delivered as it were still-born." Euseb. "Hist. Eccl.," V. i.

[1] There are two homilies on the Annunciation ascribed to this writer, which would make strongly for the cultus, but they are late forgeries, rejected by Dupin, Lumper, and other Roman Catholic critics.

[2] A homily on the Feast of the Purification is ascribed to this Father, but rejected as a forgery by Roman Catholic critics, on the very sufficient ground that the festival was not instituted till A.D. 542, two centuries after his death. It is highly Marian in tone.

Martyr mentions her twice in connexion with the Nativity, and once with the flight into Egypt. St. Clement of Alexandria once touches on her virgin child-bearing. Tertullian mentions her four times, once in connexion with the Nativity, once merely to defend the occasional interchangeableness of the words "woman" and "Virgin" by showing that both are applied to her ("De Veland. Virg." vi.), but twice actually to charge her with lack of belief and with seeking to call Christ away from His work (De Carne Christi, vii.; Adv. Marc. iv. 19), thereby arousing His indignation. Origen, very similarly, names the Blessed Virgin but casually a couple of times, and in the one place where he goes more into detail, he explains the sword of Simeon's prophecy to be unbelieving doubt, whereby she was offended at the Passion. "Through thine own soul . . . shall the sword of unbelief pierce; and thou shalt be struck with the sharp point of doubt." ("Hom. in Lucam, xvii.") St. Archelaus defends the Virgin-birth against Manes, and incidentally touches on the message to our Lord regarding His Mother and brethren. There remain only two passages from which any conclusion can be drawn. The first of these is in St. Irenæus, where he says that St. Mary's obedience counterbalances Eve's disobedience, so that she has become the "advocate" of Eve. ("Cont. Hær." V. xix.) We have only the barbarous Latin translation here, and cannot tell exactly what the Saint wrote or intended,[1] but we have his mind plainly enough expressed in another place, where he speaks of Christ having "checked the unseasonable haste of His Mother at Cana." ("Cont. Hær." III. xvi.) The other is in a fragment of St. Peter of Alexandria, where he styles St. Mary "glorious Lady, and ever-Virgin." Clearly,

[1] Except that *advocare* is used in this same translation as meaning *to comfort* [III. ix. 3, glossed *consolari* in the Benedictine edition], and thus the sense probably is, that women, whom Eve had caused to sorrow, can rejoice now because of Mary.

nothing in these scanty details supplies the justification sought for.

2. Nor does the witness of the greatest Fathers after Nicæa change.

St. Cyril of Jerusalem (A.D. 347) has left us very copious and valuable catechetical lectures, but though he dwells much on the Virgin-birth of our Lord, and gives His Mother the title of *Theotokos*, he is absolutely silent as to any religious homage due to her.

St. Hilary of Poictiers, Doctor of the Church (A.D. 350) declares that the Blessed Virgin has yet to abide the Last Judgment. "Shall we desire the Day of Judgment, in which we must undergo that incessant fire, and those sharp chastisements of a soul to be cleansed from sin? A sword shall pass through the soul of the Blessed Mary, that the thoughts of many hearts may be revealed. *If the Virgin who conceived God is to come into the severity of the judgment*, who will dare to be judged by God?"—("Comm. in Ps. cxviii.")

St. Basil the Great, Doctor (A.D. 370), like St. Hilary, explains the sword of Simeon's prophecy to be St. Mary's wavering in belief at the time of the Passion. He does this in answer to a bishop who consulted him on the meaning of that text.—(Epist. 260.)

St. Ambrose, Doctor (A.D. 370), who is very copious in his expressions of reverence for the Blessed Virgin, has not one sentence in all his works which can be so much as tortured into an address to her of any kind.

St. Chrysostom, Doctor (A.D. 407), is so far from countenancing the cultus, that he almost goes into the opposite extreme by alleging, first, that the Blessed Virgin was ignorant of the full mystery of the Incarnation ("Expos. in Ps. xlix."); and next, that she was moved by "excessive ambition" and "arrogance" in sending a message to Christ, in order to show the people her influence with Him. ("Hom. in St. Matt. xii. 48.") The Church has not followed St. Chrysostom in this view,

which is a most painful one; but the fact that his having
advanced it has in no way prevented his being regarded
as a great Saint and Doctor of the Church, is conclusive
that no worship of the Blessed Virgin Mary can have
been permitted in his day.

St. Gregory Nyssen, Doctor (A.D. 390), " That nothing
created is to be worshipped by man, the Divine word has
enacted, as we may learn from nearly the whole of the
sacred volume; Moses, the Tables, the Law, the Prophets
in succession, the Gospels, the decrees of all the Apostles,
alike forbid us to look to the creature. . . . . We, who
are taught by the Scriptures to look to the true Godhead,
are instructed to regard *every created being* as foreign
from the Divine nature, and to serve and reverence the
Uncreated nature alone."—(" Contr. Eunomium.")

But St. Epiphanius, Doctor (A.D. 403), is the most precise. Arguing against a new heresy, that of the Collyridians
(a body within the Church, not a sect outside it, and so
called from a small cake they offered in sacrifice), he says
that they began in reaction against those who showed
disrespect to the Blessed Virgin, and ran into extreme error
thereby. And he contemptuously remarks that this special
kind of "idolatrous heresy" has only women for its promoters, because they are fickle, weak, narrow-minded, and
prone to error. He goes on to argue that St. Mary was not
granted any priestly authority, nor permission to baptize,
though we might have expected that she, rather than
John the Baptist, would have baptized Christ; and continues, " Mary's body was holy indeed, but she was not a
Deity. *She was a Virgin, too, and honoured, but not given
to us for worship*, but worshipping Him born of her in
the flesh, who came down from Heaven and the Father's
bosom. Wherefore the Gospel warns us, saying by the
voice of the Lord Himself, 'Woman, what have I to do
with thee? Mine hour is not yet come.' [He says this]
in order that from the phrase, 'Woman, what have I to
do with thee?' people might understand that the holy

Virgin was not more than human. So He called her 'Woman,' as in prophecy, *because of the heresies and schisms which were to come upon the earth, lest any one, through excessive adoration for that Holy Virgin, should fall into the silly nonsense* (τὸ ληρολόγημα) *of that heresy* . .
For if Christ willeth not that the Angels should be worshipped, *how much more is He unwilling that worship should be paid to her who was born of Anna.* . . .
Let Mary be honoured, but let the Father, Son, and Holy Ghost be worshipped. Let no one worship Mary.
. . . Let women who act thus be put to silence by Jeremiah, nor any longer trouble the world, nor say, ' Let us honour the Queen of heaven.'"—("Adv. Hær." lxxix.)[1]

St. Jerome, Doctor (A.D. 418), not only lends no countenance to the cultus, but agrees with Origen, St. Basil, and St. Chrysostom, and other saints, in charging the Blessed Virgin with temporary unbelief, which pierced her as a sword.—(" Com. in Lucam.")

St. Augustine, Doctor (A.D. 430), in all his copious writings gives no support to the cultus.

St. Cyril of Alexandria, Doctor (A.D. 440), actually tells us, not only that St. Mary failed at the Cross from grief, bewilderment, and feminine weakness, but that the special reason for our Lord's committing her to St. John's care was in order that he, as a theologian, might teach her those truths of religion with which she was unacquainted. " How could He fail to know the thoughts which then perplexed her at the honoured Cross?

---

[1] Romanists endeavour to set aside this most explicit condemnation by saying that what St. Epiphanius blames is only the especial *mode* of honouring the Blessed Virgin, namely, by a sacrificial offering of cakes. In fact, after just incidentally mentioning that custom at first, he turns from it directly, and addresses himself to the main question. He does not say, " Give up those cakes of yours, and pray to Our Lady without them," but condemns the whole practice.

Knowing, therefore, the ponderings that were in her, He delivered her to the disciple who was the best instructor in mysteries, and who was well able, and not insufficiently, to explain that mystery."—("Comm. in Joann." xix. 26, 27.)

Finally, nothing in the least implying the cultus is to be found in Popes St. Leo the Great (A.D. 461) or St. Gregory the Great (A.D. 604).[1]

It is to be noticed, then, most carefully, that when we first find the cultus of the Blessed Virgin or of the angels making its appearance, it is at once *challenged and condemned as a novel* HERESY. This being so, from the nature of the Catholic Faith and the constitution of the Christian Church, no amount of later acceptance and popularity can ever whitewash it over, or make it lawful, as if it were a secular or political matter, which States and assemblies can alter as they please. The Faith cannot be added to, nor taken away from; all that is permissible is to explain it where it has been misrepresented, and to draw out its meaning more fully, as the Nicene Creed is fuller than, but yet the same as, the Apostles' Creed; and the Athanasian, again, does but expand and guard certain statements of the Nicene Creed which had been misconstrued.

Roman Arguments for Mariolatry.

XXV. What, then, are the defences put forward by Roman writers on behalf of this startling departure from Christian orthodoxy?

They are practically three. First, is an argument which perpetually crops up in the Roman controversy. It

---

[1] Many citations will be found in Cardinal Wiseman's Lectures, and other Roman controversial books, which seem to contradict these statements. But they are from notoriously spurious writings, often plainly declared to be such in the very editions to which reference is made. See Palmer's "Letters in Controversy with Wiseman."

is what is technically called the "*à priori* argument," the meaning of which is, simply, "Such a thing *ought* to be, and therefore it *is*." Because we know that God did bestow on St. Mary the unspeakable privilege of being Mother of the Incarnate Word, therefore we must conclude that He has given her every other grace, honour, privilege, and authority which He can confer, and we are bound to act on the belief that she enjoys them all.

There are two answers to this plea. First is the general one, that we, as blind and finite creatures, are quite incapable of reading the secret counsels of God, and of deciding how He must needs act when He has not given us any clue. We are as likely to go wrong in our guess, as a dog is in guessing what we think about and mean to do. And, besides, it is this very plea which is urged by some against the Incarnation and the Atonement.

Secondly; we *can* argue as to how other men and women ought to act and think; and we can therefore be sure that the Blessed Virgin, because of her love and loyalty to her Son, must needs shrink with pain and abhorrence from a worship which she feels and knows ought to be His alone, and which He has never, so far as we know, granted to her. We have her own rule to guide us, in that saying aptly called, "The Gospel according to St. Mary"; viz. "Whatsoever He saith unto you, do it" (St. John ii. 5); words which have a negative as well as a positive force.

The second argument is, that the worship of the Blessed Virgin is a strong outwork of the doctrine of the Incarnation, and is thus practically useful.

The reply is, that so far from this view finding favour with the Catholic Fathers when Arianism was powerful and threatening to conquer the whole Church, they—and especially St. Athanasius—contended that the fact of worship having been confessedly paid to Christ from the beginning was the strongest proof that He was not a mere creature, but God; because God *only* can be worshipped at all. And, in fact, St. Athanasius goes so far as to charge the Arians with idolatry, in that they worshipped Christ, while denying His Godhead.[1] If the cultus of the B. V. M. be allowed, this plea fails, and the argument for the Incarnation is seriously weakened. In truth, there is not such zeal now for the Incarnation itself in the Roman Church as to inspire confidence in its own permanent hold of that article of the Faith. For, in F. Gury's "Compendium of Moral Theology" (vol. i. pp. 124, 125), a widely-used and standard text-book in nearly all Roman Catholic clerical seminaries, and issued even from the press of the Propaganda itself in 1872, the question is asked: "Is *explicit* belief in the mysteries of the Trinity and the Incarnation matter of necessity (*i.e.* so as to be *indispensable* to salvation)?" And the answer is, that opinions are divided on this head, but the more probable one is the *negative*, because a merely implicit belief sufficed before Christ's coming, and therefore ought to suffice afterwards also. If a Roman Catholic be at liberty to believe no more than, say, Judas Maccabæus did, or than the Jesuits exacted from their Chinese converts at the beginning of the last century,[2] one does not quite see the utility of the Church as a witness to Christ's revelation of Himself. But implicit belief in the Pope is not sufficient; that must be explicit, according to many teachers now.

The third argument is from human analogy, that as Christ was subject to His mother once, He must be so

---

[1] "Orat. Cont. Arian," ii. 14; iii. 16. It may be remarked, in illustration, that the use of the pagan word *Divus* = God, to denote the saints, seemingly borrowed from the application of it to the deified Roman emperors, was once very widely common amongst Roman Catholic writers, was never censured, and has only of late dropped away. It is still in the Roman Breviary; e.g. June 4, lect. v.

[2] They did to death, in 1710, in the Inquisition of Macao, Cardinal Tournon, the Papal legate sent by Clement XI. to stop their paganization of Christianity. Cartwright, "The Jesuits," chap. xii.

still, just as every dutiful son is to his parents; and that she, as Queen, partakes all the King's privileges, and bestows all His bounties.

The answer is, that it is the Queen-*Consort*, not the Queen-*Mother*, who shares the King's dignity, so far as communicable, and that the Church, not the B. V. M., is the Bride and Wife of the Lamb; while no loving bridegroom makes his own mother the channel of the gifts and favours he bestows on his bride. The plea as to the continuance of St. Mary's maternal authority in Heaven (even if it were not disproved by our Lord's own acts and words after He entered on His ministry), so far as it is based on earthly analogy, cannot stand for a moment in England, where we are familiar with the fact that when Queen Victoria came to the throne, her mother, the Duchess of Kent, sank at once to the grade of a powerless subject, and was not even first in that rank amongst women so long as the Queen-Dowager survived; while she would have receded again to the second place, had she lived till there was a Princess of Wales.[1]

Denial of the Chalice to the Laity.

XXVI. We must now come to a further rebellion against an express Divine command, of which the Roman Church is guilty, that of its mutilation of the Sacrament of the Holy Eucharist. It is expressly recorded in the institution of that ordinance that the Lord laid a peculiar emphasis on the Cup—as though in prophetic view of a coming disobedience—which He did not lay upon the other part of the Sacrament, saying, "Drink ye *all* of it" (St. Matt. xxvi. 27); and

---

[1] It is not unfair to press Roman Catholics, who are fond of applying to the Pope language which Scripture confines to Christ, with the argument that no special attribute or authority in ecclesiastical matters has been alleged to vest in the mothers of Popes, albeit many have survived the elevation of their sons.

accordingly it is set down by another Evangelist that "they all drank of it" (St. Mark xiv. 23). Nevertheless, the existing rule of the Roman Church is that none but the celebrating priest ever does receive the chalice, so that not merely is the precedent of the first Eucharist departed from, even when others of the clergy communicate, but the laity are cut off for ever from participation in that half of the rite : albeit our Lord has said in another place, "Except ye eat the Flesh of the Son of Man, *and drink His Blood*, ye have no life in you" (St. John vi. 53); and His Apostle has added, writing to the laity of Corinth, "As often as ye eat this bread and drink this cup, ye do show the Lord's death till He come;" and again, "Let a man examine himself, and so let him eat of that bread and drink of that cup" (1 Cor. xi. 26, 28); words which cannot mean less than that St. Paul expected that lay communion in the chalice would last till the second coming of the Lord.

A Modern Novelty.

XXVII. There is no question as to usage here. Not only does the Greek Church, more ancient than the Roman, still communicate her eighty millions of believers in both kinds; and Cardinal Bona, one of the most eminent liturgical writers of the Roman body, confesses that "the faithful always and in all places, from the first beginnings of the Church till the twelfth century, were used to communicate under the species of bread and wine, and the use of the chalice began little by little to drop away in the beginning of that century, and many bishops forbad it to the people to avoid the risk of irreverence and spilling" ("Rer. Liturg." ii. 18) : but actually the Council of Constance itself, which first dared, on June 15, 1415, to expressly set aside Christ's command, confesses itself to be innovating by the very terms of its decree, wherein it not merely allows that

Christ Himself administered in both kinds to His disciples: but that "in the primitive Church this sacrament was received in both kinds by the people." Nevertheless, it rules that the contrary usage, now grown to be a "custom," is to be held as a "law," and any persons who maintain it to be sacrilegious or even illicit, are first to be censured as erroneous, and if persevering, to be condemned and punished by the Inquisition as *heretics;* while priests who dare to follow Christ's precept and example, by communicating their flocks with the chalice, are to be excommunicated and handed over to the secular arm, which then meant *to be burnt.* This is still the law of the Church of Rome, albeit she has no longer the power of carrying it into execution.

Four Arguments of the Council of Trent for Half-Communion.

XXVIII. The Council of Trent denies in set terms that there is any divine precept obliging others than the celebrant to communicate in both kinds, and defends half-communion on these grounds:

a. Christ said not merely, "Whoso eateth My flesh and drinketh My blood hath eternal life" (St. John vi. 54), but also said, "The bread that I will give is My flesh, which I will give for the life of the world" (St. John vi. 51); and not only said, "He that eateth My flesh and drinketh My blood, abideth in Me and I in Him" (St. John vi. 56), but also said, "He that eateth of this bread shall live for ever" (St. John vi. 58).

b. As a matter of practice, the usage of half-communion is defended on the ground of its having been confessedly practised by the early Church in times of persecution, and for sending to the sick, &c.; as also by the plea that all the Apostles at the first Eucharist were priests, and so might receive in both kinds.

c. Christ is received entire under each kind, so that

those who receive one kind only are "not defrauded of any grace *necessary* to salvation." And this doctrine, which is called "concomitance," is mainly based on the text, "Whosoever shall eat this bread OR drink this Cup of the Lord, unworthily, shall be guilty of the body AND blood of the Lord" (1 Cor. xi. 27); a passage where the Authorized Version (following a doubtful various reading, found in but few MSS.)[1] reads *and* instead of *or* in the first clause.

d. The Church has a right to change any details in the administration of the sacraments, and her custom is to be held as a law.

Refutation of the Plea of Honouring the Sacrament.

XXIX. These excuses will not stand inquiry. First of all, as regards the alleged desire to show greater reverence to the Blessed Sacrament by guarding against accidents to the chalice : it cannot be alleged that the Saints, doctors, and martyrs of the ancient Church were not as solicitous for its honour as the Latin clergy of the twelfth and fifteenth centuries, yet they never adopted such a precaution. But there is higher ground than that to take. Christians must confess that our Lord, as God, foreknew all the consequences which would flow from the terms of His institution, and freely willed to abide them. Therefore, any attempt to save His Sacrament from dishonour, by endeavouring to alter His will, is to incur His stern reprimand to St. Peter for exactly similar conduct :—

" From that time forth began Jesus to show unto His disciples, how that He must go unto Jerusalem, and suffer many things of the elders and chief priests and scribes,

---

[1] One of these MSS., however, is the Alexandrine Codex, and Origen had the same text before him; while *et*, not *vel*, is the reading of the oldest printed Vulgates, as the Mazarin Bible of 1450, the Bible of 1462, the Complutensian Polyglot, &c.

and be killed, and be raised again the third day. Then Peter took Him, and began to rebuke Him, saying, 'Be it far from thee, Lord : this shall not be unto thee.' But He turned, and said unto Peter, ' Get thee behind Me, Satan : thou art an offence unto Me : for thou savourest not the things that be of God, but those that be of men.' " (St. Matt. xvi. 21–23.)[1]

Refutation of the Plea from Ancient Usage.

XXX. Next, as regards the ancient custom of sending the Holy Eucharist in one kind to the sick, to hermits, and to persons in time of persecution, there are three reasons why it does not apply :—

a. All these cases, whatever they were, belong to the class of exceptional communions made *out of* church, and *apart from the Liturgy*. They supply no rule for the ordinary and normal use *in* church.

b. They were all cases of *necessity*. Imagine the Admiralty to lay down that no ship's crew should have more daily food and drink per man than one biscuit and a quarter of a pint of water, because there are many instances known of vessels formerly, where, when provisions ran short, no more could be allowed as rations.

c. The still prevalent custom in the rigidly conservative Eastern Church, of moistening in the chalice the sacrament reserved for the sick, makes it highly probable that such was the ancient use also, so that these apparently half-communions were really in both kinds.

---

[1] As a fact, nearly all the recorded acts of irreverence towards the Holy Eucharist, historical or legendary, took place in relation to the species of bread, and not with regard to the chalice, because it remains in the custody of the priest. And as regards accident, it is quite as likely that small particles of the species of bread may fall, or be blown away, as that a drop should fall from the chalice.

As to the argument from the priestly rank of the Apostles, that will not stand with the existing Roman usage, which is to exclude all priests, too, when not themselves celebrating, from the cup. To make the parallel good, our Lord, the celebrant at the first institution, should have taken the chalice Himself, and withheld it from the Apostles.

Uncertainty of the Doctrine of Concomitance.

XXXI. Touching the doctrine of concomitance, it is not a directly revealed truth, but at best a *guess*, a mere possible inference from one reading, not free from doubt, of the single text, 1 Cor. xi. 27. But there is a perfectly plain text which makes the other way, clearly distinguishing the grace conferred under each kind : " The cup of blessing which we bless, is it not the communion of the Blood of Christ ? The bread which we break, is it not the communion of the Body of Christ ? " (1 Cor. x. 16.) Moreover, the text 1 Cor. xi. 27, does not prove that the two parts of the sacrament *include* each the other, but only that they are so intimately associated, that irreverence to one involves irreverence to the other. So, in English law, though a queen-consort possesses no sovereign authority whatever, nor any share in government, yet conspiracy against or outrage upon her is high treason against the king, because of the tie of union between them. But that does not make the queen-consort identical with the king. And, with respect to the texts quoted by the Council of Trent, as qualifying each other, the well-known rule of interpretation, not only of Scripture, but of all written laws, is directly contravened, namely,—that where there are two or more statements regarding the same subject, but it is not intended that one should *repeal* the other, then the narrower statement is to be explained and governed by the wider one, not the wider by the narrower. Here is a case in point from Holy Writ. Our Lord enjoins baptism "in the Name of the Father, and of the Son, and of the Holy Ghost" (St. Matt. xxviii. 19). But baptism "in the Name of the Lord Jesus" is twice mentioned also (Acts viii. 16; xix. 5). Yet it is held all through the Catholic Church that this narrower statement must be read in the light of the wider one, and that baptism by the latter formula is invalid; while its true application is to be found in the words "and of the Son" in the fuller form. Precisely the same argument applies to the texts in St. John vi., and we are bound to read the briefer statements there by the light of the longer ones. And even if concomitance be true in itself, that will not mend the matter; for blood which is consumed in and with the flesh is always said to be *eaten* (Gen. ix. 4; Lev. xvii. 10-14; xix. 26; Deut. xii. 23; 1 Sam. xiv. 32, 33), whereas Christ's command is, *Drink*. Lastly, it is conceded as at least "probable" by many Roman theologians that there is a special grace conferred by the chalice, so that a layman is not to be blamed who desires the priesthood in order that he may communicate in both kinds.—(Liguori, "Theol. Mor." VI. iii. 227.)[1]

---

[1] Dens feebly urges that to say that more grace is conferred by reception in both kinds, is to argue as if a priest who took two or three sips of the Cup obtained more grace than if he drained it off at once. ("Theol." de Euchar. n. 58.) The two great Corpus Christi hymns, "Pange lingua" and "Lauda Sion," are both adverse to concomitance, as they clearly distinguish between the two kinds and their effects; while St. Thomas Aquinas thrice defines the effects of the two species as distinct, saying that "the Body is offered for the salvation of the body, and the Blood for the salvation of the soul." "Summ. Theol." III. lxxiv. 1, lxxvi. 2, lxxix. 1. And the Tridentine decree on Transubstantiation contradicts concomitance, saying that "there is a conversion of the whole substance of the bread into the substance of the Body of Christ our Lord, and of the whole substance of the wine into the substance of His Blood." (Sess. xiii. 4.)

Custom cannot supersede Law.

XXXII. It thus appears on the very face of things, that every priest who takes Holy Orders in the Church of Rome is bound to mutilate the administration of the Sacrament, and so to disobey that part of Christ's own command, " Do this," which relates to the mode of dealing with the chalice; while every lay convert binds himself to disobey that part of Christ's command denoted by the words, " Drink ye all of it," and that on the mere chance that a human guess as to the possible meaning of an apostolic gloss may set aside a plain direction of Christ Himself. Indeed, it might be urged as regards all English Churchmen who voluntarily secede to the Roman Church, and have not the excuse of being born in it, or of invincible ignorance, that they derive no benefit at all from the Holy Eucharist, but rather eat to their own condemnation, because they refuse to comply with the Lord's own command. And, if they raise the plea of *custom*, there are some weighty sayings of the Fathers which exactly apply :—

"A custom, beginning from some ignorance or simplicity, hardens into use by continuance, and so is defended against the truth. But our Lord Jesus Christ called Himself the *Truth*, and not the *custom*. Since Christ is for ever, and before all, so, too, truth is an everlasting and ancient thing. Let those beware, therefore, to whom that is new which in itself is old. It is not so much novelty as truth which refutes heresies. Whatever savours of opposition to the truth, this is a heresy, even if an old custom."—(Tertullian, " De Vel. Virg.," i.)

" Custom, without truth, is only antiquity of error."— (St. Cyprian, Ep. lxxiv.)

" That Christ alone has a right to be heard, the Father Himself attests from heaven, saying, 'This is My beloved Son, in Whom I am well pleased. Hear Him'

(St. Matt. xvii. 5); therefore, if Christ alone is to be listened to, we ought not to heed what anyone before our time may have thought fit to be done, but what Christ, Who is before all, first actually did. For we ought not to follow man's custom, but God's truth, seeing that God speaks and says by the prophet Isaiah, 'In vain do they worship Me, teaching for doctrines the commandments of men' (Isa. xxix. 13; St. Matt. xv. 9). And the Lord repeats this same thing again in the Gospels, saying, 'Ye reject the commandment of God, that ye may keep your own tradition' (St. Mark vii. 9). But in another place He lays down a rule, and says, 'Whosoever, therefore, shall break one of the least of these commandments, and teach men so, he shall be called the least in the Kingdom of Heaven' (St. Matt. i. 5-19). So, then, if it be not lawful to break even the least of the Lord's commandments, how much more is it impious to violate, and to change by human traditions into something different from the divine institution, such great and weighty things, and so closely pertaining to the very Sacrament of the Lord's Passion and our redemption? For, if Jesus Christ our Lord and God is Himself the High Priest of God the Father, and first offered Himself in sacrifice to the Father, and bade this be done in commemoration of Him, surely that priest truly acts in Christ's stead who imitates what Christ did. . . . But the whole discipline of religion and truth is overthrown unless there be faithful observance of that which is spiritually enjoined."—(St. Cyprian, Ep. lxiii.)[1]

"Let no man prefer custom to reason and truth, for reason and truth shut out the plea of custom."—(St. Augustine, "De Bapt. cont. Donat.," III. 11.) "The Lord in the Gospel said, I am the Truth; He did not

---

[1] St. Cyprian is here arguing for the mixed chalice, which is not expressly recorded in Scripture, so that his words apply with all the more force to what is so recorded.

say, I am the Custom. Therefore, when the truth is made plain, custom must give way to truth."—(Idem, VI. 71.)

Half-Communion declared Heretical by Popes.

XXXIII. Seeing that such is the mind of the ancient Church, we should naturally look to find half-communion, like Mariolatry and the invocation of angels, condemned as a heresy when it first crops up. And so we do, by the highest authority, moreover, which Roman Catholics acknowledge.

Pope Leo the Great declares that abstinence from the chalice is a Manichæan heresy, and says: "They receive Christ's Body with unworthy mouth, and entirely refuse to quaff the Blood of our redemption; therefore, we give notice to you, holy [brethren], that men of this sort, whose sacrilegious deceit has been detected, are to be expelled by priestly authority from the fellowship of the saints." (Hom. xli.)

Pope Gelasius I., in a letter to the Bishops Majoricus and John, embodied in the Roman canon law (Corp. Jur. Can. "Decret." III. ii. 12), says: "We have ascertained that certain persons, having received a portion of the Sacred Body alone, abstain from partaking of the chalice of the Sacred Blood. Let such persons, without any doubt (since they are stated to feel themselves bound by some superstitious reason) *either receive the Sacrament in its entirety*, or be repelled from the entire Sacrament, because the division of one and the same mystery *cannot take place without great sacrilege.*"

The Pope is clearly speaking about *laymen* here, for he not only does not name priests, but the clause about repelling must refer to the duty of the celebrant in respect of such disobedient communicants, as he clearly could not repel *himself;* and we should find, if priests were intended, some threat of suspension or deposition instead. Accordingly, in the older editions of the Canons (as those collected by Ivo of Chartres and Micrologus), the heading ran : "*No one* is permitted to receive the Communion of the Body alone without partaking of the Blood," but it has been altered in the later editions into, "The *Priest* ought not to receive the Body of Christ without the Blood." Even Cardinal Baronius rejects this gloss as foolish (*frigidam*). ("Ann. Eccl." A.D. 496.)

And the Council of Clermont, presided over in 1095 by Pope Urban II. in person, decreed, in its twenty-eighth canon, that "no one shall communicate at the altar without he receive the Body and Blood separately and alike, unless by way of necessity, and for caution."

Here then are three Popes, and on the last occasion with a council of 218 bishops and abbots, deciding one way; and, on the other hand, the first decree the other way was at Constance, after the Council had just deposed one Pope as a heretic and schismatic, but had not yet elected any other in his stead. John XXIII. was deposed on May 29, 1415, the canon enjoining half-communion was passed on June 15, 1415, and the new Pope was not elected till November 11, 1417. So that the evidence against the lawfulness of the change is overwhelming, even on Roman grounds.

Divine Service in a Dead Language.

XXXIV. Once more, the Church of Rome is in plain contradiction both to the letter and spirit of Holy Scripture, by conducting the most important parts of Divine Service in a dead language. The words of St. Paul on this topic are so pertinent that it is desirable to cite them in full :—

"If I pray in an unknown tongue, my spirit prayeth, but my understanding is unfruitful. What is it, then? I will pray with the spirit, and I will pray with the understanding also: I will sing with the spirit, and I will sing with the understanding also. Else when thou shalt bless with the spirit, how shall he that occupieth the room of the unlearned say Amen at thy giving of thanks, seeing he understandeth not what thou sayest? For thou verily givest thanks well, but the other is not edified. I thank my God, I speak with tongues more than ye all: yet in the church I had rather speak five words with my understanding that I might teach others also, than ten thousand words in an unknown tongue" (1 Cor. xiv. 14-19).

Now, the references to the "giving of thanks" (εὐχαριστίᾳ), and to the response "Amen," show plainly that the Apostle is here speaking of the [Mass or] Holy Eucharist, and is insisting on the necessity of its being celebrated in the vulgar tongue, that the people may know when and how to make the responses. And Cardinal Bona, following St. Thomas Aquinas, affirms this ("Rer. Liturg." I. v. 4). But it is precisely the Mass which Roman canon law forbids being translated from Latin for public use into any other language,[1] so that it has become necessary to employ the mechanical signal of a bell at certain points of the rite, to warn the congregation of that which they cannot, for the most part, learn from the words of the celebrant.

It may be admitted that no great harm was meant or worked by this system when it began, which was after the inroad of the barbarians into the Roman Empire, when the new Christian converts were found to be speaking a great variety of dialects, none of which had any literature, and all liable to incessant changes, whereas Latin was more or less generally understood. The fault was in not meeting the change of circumstances, when Latin dropped out of popular use, and the new languages of Europe took final shape.

[1] "This, truly [vernacular translation of the Mass], the Catholic Church abhors and always has abhorred." (Bened. XIV. De Sacrif. Miss. II. ii. 5).

Nor is the Roman case like that of the modern Jews, who use Hebrew still in their public devotions, as being the original sacred language in which their religion was Divinely revealed, and as being further a bond of tribal union to a scattered race. The most ancient Christian records are in Greek; the Epistle of St. Paul to the Roman Church itself is in Greek; and the *Kyrie Eleison*, with other Greek words, still embedded in the Missal, attest that the Mass of the Roman Church was once said in Greek too. Accordingly, the Latin translation, now held as sacred, must have been made with the intention of obeying St. Paul's precept, when Greek began to fall into disuse in Rome, and the bulk of the Christian people began to speak Latin.

No doubt this disobedience to Holy Scripture is of far less heinousness than the preceding examples, but still it *is* disobedience, and shows how Rome prefers her own will to God's will.

Nor is the usage without serious practical mischief. In the first place, it has made the act of the congregation at Mass largely mechanical and unintelligent, especially where, as the rule is in all Roman Catholic countries, the great bulk of those present are totally unlettered. Next, even for those somewhat better instructed, it has resulted in the very general employment of private and unofficial books of devotion, which are used at Mass, instead of the Missal itself, so that there is no attempt of the congregation to join directly in the lay portions of the office; and these books are usually far below the level of the Missal in tone and doctrine, so that the people are never lifted up to the ancient standard.[1] Lastly, the unknown tongue puts an ignorant

---

[1] This objection to the existing system is alleged even by the Ultramontane writer Léon Gautier, in his "Lettres d'un Catholique" (Paris, V. Palmé). And Faber says: "A man who is much given to vocal prayer is in no slight degree in the power of his prayer-book" ("Growth in Holiness," p. 278).

congregation wholly at the mercy of an infidel celebrant, who can substitute any other matter he pleases for the words he is supposed to be reciting.

Discouragement of the Bible.

XXXV. Besides these plain revolts against the clear letter of Holy Scripture and of the historical tradition of the Catholic Church, there are other respects in which the whole *spirit* of these two witnesses to the Faith is departed from, albeit there is not such express violation of the *letter*. First of these may be set the *discouragement* and slight put upon Holy Scripture by the Roman Church, not merely indirectly, by raising unwritten ecclesiastical traditions to equal rank with the Divine oracles (Conc. Trid., sess. iv.; Conc. Vatic. sess. iii. cap. 2), but directly, by restricting and disallowing the free circulation of the Scriptures in the vernacular. As this fact is often called in question, it may as well be here set down that the fourth Rule of the Congregation of the Index of Prohibited Books, approved by Pius IV., *and still in force*, runs as follows:—" Since it is manifest by experience that if the Holy Bible in the vulgar tongue be suffered to be read everywhere without distinction, more evil than good arises, let the judgment of the bishop or inquisitor be abided by in this respect; so that, after consulting with the parish priest or the confessor, they may grant permission to read translations of the Scriptures, made by Catholic writers, to those whom they understand to be able to receive no harm, but an increase of faith and piety, from such reading: which faculty let them have in writing. But whosoever shall presume to read these Bibles, or have them in possession without such faculty, *shall not be capable of receiving absolution of their sins, unless they have first given up the Bibles to the Ordinary.* Booksellers who shall sell or in any other way furnish Bibles in the vulgar tongue, to any one not possessed of the licence aforesaid, shall forfeit the price of the books, which is to be applied by the bishop to pious uses, and shall be otherwise punished at the pleasure of the said bishop, according to the degree of the offence. Moreover, Regulars may not read or purchase the same without licence had from their superiors."

So far, then, we see that permission to read the Bible is not a thing of course, but an exceptional favour, made difficult to obtain, and likely at once to be refused in every case where any man wanted honestly to know what God's revelation says upon some point of popular religion which might perplex him. But this is not all; for Clement VIII. glossing this rule, declares that the order and custom of the Holy Inquisition *have taken away from Bishops and Superiors all power to grant any such licences.*[1]

That the subjoined items are amongst the 101 Propositions of Quesnel, *condemned* by the Bull "Unigenitus" of Clement XI. in 1713, as "false, scandalous, pernicious, seditious, impious, blasphemous, and heretical," is a very pregnant fact :—

"79. It is useful and necessary at all times, in all places, and for all kinds of people, to study and learn the spirit, holiness, and mysteries of the Sacred Scripture.

"80. The reading of Holy Scripture is for all.

"82. The Lord's Day ought to be hallowed by Christians with pious reading, and above all of Holy Scripture. It is dangerous to attempt dissuading Christians from this reading.

"84. To take the New Testament out of the hands of Christians, or to keep it shut against them, by taking

---

[1] "Index Lib. Prohib." This new rule was so far relaxed in 1757 that specially authorized editions, *with notes*, might be tolerated, but no practical effect has followed.

away the means of understanding it, is to close Christ's mouth to them.

"85. To forbid Christians the reading of Holy Scripture, especially of the Gospels, is to forbid the use of light to the children of light, and make them undergo a sort of excommunication."

Pope Leo XII., in an Encyclical dated May 3rd, 1824, addresses the Latin Bishops thus :—" We also, venerable brothers, in conformity with our apostolic duty, exhort you to turn away your flocks from these *poisonous pastures* [of vernacular Bibles]. Reprove, intreat, be instant in season and out of season, in all patience and doctrine, that the faithful committed to you (*adhering strictly to the rules of our Congregation of the Index*) be persuaded that if the Sacred Scriptures be everywhere indiscriminately published, more evil than advantage will arise thence, because of the rashness of men."[1]

Pius IX., in the Papal Syllabus of Errors, groups *Bible Societies* along with Socialism, Communism, and Secret Societies, as *pests*, which have alike been often reproved by him with the severest terms in various Encyclicals.

Here, in England, where it is impracticable to forbid the Bible to such as wish to procure it, these rules are not insisted on, but it is almost an unknown book, save in Germany, to the Continental Roman Catholic. Nor are there any such Bible readings with explanations given by the clergy in church as to make amends for

---

[1] The writer has known a bonfire to be made of Anglican Bibles and Testaments by Roman Catholic clergymen at a mission in Kingstown, Dublin. If these persons knew how trifling is the difference, apart from mere style, between the Anglican version and the Douai version, what are we to think of their reverence for God's Holy Word? If they did not know it, what are we to think of their professional education, and their own anxiety to learn the truth of the matter? Imagine the like done by Anglican clergymen to Douai Bibles and Testaments.

the restriction. An explanation of the Gospel at Mass *may* be given, but is not obligatory, and there is nothing whatever analogous to the Anglican system of public lessons, for the Breviary Lessons are not only in Latin, but are part of an office which is never said in any parish church whatever, namely, the Nocturns or Night Hours.

These plain facts must be set against such titular approvals of vernacular Bibles as the Brief of Pius VI., for example, prefixed to Archbishop Martini's Italian version in 1778, which is the only solid argument cited by Roman controversialists in defence. The phrase "poisonous pastures" in the Encyclical of Leo XII., must mean one of two things, either that *all* vernacular translations are poisonous, or that such as are made by non-Romans are incorrect, corrupt, and misleading. In the latter case, obviously the duty of the Church is to provide trustworthy versions as the only sure antidote; but although there have been many translations of the Bible made by Roman Catholics into various European languages, there is, at this moment, speaking under correction, *none formally recognized and sanctioned for general use except the Douai Version*, and that for obvious reasons. All others are mere private ventures, for the most part, and certainly are not encouraged by authority;[1] nor does the great College *De Propaganda Fide*, at Rome, whose polyglot press is one of the boasts of the local Church, do anything to supply the deficiency.

---

[1] Martini's version, the one apparent exception, is not such in fact. In the first place, it is published only at a prohibitory cost; and next, an edition without the notes, issued in 1818, was promptly *put on the Index*. Moreover, Leo XII., writing forty-six years after Pius VI.'s Brief, makes no exception in favour of Martini on that ground. The edition to which that Brief applies (Turin, 1776–81) is in *twenty-three* quarto volumes; and the force of the Brief itself is seriously qualified by one clause, praising Martini chiefly for *obeying the laws of the Congregation of the Index*, by adding notes to avert the peril of misuse.

Lack of Aids to Biblical Study amongst the Clergy.

XXXVI. Nor is there any great zeal for instructing even the clergy in the Scriptures. It was actually not till Cardinal Mai published his edition of the Vatican MS. in 1858, that any Greek Testament was ever printed in Rome, though some twenty editions had appeared elsewhere, including Venice and Paris, as early as the sixteenth century, nor has any Hebrew Bible been published there even yet. And apart from the large, costly, and now partly antiquated works of Cornelius à Lapide and Calmet, severally 200 and 150 years old, there are at this moment no full commentaries on the entire Bible accessible to the Roman clergy, and very few indeed on separate portions except Maldonatus and Estius, the great majority of such as do exist being German, while little is done in France, almost nothing in Italy, and quite nothing in Spain and Portugal, for Biblical study.

What the Old Testament says about Itself.

XXXVII. Let us now see what can be gathered from Holy Scripture itself on this head. " To the Law and to the Testimony : if they speak not according to this word, it is because there is no light in them " (Isa. viii. 20). First of all, the principle of vernacular translations is Divinely sanctioned by the fact that the Apostles constantly quote from the Greek version of the Old Testament, and not directly from the Hebrew, as can be seen by comparing the LXX. and the original. Next, all through the Old Testament, there is ample evidence that the sacred writings were addressed to the whole Jewish nation, and not to the priestly caste alone ; that the lay people were expected to study them independently ; and that it was part of the duty of the teaching body to promote such study. A few examples will suffice in illustration :—

a. " And Moses called all Israel, and said unto them,

Hear, O Israel, the statutes and judgments which I speak in your ears this day, that ye may learn them, and keep, and do them" (Deut. v. 1).

b. "And these words, which I command thee this day, shall be in thine heart: And thou shalt teach them diligently unto thy children, and shalt talk of them when thou sittest in thine house, and when thou walkest by the way, and when thou liest down, and when thou risest up" (Deut. vi. 6, 7).

c. "When all Israel is come to appear before the LORD thy God in the place which He shall choose, thou shalt read this law before all Israel in their hearing. Gather the people together, men, and women, and children, and thy stranger that is within thy gates, that they may hear, and that they may learn, and fear the LORD your God, and observe to do all the words of this law: And that their children, which have not known anything, may hear, and learn to fear the LORD your God, as long as ye live in the land whither ye go over Jordan to possess it" (Deut. xxxi. 10–13).

d. "And with them he sent Levites, even Shemaiah, and Nethaniah, and Zebadiah, and Asahel, and Shemiramoth, and Jehonathan, and Adonijah, and Tobijah, and Tobadonijah, Levites; and with them Elishama and Jehoram, priests. And they taught in Judah, and had the Book of the Law of the LORD with them, and went about throughout all the cities of Judah, and taught the people" (2 Chron. xvii. 8, 9).

g. "And all the people gathered themselves together as one man into the street that was before the watergate; and they spake unto Ezra the scribe to bring the book of the law of Moses, which the LORD had commanded to Israel. And Ezra the priest brought the law before the congregation both of men and women, and all that could hear with understanding, upon the first day of the seventh month. And he read therein before the street that was before the water-gate from the morning until midday, before the men and the women, and those that could understand; and the ears of all the people were attentive unto the Book of the Law. Also Jeshua, and Bani, and Sherebiah, Jamin, Akkub, Shabbethai, Hodijah, Maaseiah, Kelita, Azariah, Jozabad, Hanan, Pelaiah, and the Levites, caused the people to understand the law: and the people stood in their place. So they read in the book in the law of God distinctly, and gave the sense, and caused them to understand the reading" (Neh. viii. 1, 2, 3, 7, 8).

What the New Testament says.

XXXVIII. So much for the Old Testament. Now let us turn to the New.

a. "And Jesus answering said unto them, Do ye not therefore err, because ye know not the Scriptures, neither the power of God?" (St. Mark xii. 24).

b. "And the brethren immediately sent away Paul and Silas by night unto Berea: who coming thither went into the synagogue of the Jews. These were more noble than those in Thessalonica, in that they received the word with all readiness of mind, and searched the Scriptures daily, whether those things were so. Therefore many of them believed; also of honourable women which were Greeks, and of men, not a few" (Acts xvii. 10-12).

c. All St. Paul's Epistles, except those to Timothy, Titus, and Philemon, are addressed to the whole body of the faithful in each place. One instance, by naming the clergy separately, emphasizes this fact: "Paul and Timotheus, the servants of Jesus Christ, to all the saints in Christ Jesus which are at Philippi, with the bishops and deacons" (Philipp. i. 1).

d. "And when this epistle is read among you, cause that it be read also in the church of the Laodiceans;

and that ye likewise read the epistle from Laodicea" (Col. iv. 16).

e. "I charge you by the Lord that this epistle be read to all the holy brethren" (1 Thess. v. 27).

f. "But continue thou in the things which thou hast learned and hast been assured of, knowing of whom thou hast learned them; and that from a child thou hast known the Holy Scriptures, which are able to make thee wise unto salvation through faith which is in Christ Jesus. All Scripture is given by inspiration of God, and is profitable for doctrine, for reproof, for correction, for instruction in righteousness: that the man of God may be perfect, throughly furnished unto all good works" (2 Tim. iii. 14–17).

g. "For whatsoever things were written aforetime were written for our learning, that we through patience and comfort of the Scriptures might have hope" (Rom. xv. 4).

There is nothing about "poisonous pastures" in all this, and indeed only one text in which the Bible is capable of being so much as cited on the other side. Here it is:—"And account that the long-suffering of our Lord is salvation; even as our beloved brother Paul also according to the wisdom given unto him hath written unto you; as also in all his epistles, speaking in them of these things; in which are some things hard to be understood, which they that are unlearned and unstable wrest, as they do also the other Scriptures, unto their own destruction" (2 Pet. iii. 15, 16).

But there is not a hint of withdrawing the Scriptures from circulation because of this abuse on the part of a few, nor in the case of these few is there any distinction drawn between clergy and laity; while, as a fact, most of the ancient heresies have had a clerical, not a lay origin.

The Fathers on Bible-Reading.

XXXIX. Let us now briefly examine the witness of the ancient Church. And it is to be remembered, at the outset, that it was to the full as much vexed by manifold sects and heresies, often appealing to the Bible, as modern Christianity, perhaps even more so, and therefore the same reason might have been pleaded then as is urged by the Roman Church now for keeping the Bible a sealed book. It will not be necessary to make many quotations, as those given shall be honestly average samples:—

a. In that august relic of primitive Christianity, the Liturgy of St. James, the following rubric occurs, whose great antiquity is attested by the absence of special reference to a collected New Testament:—" Then are read consecutively (*or* at much length, διεξοδικώτατα) the sacred oracles of the Old Testament and the Prophets; and the Incarnation of the Son of God, His sufferings and resurrection from the dead, His ascension into heaven, and His second coming with glory are set forth. And this is done every day in the holy and divine service."

b. " On the day called Sunday . . . the memories of the Apostles and the writings of the Prophets are read, so long as time permits; then, when the reader has ceased, the president verbally instructs, and exhorts to the imitation of these good things."—(St. Justin Mart. " Apol." i. 67.)

c. " We were enjoined by Christ Himself to put no faith in human doctrines, but in those proclaimed by the blessed prophets, and taught by Himself."—(St. Justin Mart., " Dial. with Trypho," xlviii.)

d. " Let the school of Hermogenes tell us where such a statement is written [in Scripture]. If it be not written, then let that school fear that Woe, awaiting those who take from or add to Scripture."—(Tertullian, " Adv. Hermogenem," xxii.)

e. " It is a manifest falling-away from the Faith, and a crime of presumption, either to annul anything in Scripture, or to introduce anything not in Scripture, since our Lord Jesus Christ has said, 'My sheep hear My voice' (St. John x. 27) . . . and the Apostle, taking an example from man's customs, vehemently forbids adding or taking anything away from the Divinely-inspired Scriptures, in these words : 'Though it be but a man's covenant, yet if it be confirmed, no man disannulleth, or addeth thereto'" (Gal. iii. 15).—(St. Basil the Great, "De Fide," 1.)

f. "*For practical purposes it is useful and necessary that everyone should thoroughly learn out of the Divinely inspired Scriptures, both for the fulfilment of piety and also in order not to become habituated to human traditions.*"—(St. Basil the Great, "Short Rules," 95.)

g. "Let us hear no more of 'You say,' 'I say,' but let us hear, 'Thus saith the Lord.' There are unquestionably books of the Lord, to whose authority we both of us give assent, submission, and obedience; let us look for the Church there, and there discuss our dispute."—(St. Augustine, "Ep. cont. Donat." iii. 5.)

h. "When impious heresy, which is the army of Antichrist, occupies the Churches, then know that there is no proof of the true faith and of Christianity, except the Holy Scriptures, for they who look elsewhere shall perish. Formerly, it was manifested in several ways which was the Church of Christ, and which was heathenism; but now there is no way of knowing which is the true Church of Christ, save only by the Scriptures. And why? Because those heresies have in their schism all things which belong to Christ in truth. They have similar churches, the same Holy Scriptures, similar bishops, and other grades of the clergy, baptism, and Eucharists, and all else; finally, Christ Himself. How, then, can anyone, wishing to know which is the true Church of Christ in such a confusing likeness, do so, save by the Scriptures?" (St. Chrysostom, "Hom. XLIX. in St. Matt." ii. 3.)

"The reading of the Scriptures is a powerful safeguard against sin, and ignorance of the Scriptures is a dangerous abyss. It is greatly to risk one's salvation to know nothing of Holy Writ; this is the source of many of the heresies and corruptions which have introduced themselves into the Church."—(St. Chrysostom, "Hom. III. on Lazarus.") This homily is not certainly his, but its witness is ancient.

"The Scriptures make use of simple words to explain the truth, in order that the learned and the ignorant, women and children, may alike learn from them . . . The heavenly oracles were written for the whole of mankind; even those who are employed in agricultural labour, and in various trades and businesses of life, profit by their clearness, and are able to learn from them in a moment what is necessary to be known, what is right and useful."—(St. Isidore of Pelusium, Epp. iv. 67, 91.)

Thus it is clear that in so important a particular as the mode of dealing with God's Word, the modern Roman Church is at fundamental variance with that Word itself and with the teaching and practice of the Catholic Church in its purest days.[1]

Indulgences.

XL. Next, let the doctrine and practical use of Indulgences be examined. This is a sore subject with Roman Catholics, and they pass over it as lightly as they can, softening and minimizing its peculiarities. Their statement, as they usually put it, is that an Indulgence is simply a remission of those temporal punish-

---

[1] It is possible to bring the evidence down much lower. In 1237, Pope Gregory IX. addressed a letter to Germanus, Patriarch of Constantinople, urging the reunion of the two Churches, and beginning with this sentence: "Whereas, according to the witness of the Truth, ignorance of the Scriptures is the occasion of errors, it is expedient that all should read or hear them, because Divine inspiration willed them to draw forth, for the warning of the moderns, whatsoever things He stored up therein for the teaching of such as should follow."—Matt. Paris, "Hist. Maj." 1237.

ments which remain due for those sins for which pardon has already been obtained through penance and confession. Now this *was* partly true once. In the early ages of the Church the penitential discipline was very severe, and persons were frequently placed under excommunication for long terms of years, besides being enjoined other penalties before receiving absolution. Of course, the authority which inflicted these censures could mitigate or remove them, precisely as the civil government now can grant a ticket-of-leave or a free pardon to a convict. But the modern Indulgence has little or nothing to do with *man's* ecclesiastical censures and penalties here on earth, and all citation of ancient usage in respect of such things is beside the question. It is now almost entirely concerned with *God's* chastisement of sin in the intermediate state of souls between death and the Last Judgment. It does not apply to cases like that of the incestuous Corinthian (1 Cor. v.; 2 Cor. ii. 6–8) which Romans quote in illustration, but to such as that of the rich man in the parable of Dives and Lazarus (St. Luke xvi. 23).

What Indulgences used to be.

XLI. Further, it is much insisted on in Roman apologetic books that Indulgences are in no sense *pardons* for sin, far less *licences to commit sin*, nor purchasable for money. This is true *now*, but it was not always true. The existing practice, whatever its errors and abuses may be, is at any rate free from the horrible scandals which attended the older method, abolished by the Council of Trent in consequence of the outcry raised on the subject at the Reformation—one proof, amongst many, that Rome *can* be forced to mend her ways by pressure from without, though she never does it voluntarily. The Roman Catholic princes of Germany, alarmed at the progress of Lutheranism, met in Diet at Nuremberg in 1522, and addressed a petition to Pope Hadrian VI. for the remedy of a "Hundred Grievances of the German Nation" which they set forth in that document. Amongst these occur

No. 5. How licence to sin with impunity is granted for money.

„ 67. How more money than penitence is exacted from sinners.

„ 91. How bishops extort money from the concubinage of priests.

They re-stated these grievances more at length, classifying them in chapters, and alleged that the vendors of Bulls of Indulgence "declare that by means of these purchasable pardons, not only are past and *future* sins of the living forgiven, but also those of such as have departed this life and are in the purgatory of fire, provided only something be counted down. . . . . Everyone, in proportion to the price he had expended in these wares, promised himself impunity in sinning. Hence came fornications, incests, adulteries, perjuries, homicides, thefts, rapine, usury, and a whole hydra of evils. For what wickedness will mortals shudder at any longer, when they have once persuaded themselves that licence and impunity for sinning can be had for money, however extravagant the sum, not only in this life but after death also, by means of these marketings of Indulgences?" Then, speaking of "Reserved Cases,"[1] the princes add : " But if any one have the means of paying, not only are present breaches of these constitutions allowed, but by the indulgence he has permission to transgress them with impunity for the future. Whence it happens that they who have got such a dispensation lay hold of it as a handle for committing perjury, murder, adultery, and similar atrocities, since any common priest can give them

[1] That is, sins which ordinary confessors are not allowed to absolve, but which are kept for the bishop, or, in some instances, for the Pope.

purchasable absolution by virtue of the indulgence."[1] And the Pope, instead of indignantly denying the truth of these horrible charges, implicitly admitted the facts to be as stated. Indeed, he could not deny it, for the book entitled, "Taxes of the Sacred Apostolic Penitentiary," was then, and is still, extant, with a regular tariff for the absolution of all kinds of sins, including simony, murder by a priest, parricide, incest, arson, &c.[2] There is even, in some copies of the Taxes, a special note, stating that dispensations of this sort are not to be given to poor persons. The whole question is fully treated in the reprint, by Professor Gibbings, of the Roman and Parisian editions (1510 and 1520) of the "Taxes of the Apostolic Penitentiary" (Dublin, McGee, 1872). This kind of thing had been steadily growing up for some centuries, till it reached its highest pitch under Pope Alexander VI., and then the outcry began which ended in the comparative reformation of the abuse in 1563. Nevertheless, even as reformed, the practice and doctrine are altogether diverse from those of the ancient Church, and the assertion made by Dr. Milner, Cardinal Wiseman, and others, that nothing more is intended by indulgences than the relaxation of outward guilt, or of such penances as are enjoined by canonical discipline, is untenable. In fact, when they say so, they are actually

---

[1] See the whole document in Brown's "Fasciculus Rerum." London, 1690, vol. i. pp. 334-393.

[2] Some items read very curiously. Thus, the price of absolution for the murder of a father, mother, brother, sister, or wife, if the murderer be a laic, is 1 ducat and 4 carlini. But if more than one of these victims have been murdered, and a single absolution be taken out for all, then only half rates are charged after the first name on the list, for which the full price must be paid. A clerical murderer, in like circumstances, is required to make a journey to Rome. No doubt these charges began as mere legal costs in the ecclesiastical courts, in suing out pardons, but there is no avoiding the conclusion that they were perverted into a tariff for sins themselves, though probably never by any lawful and binding authority.

reproducing in substance two of the propositions of Luther on Indulgences, condemned, as "pestiferous, pernicious, and scandalous," by Leo X., in the Bull "Exurges" of June 25, 1520, namely, that " Indulgences do not avail, for those who truly acquire them, to the remission of punishment due to Divine justice for actual sins," and that "graces of this sort have relation only to the penalties of sacramental satisfaction, of man's appointment."

The Roman Doctrine of Indulgences.

XLII. The actual Roman doctrine is this. There are two penalties annexed to all sin, *Culpa*, or eternal punishment; *Pœna*, or temporal punishment, including that of purgatory; and even after *Culpa* has been remitted by absolution of the penitent, *Pœna* still remains uncancelled. However, as one drop of Christ's blood was sufficient for the redemption of the whole world, all the rest that He shed, together with the merits and prayers of all the saints, over and above what were needed for their own salvation, technically called "works of supererogation," constitutes an inexhaustible treasury or bank on which the Pope has a right to draw, and apply the drafts in payment for the release of souls in purgatory,[1] so that anyone who obtains an Indulgence can apply its merits to himself, or transfer it to some other, living or dead. When an Indulgence of a hundred days, or of seven years, is spoken of, it means that so much guilt is bought off as would be expiated by undergoing a penance extending over the whole of that time; while a *plenary* Indulgence means the entire remission of all purgatorial chastisements. Two plain facts will show the entire unlikeness of this theory to the ancient discipline of the Church. First, the enormous majority of Indulgences are now acquired by persons who are not under canonical penance at all, but are in full com-

[1] Bellarmine, " De Indulg." i. 14.

munion; nay, regarded as specially devout and obedient.[1] Next, whereas a hundred years is the extreme limit of human life, yet in the "Hours of B. V. M., according to the Use of the Church of Sarum" (Paris, 1526), indulgences are promised for 500, 11,000, 32,755, and 56,000 years. Modern indulgences are more cautiously granted, and the highest number specified in the "Raccolta" is seven years and seven quarantines, *i.e.*, 280 days; though there are longer periods to be had, as will be shown presently; and thus the popular notion often is that so many years in purgatory itself are remitted by the Indulgence.

Novelty of this Doctrine.

XLIII. The first thing to remark upon as to this doctrine is its novelty. The system cannot be traced back earlier than the quarrel of Gregory VII. with the Emperor Henry IV., when remission of sins was offered in 1084 to such as would take up arms against the Emperor. Then it was used for the Crusades, and it was extended by Innocent III. to all who took up arms against the Albigenses and other heretics. Since then it has been applied indiscriminately. The Eastern Church has never had anything even remotely like it. Next, the whole doctrinal basis on which it rests was denied as late as 1141 by Peter Lombard, Bishop of Paris, in that famous work, for centuries a text-book in the theological schools of Western Christendom, which earned him his title of "Master of the Sentences." He lays down there explicitly that God only can remit either the *Culpa* or the *Pœna* of sin ("Sentt." iv. 18); while man can dispense only with the penalties man has instituted.

---

[1] "The use of indulgenced devotions is almost an infallible test of a good Catholic." Faber, "Growth in Holiness," p. 278.

Indulgences destroy Devotion.

XLIV. Next,—and here is an objection which, fatal as it is, curiously enough rarely seems to be raised against Indulgences—the system entirely eats out all that spontaneity and freewill offering of devotion without which prayer cannot please God, Who "loveth a cheerful giver" (2 Cor. ix. 7). It assumes as certain that people will not pray unless they be bribed to do it by a certain fixed tariff of so much direct advantage and profit for so much prayer; and thereby it changes prayer from a freewill offering into a coarse attempt at making a huckstering bargain with Almighty God. And by holding out this inducement to certain specified religious exercises, it thereby directly discourages the use of all others, so that freewill prayers and praises are becoming almost unknown to the bulk of Roman Catholics. Indeed, Faber says: "Why should we have *any* vocal prayers which are not indulgenced devotions?" ("Growth in Holiness," p. 282). Nothing can be more profoundly unspiritual, or tend more to quicken and bring back that original sin of selfishness, which it is the aim of Christ's example and teaching to slay and cast out of man's heart and soul.

Their Inconsistency with Scripture.

XLV. There are other grave religious objections to the whole theory, even if we do not dwell on the entire absence of Scriptural proof of such a theory of purgatory as is prevalent in the Roman Church, and the absence of anything either in Scripture or in ancient Christian writers which can be tortured into a semblance of the alleged Treasury of Merits. First, then, since Christ's merits are *infinite*, the merits of all Saints together, which at best are *finite*, cannot make His merits *greater* or more efficient. It is like adding on a farthing to ten thousand millions of pounds. And next, whereas no man, not even the holiest saint, has ever achieved perfect conformity to God's holiness and Christ's example (though no less pattern is set before us), yet the Lord Himself says:—"When ye have done all those things which are commanded you, say, We are unprofitable servants: we have done that which was our duty to do" (St. Luke xvii. 10). And He who is the Truth would not have put a lie in the mouths of His Apostles merely to practise them in humility. We have thus one illogical inconsistency, and one explicit denial of Christ's truth, in the doctrine of the Treasury of Merits.[1]

Their Mischievousness, even if Valid.

XLVI. Again, Christ came to save us from sin itself, not from the mere punishment of sin. And He did not come to spare His saints any suffering which He, the Great Physician, judges to be needful for their perfection. Now, it is quite true that we can, perhaps, see through the thick veil which lies between us and the world of spirits a few glimpses in Scripture of some process of gradual improvement and fitting for heaven which goes on after death; which, it is possible to conjecture, may be attended with the twofold pain of horror at past sin and longing for the deferred presence of God. Very little, indeed, is told us, but we can just guess at so much. However, in the plainest of all those passages alleged by Roman Catholics, Our Lord overthrows with one sentence the whole theory of Indulgences, "Verily, verily, I say unto thee, thou shalt by no means come out thence, till thou hast paid the uttermost farthing" (St. Matt. v. 26).

For even on Roman principles, purgatory is reserved exclusively for *pious* and *justified* souls, which have departed in a *state of Grace* ("Catechism of Trent," I. v. 5;

---

[1] Christ's Parable of the Ten Virgins also contradicts this doctrine, for He makes the Wise Virgins refuse to share their oil with the foolish, on the express ground that there would not be enough for all. St. Matt. xxv. 8, 9.

Perrone, "Præl. Theol."). God cannot but love such souls, and purgatory can only be intended to *purify* and *cleanse*, not to *punish* them. And He must be trusted to cleanse them in the most merciful and tender, as well as in the most effectual, way. Surely, then, to take them out of purgatory before their time be come, must be bad for them; unless we fall back on the theory that the Roman Church is wiser and more merciful than God Himself, and, so to speak, delivers His victims out of His hand! Put a parallel case in human affairs. What should we think of an association intended to beg off all boys sentenced to detention in a reformatory, and to send them straight away, without the corrective training which they would have received there, into good society as finished young gentlemen?

Roman View of Purgatory contradicts Scripture.

XLVII. But, in fact, the modern Roman doctrine of Purgatory is dishonouring to the mercy, justice, and love of God. That doctrine is, that the pains of purgatory, both physical and mental, are the same, except in mere duration, with the pains of hell (Benedict XIV., "De Sacrif. Missæ," II. ix. 3, 6; xvii. 3). Now here is what the Book of Wisdom, *which the Roman Church accounts canonical*, has to say on that head:—

"But the souls of the righteous are in the hands of God, *and there shall no torment touch them.* In the sight of the unwise they seemed to die: and their departure is taken for misery, and their going from us to be utter destruction, *but they are in peace*" (Wisd. iii. 1–3).

So, too, St. John: "And I heard a voice from heaven saying unto me, Write, Blessed are the dead which die in the Lord from henceforth. Yea, saith the Spirit, that they may *rest from their labours*" (Rev. xiv. 13).[1]

---

[1] It is very noteworthy that St. John's own word for "labours" here is κόπων, which strictly means "beatings," and then any kind

But the received Roman doctrine is that these are *justified* souls; and justification, in the Tridentine sense, includes *sanctification, union with Christ*, and the full enjoyment of faith, hope, and charity (Conc. Trident. sess. VI. cap. vii.); and yet Rome represents those who are in this state as not merely subject to the *justice*, but as pursued by the *wrath, anger*, and *vengeance* of God (see Cardinal Wiseman's "Lectures," ii.), which is an implicit denial of the whole Gospel dispensation, and, what is more to Roman Catholics, a flat contradiction of received Roman doctrine on two points.

And Contradicts other Roman Doctrine.

XLVIII. These points are: (1.) Venial sins are punished in purgatory, and, indeed, form the bulk of those chastised there. But, although Rome teaches that penance, confession, and absolution, are the remedies for post-baptismal sins, yet it is laid down that venial sins are so trifling that *no one is bound to confess them at all*, and may communicate without confession; while they may be remitted in many ways besides that of penance (Liguori, "Theol. Mor." vi. 318, 319; Conc. Trident., sess. xiv. c. 5), although the Council of Lateran requires *all sins* to be confessed at least once a year. Therefore, the conclusion is, that God visits with wrath and vengeance what the Church looks on as not really sins, but as too insignificant to require formal censure. (2.) It is argued by Roman Catholics that the right to grant indulgences is part of the Power of the Keys, granted to the Apostles and continued to the Church, for remitting or retaining sins. But the very doctrine of purgatory is that *after* the Power of the Keys has been exercised by absolution, there *remains* a temporal penalty *untaken away*, and consequently *unaffected* by the Power of the Keys.

of hard toil or *suffering*. How could it be said of souls "tortured (*cruciatæ*) in the fire of purgatory," as the Council of Trent declares, that they *rest* from sufferings?

It now remains to compare a modern Roman hymn on the state of the departed with one or two passages from the works of Saints and from the office-books of the Eastern Church, which, while retaining prayers for the dead, utterly rejects the Roman doctrine of Purgatory, though unjustifiably quoted by Dr. Faa di Bruno as maintaining that doctrine.

> (1.) "In pain beyond all earthly pains,
> Favourites of Jesus! there they lie,
> Letting the fire purge out their stains,
> And worshipping God's purity."—FABER.

(2.) "Where there is grace, there is remission; where there is remission, there is no punishment."—(St. John Chrysostom, "Hom. VIII. in Epist. ad Rom.")

(3.) "God acts with liberality. He forgives entirely."—(St. Bernard, "Serm. de Fragmentis.")

(4.) "Grant rest unto the souls of Thy servants, O Lord, together with Thy saints, where there is no pain, nor sorrow, nor sighing, but life without end."—(Greek Office for All Souls' Saturday.)

Lastly, here is the witness of eminent Roman Catholic divines as to Indulgences:—

"We have no testimony in the Scriptures, nor amongst the Fathers, in favour of Indulgences, but only the authority of some modern authors."—(St. Antoninus, Abp. Florence (1459), "Summ. Theol." I. 3.)

"Since it was so late before purgatory was admitted into the Universal Church, who can be surprised that at the earlier period of the Church, no use was made of Indulgences?"—(Cardinal Fisher, Martyr (1535), "Adv. Luther," 18.)

"There is nothing in the Scriptures less clear, or of which the ancient Fathers have said less, than Indulgences; it would appear that this system has only lately been received into the Church."—(Alfonso de Castro, Abp. of Compostella (1558), "Adv. Hæres.")

The Mass Traffic.

XLIX. But even though one of the worst features of the old Indulgence system, its shameful venality, has been ended, and the Council of Trent has forbidden "disgraceful gains" of the kind to be any longer trafficked in (Sess. XXI. 9), nevertheless the same greedy spirit exhibits itself still in a manner which, if not quite so scandalous on the very surface, is just as revolting when viewed more closely.

It is still true in a very frightful way that the Church of Rome, which boasts itself as being in an especial sense the "Church of the Poor"—thereby too often really meaning that it has alienated all educated people, and has none but ignorant clients left—lies justly under the accusation of being what it is called in France, *La réligion d'argent*, "the creed of money"—which our own forefathers implied by their proverb, "No penny, no Paternoster."[1]

It is perhaps *the* most distinctive peculiarity of the Gospel that it puts the poor in such an honourable position, not in the mere way of studiously recommending them to the charity of the rich (as even the Law did), but in that the Gospel itself is in a very special way addressed and "preached to the poor" (St. Matt. xi. 5; St. Luke iv. 18, vii. 22), and that "God hath chosen the poor of this world, rich in faith, and heirs of the kingdom which He hath promised to them that love Him" (St. James ii. 5). And one practical interpretation put on these and like sayings of Scripture in Roman Catholic countries is the encouragement of idle mendicants, to relieve whom is accounted a religious

---

[1] For the shameless competition of rival shrines in France, with their advertisements of advantages, from privileged Masses up to miracles, to be had by customers at prices ranging from 5 centimes to 10,000 francs, see Parfait, "Le Dossier des Pèlerinages," Paris, 1877, who gives extracts from circulars and pamphlets in proof.

duty and merit, albeit St. Paul has said, "If any work not, neither should he eat" (2 Thess. iii. 10).

But when we come to the Roman Church's own dealings with the poor, the spirit is changed entirely. It is to be remembered that the practical, encouraged, and authorized belief of Roman Catholics is that the incalculable majority of their own co-religionists who are saved at all, pass at once after death into hideous tortures of undefined duration, while the received opinion is that this duration is very long, and may extend to thousands of years. Next, the Sacrifice of the Mass, as propitiatory for the sins of the living and the dead, is held to be the *chief* means of relieving souls in purgatory, to which Indulgences are but subsidiary in operation; and Masses for the dead are consequently a very prominent feature in all Roman Catholic Churches. But, except on comparatively infrequent occasions, such as All Souls' Day and the anniversaries, or month's-minds, of purgatorial guilds, &c., these Masses are said, not for the faithful departed in general, but for private individuals, and are paid for according to a fixed tariff. The result of this usage, and of the doctrine inculcated in connexion with it, is that rich people purchase thousands of Masses to be applied for the repose of their own souls or those of their kindred and friends. Thus, only the other day, Queen Christina of Spain left money by will for ten thousand Masses to be said for herself and her husband, five thousand for each of them.

Now, by accepting this money, the Roman clergy plainly undertook to give full value for it, and that value must of course be measured by the supposed cumulative power of Masses in proportion to their number. This means, then, that a rich man, who may be just barely capable of being saved, and who, according to Roman *theory*, ought to remain longest and suffer most in purgatory, is to be released unspeakably sooner than the poor man whose friends cannot afford to pay for Masses.

And not only so, but by pre-engaging such vast numbers of Masses, the rich prevent there being time or opportunity to say gratis Masses for the poor, even if there were any inclination to do so, seeing that by a rule, very seldom relaxed, each priest can say but one Mass daily. Take a village church, then, where the rich family of the neighbourhood has ordered several hundred Masses for a dead member, which the priest from poverty cannot afford to refuse, how about all the poor of the parish who die while these have the priority?

If their souls be worse off, as compared with those of the rich, in consequence of the lack of Masses, is it not plain that money is made the key of the kingdom of heaven?

If their souls be no worse off, have not the clergy swindled the rich by taking money under false pretences, to do that which makes no practical difference?[1]

Put the case of one of the worst kinds of railway accident, where the shattered carriages are also on fire, and the sufferers are being slowly burnt as well as crushed and maimed; what would be said if it were to become known that the railway officials had extricated from the wreck only such passengers as seemed able to pay for the attention, and left all the third-class travellers to lie there without any help till the next day? And yet there is no proportion between the cruelty of such conduct and that of the Roman clergy, if they believe what they say.

Uncertainty of the Mass Traffic.

L. If such be the state of things on the supposition that the Masses ordered are duly said, and without

---

[1] Faber has tried to evade this dilemma by urging that earthly poverty, as entailing suffering, is equivalent to purgatory. But (a) there is no proof that this is the received doctrine; and (b) it does not apply to those vast numbers who, living in reasonable comfort, have yet no savings available to pay for Masses, but applies only to the starving or diseased poor.

opening up the uncomfortable doubt as to Intention, whether the celebrant really meant to say a valid Mass, and to apply it to the particular person paid for, what is to be said when there is reason to suppose that the contract has not been fulfilled in any sense, nor any value given for money received? Yet that such not only might be, but has been more than once, and may at any time again be the case, has been established by more than one scandalous trial in France of late. The cases have been of this sort:—Certain of the Parisian clergy, having contracted to say an enormous number of Masses, amounting to a couple of hundred thousand, found that the work simply could not be got through, and instead of saying so and returning the money, arranged with a middle-man to farm out a large proportion of them to country priests at a lower rate of pay per Mass, so as to leave a margin of profit to the original contractors and a commission for the agent. It was shown by a couple of lawsuits that the agent had not carried out his part of the engagement, but had simply pocketed the money, no Masses had been said (though in other instances the process of sub-letting was carried on, ending in the Masses being said for the barest pittance by starveling curates), and the customers had been defrauded on a very large scale. Imagine the working of a system which thus makes possible a Glasgow Bank fraud in the spiritual world, affecting in the profoundest way the agonized souls of the departed and the feelings of their sorrowing kindred; that the future condition of souls which Christ died to ransom should be thus at the mercy of any grasping priest or swindling commission-agent!

Necessary Result of the System.

LI. It is clear that one all but inevitable result of the system must be the encouragement of rich people to continue in the habit of committing any or all sins, short of mortal ones, to which they have a mind, in the belief that they can buy themselves out of purgatory by a sum of money expended on requiem Masses; and contrariwise, to strike dismay and terror into the hearts and souls of those who are too poor to pay for such luxuries for themselves or their friends. And accordingly the Church of Rome, so long as she persists in this course, incurs the Divine threat uttered by the Prophet:—

"Because with lies ye have made the heart of the righteous sad, whom I have not made sad; and strengthened the hands of the wicked, that he should not return from his wicked way, by promising him life:

"Therefore ye shall see no more vanity, nor divine divinations: for I will deliver my people out of your hand: and ye shall know that I am the Lord" (Ezek. xiii. 22, 23).

Marriage Dispensations.

LII. There is another scandal, akin to that of the old Indulgences, still prevalent in the Roman Church, namely, that of dispensations for marriages within the prohibited degrees, which are very much more numerous than in the Church of England, including not only first, second, and third cousins, but also "spiritual affinities" created by sponsorship at baptisms. Nevertheless, dispensations are to be had for marriage with a brother's widow, with a wife's sister, or between an uncle and niece: though in Leviticus xviii. 12–14, the marriage of a nephew and aunt is declared incestuous, and there is no difference in principle between the two cases.[1] (André, "Droit Canon," s. v. "Empêchements.") Practically, some of these dispensations mean simply the payment of certain fees by persons rich and influential enough to get

---

[1] Even this union is sometimes permitted, and there is a case of a marriage of a nephew and aunt in the Portuguese Royal family in 1777.

the matter expedited for them. Now here is a very grave scandal. Either marriages of these kinds are permissible by God's law, or they are not. That is a fairly arguable matter. But if they be permissible and expedient, the Roman Church has no right to set up toll-bars and block the way against those who desire to contract them, unless they undertake an expensive process meant to bring gain into the coffers of the Datary. Contrariwise, if such unions be forbidden or inexpedient, then to relax a moral and religious prohibition is an indefensible abuse, a playing fast-and-loose with holy things which cannot be too severely condemned. And, accordingly, Scipio de' Ricci, Bishop of Pistoia and Prato, denounced the whole system in 1780 as *una infame bottega*, "a shameful traffic."[1]

Roman Untrustworthiness.

LIII. The next valid reason (and especially for the unlearned) against joining the modern Church of Rome, is the entire disregard for truth exhibited in its polemics, in its claims, its cults, relics, legends, and even its very office-books. This is, in fact, that peculiarity of its practical system which brings it most definitely into collision with the Word of God. Not only can the Christian religion have no claim whatever on our acceptance unless it be true, but the moral tone of the Bible is throughout one, indivisible, and clear, on the hatefulness of all falsehood in God's sight. The law given on

---

[1] The practical use of keeping up this system in the modern Roman Church is this : Bishops in their dioceses are the ordinary ministers through whom such dispensations as are gratis are issued. Their faculties for doing this last only five years, and have to be periodically renewed. By depriving any bishop of this power, all the laity of his diocese are roused against him, because they are prevented from contracting such marriages, and all the clergy, too, because they lose the bridal fees, and accordingly his submission to Rome in any emergency can be secured by a turn of this screw, as Bishop Hefele of Rottenburg learnt not long ago to his cost.

Sinai, "Thou shalt not bear false witness," is echoed again and again through the sacred writings down to the last book in the canon. So Job rebukes his friends: "Will ye speak wickedly for God, and talk deceitfully for Him?" (Job xiii. 7). So the Wise Man speaks: "The Lord doth hate . . . . a false witness that speaketh lies" (Prov. vi. 16-19); and again, "Lying lips are an abomination to the Lord" (Prov. xii. 21). So the Lord Himself spake by His Prophet: "And of these shall be taken up a curse . . . . because they have spoken lying words in My Name, which I have not commanded them" (Jer. xxix. 22, 23). So the Apostle counsels his flock, "Wherefore, putting away lying, speak every man truth with his neighbour" (Eph. iv. 25); so the Apocalypse warns us that "all liars shall have their part in the lake which burneth with fire and brimstone, which is the second death" (Rev. xxi. 8); and that "whosoever loveth and maketh a lie" is left outside the gates of the heavenly city, along with sorcerers, murderers, idolaters, and the like. (Rev. xxii. 15.)

Nevertheless, the Roman Church, which professes to worship Him Who has said, "I am the Truth," is honeycombed through and through with accumulated falsehood; and things have come to this pass, that no statement whatever, however precise and circumstantial, no reference to authorities, however seemingly frank and clear, to be found in a Roman controversial book, or to be heard from the lips of a living controversialist, can be taken on trust; nor accepted, indeed, without rigorous search and verification. The thing *may* be true, but there is not so much as a presumption in favour of its proving so when tested. The degree of guilt varies, no doubt, from deliberate and conscious falsehood with fraudulent intent, down through reckless disregard as to whether the thing be true or false, to mere overpowering bias causing misrepresentation; but truth, pure and simple, is almost never to be found, and the *whole* truth, in no case whatever.[1]

[1] "Do you know, Monseigneur, in the history of the human

Proofs of the Charge.

LIV. And now to offer a few proofs in support of so heavy an accusation. The process began early :—

a. In A.D. 419, a Council of the whole African Church was held at Carthage, and Faustinus, Bishop of Potenza, who was legate of the Pope there, tendered, in proof of the Pope's right to hear appeals from foreign Churches, certain Canons of the local Synod of Sardica, held in 347, and not received either in Eastern or Southern Christendom, as if they were canons of the General Council of Nicæa in 325, and universally binding. The Council had a search made in the archives of Alexandria, Antioch, and Constantinople, of course vainly, save that authentic copies of the Nicene Canons were sent to it; whereupon it rejected the Sardican Canons, had the genuine Nicene Canons read and affirmed, and wrote to the Pope, complaining of the attempted fraud, and told him that nothing should make them tolerate such insolent conduct on his part.[1] This letter was signed, amongst others, by the illustrious St. Augustine. Nevertheless, the same use was made of them by Pope Leo 'the Great only thirty years later when the matter was still fresh;[2] and yet a third time by Felix III., to coerce Acacius of Constantinople.

b. The Roman legates at the Council of Chalcedon in 451, produced a forged copy of the Nicene Canons, containing, in the Sixth Canon, the words, "The Roman See has always had the Primacy," which were promptly repudiated by the Council.[3]

---

mind, any question, theological, philosophical, historical, or otherwise, which has been so disgraced by falsehood, bad faith, and the whole work of the forgers, [as Papal authority]? I say it again, *It is a question utterly gangrened by fraud.*" (Gratry, "Letter II. to Déchamps.")

[1] "Non sumus jam istum *typhum* passuri." Cod. Ecc. Afri. cxxxiv.
[2] Fleury, " Hist. Eccl." xxvii. 43.
[3] Fleury, " Hist. Eccl." xliii. 17. This forgery is quoted as genuine in Dr. Di Bruno's " Catholic Belief," p. 112.

c. It is matter of history, recorded by St. Jerome, that the Emperor Constantine the Great was baptized on his death-bed in Nicomedia, an Asiatic city, by Eusebius, its bishop. Nevertheless, a fable was invented in the fifth century that this emperor was a leper, and was healed of his disease at Rome by means of baptism administered to him there by Pope Sylvester, in gratitude for which he made over to the Popes all right of sovereignty over Rome itself, and much adjacent territory (the famous so-called Donation of Constantine); and this falsehood, invented for a political purpose, which it effectually served, holds its place still in the Roman Breviary, and is read by every priest on December 31st each year.[1]

d. In 754 Pope Stephen III. forged a letter in the name of the Apostle St. Peter, and sent it to Pippin, King of France, calling on him to come to the defence of the Pope and the city of Rome against the Lombards; which he accordingly did, and bestowed on the Pontiff a great territory, containing more than twenty cities, the first beginning of the temporal power. Fleury, in recording this event, describes it as "an artifice without parallel before or since in Church history." ("Hist. Eccl." IX., xliii. 59.) That is how the Pope first became a king.

e. In the middle of the ninth century came the greatest of all the forgeries, the famous "False Decretals," that is, a collection of about a hundred formal official letters

---

[1] There are many other falsifications in the Breviary (for the most part in those lives of Saints which occupy the second set of Lessons in the "Night Hours," whence a French proverb: "He lies like the Second Nocturn"), but this one is here singled out because of the impossibility of disputing the fact that it is a lie, and is known to be such by the Roman authorities. Perhaps it is more curious that the offer of Satan to Our Lord, of giving Him all the kingdoms of the world, has been adapted as if spoken by God to St. Peter, and is worked into the responsory to the sixth lesson for the feast of SS. Peter and Paul. "The single fact of systematic falsifications of the Roman Breviary . . . is sufficient to prevent us from proclaiming before God and man, in the teeth of good faith and honour, anything under this pretence, . . . because it has falsehood for its ally." (Gratry, "Letter I. to Déchamps.")

and decrees of a number of early Popes and Councils, on points of doctrine and discipline, all intended to augment the Papal authority; which were fabricated in Western Gaul about 845, and were eagerly seized on by Pope Nicolas I., an ambitious and perfectly unscrupulous pontiff (858–867), to aid in revolutionizing the Church, as he, in fact, largely succeeded in doing. Here are a few specimens of the sort of thing with which they teem:

"Not even amongst the Apostles was there equality, but one was set over all."

"The Head of the Church is the Roman Church."

"The Church of Rome, by a unique privilege, has the right of opening and shutting the gates of Heaven for whom she will."

It is usually alleged by Roman controversialists that the Popes had nothing to do with inventing these forgeries, and that the worst with which they are chargeable was having, like everybody else, accepted them as genuine in an uncritical age, especially as they did but codify and register what was actually believed much earlier. These pleas are untenable; for the very simple reason that the Popes have always had what no one else had, full means of ascertaining the facts by referring to the Roman archives. But Pope Nicolas I. solemnly and publicly lied on this head to some of the Frankish bishops, assuring them that the Roman Church had long preserved all these documents with honour in her archives, and that every writing of a Pope is binding on the whole Church, knowing, as he did, that not one of the forgeries was or ever had been laid up in those archives. (Mansi, "Concil." xv. 695.)[1] Not only so,

[1] An attempt has been made to acquit Nicolas, on the ground that he does not expressly cite the False Decretals, and therefore may not have cited them at all; but (*a*) Baronius and most other historians agree that he did cite them; (*b*) it was precisely against Decretals not to be found in the acknowledged Canons that Hincmar of Reims protested; and (*c*) the latter clause of the Pope's statement is a fraudulent gloss on the legal fact, which is that *extracts from duly enacted Canons* may be authoritatively issued as

but though the forgeries have been now known as such for more than three centuries, and are admitted by Cardinals Baronius ("Ann." A.D. 865, sect. 8) and Bellarmine ("De Pontif. Rom." ii. 14), the two greatest of Ultramontane writers, nay, by Pope Pius VI. himself, who in 1789 said they ought to be burned[1] ("Letter to Four German Metropolitans," quoted by F. Gratry); yet they are still wrought into the whole texture of the Roman canon law, which is very largely made up of them; they are quoted as genuine in Liguori's "Moral Theology," i. 114, the chief text-book on its subject in the Roman Church, to prove Papal Infallibility; and they have been inserted as genuine several times in the Breviary itself at the last revision, by those two very cardinals just named, who knew the truth; as on January 16, where Pope Marcellus I. is represented as having written to the Bishop of the patriarchate of Antioch to the effect that Rome is the Head of the Church, and that no council can lawfully be held without leave of the Roman Pontiff.

f. Baronius has also falsified the Roman Martyrology, by inventing statements that various early bishops, whose mere names stand in the old editions, were consecrated and given mission to different Churches by St. Peter from Rome, so as to make Rome appear the Mother Church of these places. And he has altered the date of St. Denis of Paris by 200 years with this same view.[2]

Falsification of the Fathers.

LV. As the genuine writings of the Fathers bear constant testimony against the Papal doctrines and usages, a regular system of forgery has gone on in respect

---

injunctions by Popes; not that their own personal decrees are law. Richer, "De Eccl. et Polit. Potest." viii. 3.
 [1] "Let us put aside this collection, to be burnt with fire, if you like." Gratry, Second Letter to Mgr. Déchamps.
 [2] Janus, "The Pope and the Council," pp. 399, 400.

of them also; sometimes by the falsification of whole works, at other times by interpolations in the text of genuine works. Here are a few samples:—

St. Irenæus is quoted, and by Liguori amongst others, as saying: "It is necessary that all should depend on the Church of Rome, as on a well-spring or fount." No such passage exists.

St. Cyprian is one of the chief authorities against Papalism, and accordingly he has been made to say: "Upon him [Peter] He builds His Church, and commits His sheep to be fed .... and the primacy is given to Peter, that it might be shown that the Church is one and the Chair one." .... "He who opposes and resists the Church, who forsakes the Chair of Peter, upon which the Church is built, can he trust that he is in the Church?" "De Unitat. Eccl." 4. This impudent forgery, absent from almost every extant MS. of St. Cyprian, and from every printed edition till one in 1563, was first adduced by Pope Pelagius II. in a letter to the Bishops of Istria. But it is inserted still in the Roman editions of St. Cyprian's works, besides being constantly quoted by Ultramontanes, though Baluze's note, giving the facts, stands in the Benedictine edition, which was falsified after his death while he was busy on it.

St. Augustine is still incessantly quoted as having said: "Rome has spoken, the cause is ended." *Roma locuta est, causa finita est.* He never said anything of the sort. The passage which has been quoted thus runs in this manner: "The results of two Councils on the matter (Pelagianism) have been sent to the Apostolic See, and replies have come thence. The cause is ended. Would that the error may end some time!" Serm. CXXXI. It did not end then, for Zosimus, the new Pope, immediately afterwards sided for a time with the Pelagians, and the controversy was not terminated till the Council of Ephesus.[1]

[1] Fleury, "Hist. Eccl." V. xxiii. 44.

Forged Greek Catena.

LVI. A forgery, only second to the False Decretals in extent and audacity, was made in 1261 by a Dominican friar, consisting of a spurious catena of Greek Councils and Fathers, in support of a new claim set up by the Pope to rule the other four Patriarchs. Pope Urban IV., who seems to have known something of the truth about it, at once used it in a letter to the Greek Emperor, keeping carefully back the names of the alleged witnesses, and also sent it to St. Thomas Aquinas, who embodied large extracts of it into his work against the Greeks, without any suspicion. And it passed at once into the formal authoritative teaching of the theological schools of the Roman Church, nor has it ceased to be appealed to even now, for Liguori again uses it to prove the Pope's supremacy. The two great tenets developed in this forgery are, that the Pope is the infallible teacher of the whole world, and the absolute monarch of the Church. (Janus, "The Pope and the Council," pp. 264–268.)

Faith not to be kept with Heretics.

LVII. Further: it is the received principle of the Roman Church, that no faith need be kept with heretics; and no oath, however solemn, observed which is against Roman interests.

Here are proofs:—1. John Huss went to the Council of Constance under a safe-conduct from the Emperor Sigismund, to go, stay, and *return*.[1] When he got there he was at once imprisoned, tried, and burnt, despite his protest to Sigismund in person. This great crime shocked the public opinion of the day, and aroused a

---

[1] The exact words of the safe-conduct are: "Omni prorsus impedimento remoto, transire, stare, morari, et *redire* libere permittatis."—(Von der Hardt, "Conc. Constant." iv. 81.)

general outcry, to which the Council responded by passing the following *ex post facto* decrees : (*a*) " Notwithstanding safe-conducts . . . the competent judge may inquire into cases of heretical pravity, and by such safe-conducts no prejudice can be created against the Catholic faith or against the jurisdiction of the Church, and, notwithstanding such safe-conduct, the ecclesiastical judge may inquire concerning the errors of such persons, and proceed duly against them, and punish them . . . *even though they have come to the place of trial relying on the safe-conduct, and otherwise would not have come.*" (*b*) " The said John Huss, by obstinately impugning the orthodox faith, forfeited all safe-conduct and privileges, and *no faith or promise was to be kept with him by natural law, either human or divine*, to the prejudice of the Catholic faith."[1]

2. Here are some maxims from the Roman canon law :—

" An oath taken against ecclesiastical interests does not bind."

" Those are to be styled perjuries, not oaths, which are taken against the advantage of the ecclesiastical body "—(" Decret. Greg. IX." II. xxiv. 27).

" No one is obliged to keep faith (*fidelitatem servare*) with excommunicated persons until they have been reconciled."—(" Decret." II. Caus. xv. quæst. vi. 4, 5.) This is a decree of Pope Gregory VII., and refers primarily to oaths of allegiance taken by vassals to their feudal superiors, but covers much more ground, and is more

[1] The genuineness of these decrees has been questioned; but that fact will not help Roman controversialists; for the Council of Trent has accepted them by the very act of granting a temporary suspension of their force. Finding that no use was made of the safe-conduct to Protestants it had proclaimed in its thirteenth session (1551), it issued another in the eighteenth (1562), solemnly promising not to avail itself, *for this time*, of any law, statute, or canon of any Council, *especially Constance*, for the violation of its own pledge.

bluntly worded by Innocent III. : "Faith (*fides*) is not to be kept with him who does not keep faith with God."

That is what the Church of Rome says. Here is what the Word of God says :—" Lord, who shall dwell in Thy tabernacle, or who shall rest upon Thy holy hill? . . . He that speaketh the truth from his heart . . . that hath used no deceit in his tongue . . . he that sweareth unto his neighbour, and disappointeth him not, though it were to his own hindrance" (Ps. xv. 1, 2, 3, 5).

Roman Divines and Controversialists.

LVIII. And in the full spirit of these Roman principles, the controversial and theological writings of Roman divines perfectly swarm with falsehoods. A very few instances will suffice in illustration : and they are fair average specimens.

a. Liguori, in his "Glories of Mary," (Fr. Coffin's translation : Burns & Oates, 1868), p. 112, quotes St. Anselm as saying, that it is safer and better to call on the Blessed Virgin than on Christ. The passage is from a notoriously spurious treatise. At p. 123 he quotes St. Bernard as saying, "At the name of Mary every knee bows," with a false reference to the Annunciation sermons, wherein the passage does not occur, nor anywhere else in St. Bernard. At p. 197 he quotes St. Ignatius of Antioch, as saying that no one can be saved without Mary's help and favour; and, allowing that the passage has been doubted, alleges that at any rate St. Chrysostom acknowledged its genuineness, and adopted it. Both statements are wholly false. And if it be pleaded that Liguori erred through ignorance,[1] the reply is that his editors do not correct him, though they, at any rate, know the facts.

b. Cardinal Wiseman, in his "Lectures on the Catholic Church," systematically quotes doubtful, spurious, and

---

[1] In that case, what are his qualifications as a "Doctor of the Church"?

forged writings of Fathers as genuine; besides being guilty of other falsifications. Here are a few examples: —He quotes long extracts from the "Christus Patiens," attributing it to St. Gregory Nazianzen, in the fourth century. It is rejected as spurious by Baronius, Tillemont, Dupin, Labbe, Bellarmine, and Natalis Alexander, six of the most eminent Roman Catholic scholars; and the Benedictine edition of St. Gregory assigns it to the ninth century, five hundred years after his time. He produces an inscription in favour of invoking Saints, and alleges that the great scholar Muratori assigns it to the fifth or sixth century. When the reference to Muratori is verified ("Antiq. Med. Ævi," v. 358), it turns out that he names *three* writers as ascribing it to the ninth century, *one* as referring it to the fifth or sixth, and gives no opinion himself. Wiseman also quotes as genuine a sermon by St. Methodius, intended for use on a festival not instituted till that Saint had been dead more than two hundred years.[1]

c. In a small tract, called, "What do Catholics really believe?" edited by W. H. Anderdon, S.J. (Burns & Oates, 1878), the following statements occur, which may be profitably compared with some of the evidence given earlier in this treatise :—

1. "Protestants are quite right in saying the Catholic Church teaches that every one cannot understand the Scriptures by themselves [*sic*], but *it is false to say that she forbids the reading it in the true and correct translation.*"

2. "When Protestants invented their religion, they split the commandment [*i.e.* Com. I.] and the explanation [*i.e.* Com. II.] in two, by way of being different from the Church." The English division of the Ten Commandments, according to which polytheism is forbidden in the First Commandment, and idolatry in the second, *is that of the Jews*, of the Eastern Church, of Origen, and

[1] For these and many similar instances see Palmer's "Letters in Controversy with Wiseman," London, 1851.

of St. Jerome. The Roman division first appears in St. Augustine, so we can be certain which is the older.

3. The title "Worshipful" given to mayors in this country is cited as showing that Roman Catholics mean no more than high respect to saints and images when "worshipping" them,—as if any people ever went down on their knees to a mayor, and prayed to him to save their souls! or knelt and burned incense before his picture in a church!

d. In Dr. Faa Di Bruno's "Catholic Belief" (Burns & Oates, 1878), it is alleged that "the Catholic belief in Purgatory rests especially on the Apostolic traditions of the Church, *recorded in all ancient Liturgies*" (p. 179). The truth is, that though prayers for the dead *are* found in all ancient Liturgies, not one syllable in those prayers hints at a state of suffering. They are the same in spirit (though fuller in form), as the petitions of the English Prayer Book in the Church Militant Prayer and the Burial Service: that is, thanking God for the departed, and asking that we and they together may enter into the kingdom of heaven.[1] It no more follows that the ancient Church, when praying for departed Christians, thought they were suffering tortures in purgatory, than we now, when praying for living friends whose whereabouts and circumstances we do not know, take for granted they are in penal servitude. And whereas the Greek Fathers are appealed to as teaching purgatorial doctrine, here is the formal judgment of the Eastern Church, which lays great stress on prayer for the dead: "No part of Scripture touches on it, nor is there found any temporary purgative chastisement for sin after death. Above all, Origen's opinion was condemned just for this very reason in the Second Council of Constantinople. . . . As to the fables which certain men utter about souls, that when they have left this world without sufficient penance, they are

[1] For proofs in full see "Translations of the Primitive Liturgies," by Neale and Littledale (Hayes).

tortured . . . *the Church has never received them."*—
("Orthodox Confession," xlvi.)

e. The "Nag's Head Fable," against Anglican Orders, though exposed and rejected by Roman Catholics like Dr. Lingard and Canon Estcourt, is brought up every now and then quite fresh, when it is thought that there may be ignorance of the truth to trade upon. And this, though there is one lie in the account which alone disproves it; namely, that it represents Scory, the alleged sole consecrator of Parker and others, as having been himself then consecrated by the very man on whom he had himself first laid hands; though the record of his own consecration nine years before (1551) is extant, and also that of his having acted as Bonner's assistant in Queen Mary's reign, which, as he was ordained by the Edwardine rite, settles the validity of that form on Roman authority.[1]—(Bonner's Register, fol. 347, July 14, 1554.)

f. It might be thought that if we were safe in trusting any Roman Catholic writer without hesitation, "the noblest Roman of them all," Cardinal Newman, is that man. And yet, not to cite what he wrote in the first acerbity of his revolt from the Church of England, but looking to his attractive story, "Callista, a Sketch of the Third Century," we find him pledging himself in the Advertisement, that "it has not admitted any actual interference with known facts without notice of its having done so." Yet in this very story he describes a picture in a cottage thus: "In the centre stood the Blessed Virgin with hands spread out in prayer, attended by the holy Apostles Peter and Paul on her right and left. Under this representation was rudely scratched upon the

---

[1] "Whereas our beloved brother John, lately Bishop of Chichester . . . hath declared himself deeply penitent . . . we have restored, etc., our said brother to exercise within our diocese of London the public function and discharge of his ecclesiastical ministry and pastoral office, as far as by law we are able."

walls the word 'Advocata,' a title which the earliest antiquity bestows upon her" (chap. iii.). And, again, describing the altar of a Christian church where St. Cyprian is officiating: "At the back is a painting on the wall . . . The ever-blessed immaculate Mother of God is exercising her office as the Advocate of sinners, standing by the Sacrifice as she stood at the Cross itself" (chap. xxix.); all which implies the cultus of B. V. M. as then usual.

No one would gather hence the real facts, that pictures such as the first-named are unknown till the *fourth* century (Northcote and Brownlow, "Roma Sotterranea," vol. ii. p. 136; Hemans, "Ancient Christianity and Sacred Art," p. 41); that those like the second are later still (Hemans); that the epithet "Advocate," used in a strictly limited sense by St. Irenæus (see above, p. 67), does not appear detached from its original context, and as an independent title of St. Mary, till very late indeed—the first instance known to the present writer is the *Salve Regina* (see page 30), ascribed to Hermannus Contractus about A.D. 1050,—and, above all, that *there is not one solitary mention, direct or indirect, of the Blessed Virgin* in any treatise or letter from St. Cyprian's copious pen.

When even Cardinal Newman, whose natural love for truth few will question, can so yield to the subtle influence of bias, it is vain to look for better things in his communion, especially from men standing on a lower moral level.[1]

---

[1] Perhaps the most curious example of all is a French New Testament, printed at Bordeaux in 1686, with archiepiscopal approval. Here are two instances of its renderings: "He himself shall be saved, yet in all cases as by the *fire of purgatory*" (1 Cor. iii. 15). "Now the Spirit speaketh expressly, that in the latter days some will separate themselves from the *Roman Faith*" (1 Tim. iv. 1). The outcry at this audacity led to the destruction of the edition, now excessively rare; but there is a copy in the British Museum, another in the Library at Lambeth and a third in the Chapter Library at Durham. [I have since learnt that a yet scarcer

The way *to* Truth must be *through* Truth, and therefore a straight, not a *crooked* road, and as Roman controversialists go crooked in the points above mentioned, there is no likelihood whatever of reaching Truth under their guidance.

Stifling Intellect and Conscience.

LIX. The Holy Scriptures dwell much on the duty of serving God not with the heart only, but with the mind and understanding: of giving Him a reasonable service; of following the guidance of an enlightened conscience. And in the New Testament this duty becomes more binding, because of Christ being our example; and He is not merely the Man of Sorrows, but the Eternal WISDOM of God. Consequently, if we wilfully fail to use the intellectual talents with which God has intrusted us, we cannot be like Him. A few citations from the Old and New Testaments will be useful.

"If thou criest after knowledge, and liftest up thy voice for understanding; if thou seekest her as silver, and searchest for her as hid treasures; then shalt thou understand the fear of the Lord, and find the knowledge of God" (Prov. ii. 3-5).

"The spirit of man is the candle of the Lord" (Prov. xx. 27).

"The man that wandereth out of the way of understanding shall remain in the congregation of the dead" (Prov. xxi. 16).

"Be ye not unwise, but understanding what the will of the Lord is" (Eph. v. 17).

"Let the word of Christ dwell in you richly in all wisdom" (Coloss. iii. 16).

one, issued by the Doctors of Louvain at Paris in 1662, has still bolder forgeries; *e.g.* to exclude the lay use of the chalice, St. Matt. xxvi. 27, is made to read: "Drink ye all *twelve* of it," and St. Mark xiv. 23: "And all the *twelve* drank of it."]

"Prove all things; hold fast that which is good" (1 Thess. v. 21).

Now, contrariwise, the current Roman teaching directs all lay folk to "sacrifice their intellect," and to subject it not to God, but to a man; not on the ground of that man's superior wisdom or holiness, but purely on that of his official position as an ecclesiastic; while the ecclesiastic in turn is to submit himself in the same spirit to his superior, with the Pope at the head of all. And, somewhat inconsistently, it is urged as the solemn duty of every man outside the Roman Church to use his reason and private judgment to study points *against* his own communion, and *in favour* of Rome, till this one-sided process has caused his conversion; but this same exercise of reason, once it has landed him in Rome, becomes a sin, and no further inquiry into or canvassing of religious topics is to be pursued.

Now there is one very simple answer to this teaching, which is, that in Roman theology, Sloth is one of the seven deadly sins; and as the mind is higher than the body, so mental sloth must be a worse sin than bodily sloth. Yet so little is the Roman Church hostile to this sin, that wherever she has had a monopoly, as in Italy and Spain, the lower classes have been left in a state of babyish ignorance, and the ordinary clergy discouraged from such studies as might give them too great an insight into facts, and foster a spirit of independence. Authority must come first, of course, in the human order, to teach the ignorant; but if authority do its duty, the ignorant will soon become learned enough to judge for themselves, as daily experience with children shows us. And so St. Augustine aptly says, "Authority is first in *time*, but Reason in *fact*. The learner must believe, but when taught, he ought to judge" ("De Ordine," ii. 9). That is, all teaching is meant to quicken the understanding; and if religious teaching, the conscience also, not to choke it. Not to be tedious on this point, it will suffice to quote Cardinal Bellarmine, as showing the real goal of Roman teaching :—" If the Pope should err by enjoining vices or forbidding virtues, *the Church would be obliged to believe vices to be good and virtues bad,* unless it would sin against conscience." ("De Pontif." iv, 5.)— Contrast this with St. Paul, " Be ye followers of me, even as I also am of Christ" (1 Cor. xi. 1). " If we, or an angel from heaven, preach any other gospel unto you than that which we have preached unto you, let him be accursed" (Gal. i. 8). For when authority, or any superior, bids us disobey God's law, the right to command is forfeited, so far as that injunction is concerned, and disobedience becomes a duty, in order to obey the higher law ;[1] a truth impressed on us by the fact that while the Jewish Church was still the one true Church on earth, its constituted authorities rejected and crucified the Messiah.

Private Judgment.

LX. Then, as regards Private Judgment, against which Roman teachers are always declaiming, it is simply impossible to get rid of it, except through mental infirmity or bodily coercion. A baby, an idiot, or a convict

---

[1] Bellarmine, it is true, assumes the case he puts to be impossible, but so does St. Paul that which he puts, while deciding quite otherwise. And St. Bernard says very well of the plea of blind obedience to superior orders : "If that be right, the Church has no business to read, 'Prove all things, hold fast that which is good.' If that be right, we may as well blot out at once from the Book of the Gospels, 'Be ye wise as serpents,' since what follows is enough, 'and harmless as doves.' I am not saying that subjects are to sit in judgment on the commands of their superiors, where nothing is noticed as enjoined contrary to God's laws ; but I do assert that both prudence is needful to mark if there be anything thus contrary, and freedom to set it boldly at nought in that case. . . . For what a man commands, God forbids, and shall I listen to man, and be deaf to God ? Not so the Apostles, for they cry out and say, 'We ought to obey God rather than man.'"—S. Bern. Ep. vii. ad Adam. Mon.

in prison, cannot exercise private judgment, but a person of ordinary understanding and liberty of action can no more get rid of private judgment than he can jump off his own shadow. It is just as much an act of private judgment to say, " I will believe implicitly everything my director tells me, and will check all doubts as sinful," as it is to say, " I will test, to the best of my power, every statement he makes, and will not accept what I cannot get proof for." Our own conscience *must* be the final court of appeal in the last resort for each of us.[1] The only real question in the matter is, " What ought to influence and direct our private judgment ?" And no more perfect refutation of the Roman system is needful than simply to point out that it says in fact : "God's Holy Word, and the teaching of His most illustrious servants, are to go for little or nothing in the inquiry."

Cruelty and Intolerance.

LXI. Once more : whereas the Gospel is the religion of love and mercy, full of tender compassion for sinners, and employing only spiritual weapons for the defence of the truth or the chastisement of the unfaithful and rebellious children of the Church itself; contrariwise, the spirit of the Roman Church for many centuries has been that of hate and cruelty, and wherever it has been feasible, physical force and coercion have been freely employed for the suppression of opinions contrary to those she chose to propagate or encourage ; albeit God Himself uses no such means for constraining man's conscience. The horrors of the religious wars of Europe, from the crusade against the Albigenses in the thirteenth century, down to the campaigns of the Cevennes in the eighteenth; and the yet more revolting atrocities of

---

[1] See Cardinal Newman, "Letter to the Duke of Norfolk," sections 4 and 5.

the Inquisition, with its tens of thousands of victims, its armies of spies, its secret trials, its hideous tortures, and its merciless slaughters ;[1] the massacres of theological opponents—amongst which the St. Bartholomew holds a bad pre-eminence; many revolts and rebellions against legitimate civil authority, instigated on religious grounds, from the excommunication of the Emperor Henry IV. to that of Queen Elizabeth; the employment of assassination when open force could not be safely used, as in the successful cases of William the Silent of Orange, Henry III. and Henry IV. of France, and the unsuccessful ones of Queen Elizabeth and the Gunpowder Plot, all lie at the door of the Roman Church, or of its most devoted champions, the Jesuit Order.[2] Nor can

[1] In the first eighteen years of the Spanish Inquisition under Torquemada, 10,220 persons were burnt, and 97,321 imprisoned, banished, or reduced to want. In the Netherlands, under the Emperor Charles V., who was not a bigot, and before Philip II. began his harsher measures, the victims of the Inquisition burnt, strangled, buried alive, &c., were estimated from a minimum of 50,000 to a maximum of over 100,000. (Motley, "Revolt of the Netherlands.") Eating meat on fast-days was punishable with death by the rules of the Inquisition. Deslois, "L'Inquisiteur de la Foy." Besançon, 1630.

[2] The "Medulla Theologiæ Moralis" of Hermann Busembaum, S.J., has been charged with defending regicide on theological grounds. This book, which appeared first in 1645, was republished with additions by other Jesuits, and has appeared in more than fifty editions, down to the last at Louvain in 1848. It was publicly burnt in 1757 and 1758 by order of the Parliaments of Toulouse, Paris, and Rennes, as contrary to the laws of God and man; but it is not on the Roman Index even now, though some of its maxims have been condemned. As regards the specific crimes named above, Jacques Clement, assassin of Henry III., was a Dominican friar; Ravaillac, assassin of Henry IV., declared his motive to be "that the king was a Huguenot, and preparing to make war on the Pope" (Lavallée, "Hist. des Français," vol. iii. p. 65); while Balthazar Gérard, assassin of William of Orange, was like John Jaureguay, his precursor two years earlier in a like attempt, directly instigated by the Roman clergy (Motley, "Rise of the Dutch Republic.") After the execution of Jaureguay and two of his accomplices, the

it be alleged with truth that the crimes referred to had not the fullest sanction of the highest ecclesiastical authority; for Pope Urban II., for instance, lays down the maxim: "We do not account them as murderers who, burning with zeal for their Catholic Mother against excommunicate persons, have happened to slay some of them."—("Epist. xxii." ed. Migne.)

Pius IV., when the Government of Lucca had enacted a law, offering a reward of three hundred crowns and the reversal of any sentence of outlawry, or the power of transferring any such pardon, to all persons who should succeed in murdering any of the Protestant refugees who had fled from that city, described it as "a pious and praiseworthy decree, piously and wisely enacted, and that nothing could redound more to God's honour, provided it were thoroughly carried into execution."[1]

Pius V. plotted with Ridolfi, a Florentine, the assassination of Queen Elizabeth,[1] and sent the consecrated hat and sword of honour (the masculine equivalent of the Golden Rose, sent to queens, &c.) to the Duke of Alva, as a reward for his savage cruelties in the Low Countries.[2] Gregory XIII. not only caused a medal to be struck, and a painting executed, in honour of the Massacre of St. Bartholomew, but issued a Bull to Charles IX. urging him "to persevere in so pious and wholesome a measure, till his once most religious kingdom should be thoroughly purged of blasphemous heresies."[1]

And it is instructive to read the decrees of the Council of Trent, with the indiscriminate copiousness of its anathemas, which, it must be remembered, carry with them, if ratified in heaven, the pain of everlasting damnation. It is perhaps not a legitimate subject of blame that these

Jesuits collected their remains and exposed them to veneration as the relics of holy martyrs. (D'Ewez, "Hist. Gen. des Pays Bas.")

[1] See the letters of Lord Acton, a learned Roman Catholic peer, in the *Times* of Nov. 9 and 27, 1874.

[2] Ranke's "Life of Pius V."

anathemas should be affixed to propositions clearly striking at the fundamental articles of Christian belief, but they are just as freely bestowed on those who hold that Bishops ought not to reserve certain cases of sin for their own decision, nor forbid priests to pronounce absolution in such cases; on those who think that the cup at the first Eucharist was of pure wine without water; on those who, with the Eastern Church, hold that little children must needs receive the Holy Communion (a sentence which strikes not only St. Augustine, but Pope St. Gelasius);[1] on such as teach that Mass ought to be said in the vulgar tongue only; or who deny that a valid marriage, even if not consummated, is voided and dissolved by the entering of either of the parties into a monastic order, &c.

Now, whereas the guilt of religious intolerance and persecution may justly be charged against other Christian bodies besides the Roman Church, and notably the Church of England has not been free from blame in the matter, there is this broad distinction between the cases: All others confess their past guilt, have amended their practice, and reprobate the notion of a return to their former usage. Rome alone refrains because she is not strong enough to do what she would like to do, but openly avows the principle of religious persecution still; not merely by the entire absence of any expression of regret, much more any formal condemnation of her former policy, but by the denunciation of liberty of conscience and of the press in Gregory XVI.'s Encyclical "Mirari vos" in 1832, and by the insertion of the two following clauses in the Papal Syllabus (1864) of Condemned Errors, which denotes that the exactly *opposite* propositions are binding on Roman Catholics :—

"77. In the present day, it is no longer expedient

---

[1] St. August. "Epist. xxiii. cvi. ad Bonifac., Serm. 8 de Verb. Apost." &c. St. Gelas., "Ep. vii. ad Episcopos Umbriæ."

that the Catholic religion shall be held as the only religion of the State, to the exclusion of all other modes of worship.

"78. Whence it has been wisely provided by law, in some countries called Catholic, that persons continuing to reside there shall enjoy the exercise of their own worship."

These words must be read in the light of those in the Catechism of the Council of Trent :—"It is not to be denied that heretics and schismatics are within the power of the Church, and may be called to trial by her, be punished, and condemned by anathema."—("Cat. ad. Par." I. x. 8.) And they in turn, by strict Roman law, binding on all Roman Catholics in virtue of the eleventh clause of the Creed of Pius IV., involve the third Canon of the Fourth Council of Lateran, because accounted a General Council by the Roman Church; which Canon orders all secular princes to extirpate every heretic in their States; and in the event of failure to comply with this injunction, such princes are to be excommunicated, their subjects released from their oath of allegiance, and their territories are to be given over to Catholics, who are to destroy the heretics, and possess the country as their reward, besides acquiring, in virtue of their exterminating zeal, all the indulgences granted to Crusaders in Palestine. This is still unrepealed and unrepented—indeed, there is a similar clause in Paul IV.'s Bull, "Cum ex Apostolatûs officio," of 1559, with this further touch, that heretics are "to be deprived of every consolation of humanity"—and shows to what a spirit the converts to Rome give themselves over.[1] Contrast it with the example and precept of the Master:

"And it came to pass, when the time was come that He should be received up, He steadfastly set His face

[1] This is not a piece of mere antiquarianism, for Pius IX. made every effort to persuade Alfonso XII. to cancel the very scanty measure of toleration allowed to non-Romans in Spain by recent laws.

to go to Jerusalem, and sent messengers before His face: and they went, and entered into a village of the Samaritans, to make ready for Him. And they did not receive Him, because His face was as though He would go to Jerusalem. And when His disciples James and John saw this, they said, Lord, wilt Thou that we command fire to come down from heaven, and consume them, even as Elias did? But He turned, and rebuked them, and said, Ye know not what manner of spirit ye are of. For the Son of man is not come to destroy men's lives, but to save them" (St. Luke ix. 51–56).

Compare also the Apostle's words: "Though we walk in the flesh, we do not war after the flesh; for the weapons of our warfare are not carnal, but mighty through God to the pulling down of strongholds" (2 Cor. x. 4).

Superstition.

LXII. Yet again: one unchristian peculiarity of popular Romanism is that it is fast ceasing to be a Faith;[1] and is degenerating into a mere *Superstition*. This word does not mean, as people commonly fancy, over-readiness to swallow marvels. That is *credulity*, about which we are not now concerned. But "superstition" means that form of religion in which *fear* is stronger than love

---

[1] In truth, the active principle of Faith has for most practical purposes been banished from modern Romanism. The passive habit of Obedience to a visible human authority has been substituted for it, and called by its name, though Obedience and Faith are perfectly distinct qualities. Modern Romanism has this in common with atheistic Secularism, that they are both impatient of the unseen and spiritual, and crave after the visible and material. Hence Romans must have human objects of worship instead of God, and must have images of even these; must have amulets instead of belief in Providence; must have a regular tally account with Heaven instead of trust in God's love, mercy, and justice. All this not only is not Faith, but directly contradicts Faith, which is "the evidence of things *not* seen." Heb. xi. 1.

and trust. Its leading characteristic is the belief that the Powers above man are unfriendly, jealous, and vindictive; or at best stern and relentless; and that they must be baffled by mechanical amulets and magical charms, or bought off by being gratified with the sight of those sufferings which they delight to inflict. That is the sentiment which is at the root of African Fetishism and of Hindoo Fakirism alike. And now it has got almost entire possession of Romanism. Already it has been shown how the Father and Christ are avoided and shrunk from, as stern and pitiless judges, and Mary turned to as the one merciful hope of sinners; and also how God is supposed to pursue with hideous tortures the souls of even the holy dead. These ghastly distortions of Christianity are not to be found in the Missal at all, and scarcely a trace of them in the Breviary, but they form a very large part, often the larger part, of the popular creed in Roman Catholic countries now.

Cultus of the Sacred Heart.

LXIII. Even the chief remaining portion, namely, the modern worship of the Sacred Heart, is sheer heresy, condemned beforehand by the two General Councils of Ephesus and Chalcedon, which forbad any worship being paid to a divided Christ—even the separate adoration of our Lord's Sacred Humanity apart from His Godhead being heretical—and teach that *whole Christ* alone is the object of worship. When the Heart of Christ is mentioned by old writers, such as St. Bernard, before the invention of the new cult about two centuries ago, it always is a figure of speech for the *human affections and tenderness* of our Blessed Lord, and thus as a cause of love and confidence on our part; but not as a separate object of worship. Now, however, what is meant by it is the physical bodily organ of our Lord's human Body; and since even the worship of that Body entire, unless as united with the Second Person of the Most Holy Trinity, is unlawful for Christians, of course the separate adoration of a single part of it is all the more forbidden.[1] And there is not even the poor satisfaction that this worship, heretical though it be, is from its popularity redressing the balance a little, and giving Christ back in some fashion that amount of service which is His due, but of which He has been defrauded through the preference for other shrines than His. For the "Immaculate Heart of Mary" is already united with His in the cult, and has, besides, its own separate confraternity, offices, and indulgences. Here they are, on an absolute level: "May the Divine Heart of Jesus and the Immaculate Heart of Mary be known, praised, blessed, loved, worshipped, and glorified, always and in all places. Amen." ("Raccolta," v. 81.) They are on different levels, St. Mary's being much the higher, in these two indulgenced ejaculations :—

1. Sweet Heart of my Jesus, make me love thee more and more.—(" Racc.," v. 64.)

2. Sweet Heart of Mary, *be my salvation*.—(" Racc.," v. 82.)

Moreover, this second one is much more easily indulgenced. The ejaculation to our Blessed Lord cannot

---

[1] See "The Sacred Heart; Letters in Correspondence with Cardinal Manning," by Dr. Nicholson. (London : Simpkin & Marshall, 1873.) St. Athanasius reproaches the Pagans with superstition of this very kind: "Others, dismembering the parts of the body, took the head, the shoulders, the hands, the feet, and made gods of them, serving them with divine worship, as if it were not enough for them to pay devotion to the whole undivided body." "Cont. Gent." Opp. S. Athan. I. 10. (Paris, 1627.) St. Thomas Aquinas lays down that only *dulia* is due to the Sacred Humanity in itself. (Summa, III., xxv. 2.) It is a curious fact that F. La Colombière, the inventor of the cult of the Sacred Heart, borrowed it from a book he met during his two years' stay in England, namely, "The Heart of Christ in Heaven towards Saints on Earth," by Thomas Goodwin, an Independent divine, who had been Cromwell's chaplain

alone win an indulgence. It must be recited along with a Pater, Ave, and Credo, and these together gain *one hundred* days for each time of recitation, besides certain plenary ones twice monthly.

But the ejaculation to the Blessed Virgin Mary is valid *by itself*, and wins *three hundred* days for each repetition, with a plenary one monthly. A rapid speaker could say it more than a hundred times in a minute: thus gaining about ninety years' indulgence in that short space.

Amulets and Charms.

LXIV. The mechanical appliances (in no respect differing in theory or principle from the charms worn by an African savage) which are intended either to avert temporal dangers which God's love or providence will not avail to keep aloof without them, or to secure the salvation of those who wear them, are very numerous, and only a small sample can be offered here.

a. The Carmelite Scapular, miraculously bestowed on St. Simon Stock by the Blessed Virgin, which consists of two small pieces of stuff bearing her image and device, confers on its wearers (1) a share in the merits of all good works done throughout the whole Church, and in those of all confraternities in existence up to the reign of Sixtus IV. (2) Absolute immunity from hell, for those who wear it when dying, save in the case of such as die in wilful and obstinate rebellion against religion. (3) The Blessed Virgin Mary promised Pope John XXII. that she would go herself every Saturday to Purgatory, take out any Scapularists who, having died in the previous week, might be there, and bring them straight to heaven.[1] This is vouched for by that Pope in the *Bulla*

---

[1] The exact words of the vision were: "Ego Mater gratiose descendam sabbato post eorum obitum, et quos in purgatorio invenero liberabo, et ad montem sanctum vitæ æternæ perducam." —Guglielmi, "Recueil des Scapulaires," p. 143. (Paris, 1862.)

JOINING THE CHURCH OF ROME.   139

Sabbatina of 1322, and confirmed by Popes Alexander V., Clement VII., Pius V., Gregory XIII., and Paul V. ("Glories of Mary," p. 208.) If this be true, why do not the Roman authorities *oblige* every one to have a Scapular—as in Spain every one *must* take out the "Bull of the Crusade" in order to gain any indulgence,—[1] and so keep Purgatory practically empty, besides filling Heaven with continuous rapidity? This Scapular is popularly used to protect from drowning also, and various other perils.

b. The Cord of St. Francis (the only *obligation* of which is the actual wearing of the cord—which may be of thread, cotton, linen, or hemp—though certain prayers *may* be added) obtains for its wearers (1) every time they say six Paters, Aves, and Glorias, *all* the indulgences of the Holy Land, of all the churches of Rome, Assisi, &c., that is, "thousands of years of plenary indulgences, and more than a hundred thousand years of partial indulgences";[2] "more than enough," we are told, "to deliver thousands and thousands of souls from purgatory every day." (2) Every time of communicating, plenary indulgence; and if Psalm xx., *Exaudiat*, and a few short prayers be added, "*all the indulgences, plenary or partial, of all the sanctuaries of the earth*"; while people who are too ignorant to say or read the Psalm and prayers may compound by saying three Paters and Aves for the Pope's

---

[1] This Bull costs two reals, = 5½d., and its possession confers amongst other privileges the right to eat meat on nearly every fast-day in the year, except certain days in Lent, and four vigils. See Meyrick's "Practical Working of the Church in Spain," pp. 310-314.

[2] Véron—who tells us ("Rule of Catholic Faith") that the Treasury of Merits is not an article of the Faith, and that no indulgence whatever is of certain validity, or certainly remits, or is even intended to remit, the temporal penalties of sin, so that this doctrine, too, cannot be matter of faith—is precise in rejecting all Indulgences which run to thousands of years, or even beyond the extreme limits of human life.

intention. (3) Six times a year a general Absolution can be obtained, which secures the "*complete restoration of Baptismal innocence.*"[1] Here it may fairly be asked, how it is, between this cord and the Scapular, any souls are left in purgatory at all? (for Mgr. de Ségur says that "the zeal of *one* Tertiary of St. Francis is able to empty purgatory") and what is the object of encouraging pilgrimages to La Salette, &c., if all the indulgences of those shrines can be gained in five minutes in one's own room?

c. The Medal of St. Joseph arrests conflagrations, and works miraculous cures on those who wear it.[2]

d. The Medal of St. Benedict secures from all diabolic and magical attacks, cures surgical cases, purifies the water of an undrinkable well, fructifies barren fruit-trees, and saved from shells during the siege of the Commune all the houses in Paris where people hung it up in the windows, &c.[3]

e. The *Agnus Dei*, a small wax medallion, obtains for those who wear it security from spiritual languor, purges venial sins, and cleanses the last traces left by confessed sins. It puts devils to flight, protects from sudden death, confers temporal prosperity, assures safety and victory in battle, is an antidote against poison, checks the spread of epidemics, lulls storms and hurricanes, rescues from shipwreck, and delivers safely in child-birth. Unfortunately this valuable article is rather expensive, and confined chiefly to the richer class of purchasers, as only the Pope can bless it, and that usually at long intervals, so that the supply is limited.[4]

---

[1] "Le Cordon Séraphique," by Mgr. de Ségur (Paris, 1875); "Funiculus Triplex," by F. Francis Welsh, O.S.F. (Dublin, 1869.)

[2] Huguet, "Vertu Miraculeuse de la Médaille de St. Joseph." (Paris, 1869.)

[3] Dom Guéranger, "Essai sur la Médaille de St. Bénoît" (Paris, 1869); D'Arrainville, "Origine et effets de la Médaille de St. Bénoît."

[4] Montault, "De la dévotion aux Agnus Dei."

f. But a little model of St. Peter's Chains, which has touched the original relic, and thereby imbibed part of its virtue, can be had for a shilling, and worn as a watch-guard, bringing its wearer the benefit of many indulgences . . . (Lafond, "Histoire des Chaines de St. Pierre." Paris, 1868.)

g. Another little model of the chemise of the Blessed Virgin, preserved at Chartres, according to Cardinal Pie, will protect the duellist who wears it from his adversary's sword . . . (Huguet, "La Dévotion de Marie en exemples," II., 530. Paris, 1868.)

h. Articles which have touched the stole of St. Hubert preserve from insanity and hydrophobia.[1]

i. The water of Lourdes not only works miraculous cures, but a number of students at a competitive examination, who had taken the precaution to *dip their pens in the fountain*, all passed, and several with honours, by means of the papers written therewith (" Miracles de N. D. de Lourdes," p. 85); while the water of La Salette is not less vaunted, albeit Mgr. Gaume has written a book on "Holy Water in the XIXth Century,"[2] to which Pius IX. accorded a brief of approval, and which goes far to show that any ordinary village priest can manufacture an article just as efficacious as the miraculous springs of Lourdes and La Salette, besides being very much cheaper. One cannot fairly ask for more than restoration from sickness, resurrection from the dead, remission of venial sins and of temporal penalties due to sin, complete baffling of evil spirits, and expulsion of epidemics. And all this, we are informed, holy water can do.

With regard to the numerous miracles alleged as having been wrought at Lourdes and other places, it is to be observed that, without any inquiry into the reality

[1] Bertrand, "Pèlerinage de St. Hubert en Ardennes," pp. 195-198.
[2] "L'Eau bénite au XIXe Siècle." (Paris, 1866.)

of the alleged events, or their cause, natural or supernatural, if that reality be attested, they altogether fail to conform to St. Paul's canon on tongues, namely, that "they are for a sign, not to them that believe, but to them that believe not" (1 Cor. xiv. 22); whereas these Roman miracles are always wrought amongst enthusiastically credulous believers, and largely aid in the generation of unbelief amongst all others.

Roman Penances.

LXV. So much will suffice to have said on Roman fetishes, charms, and amulets, with the profound disbelief in an omnipresent, omnipotent, and all-merciful God which underlies their use. Let us now turn to the question of Roman penances. If these did but fairly represent the ascetic and self-denying side of Christianity, the subjugation of flesh to spirit (not the injury of the first to the injury of the second), and desire to be conformed to Christ's suffering life, no thoughtful Christian could censure them. But they stand on a very different footing.

The penances of the primitive Church were all inflicted before absolution was conferred. That once granted, and the penitent restored to Church communion, they ceased. Their object was, on the one hand, to be tests of sincerity; and on the other, to associate suffering with sin in the penitent's memory. And this is the Scriptural doctrine, too—

"Therefore also now, saith the LORD, turn ye even to Me with all your heart, and with fasting, and with weeping, and with mourning:

"And rend your heart, and not your garments, and turn unto the LORD your God: for He is gracious and merciful, and repenteth Him of the evil.

"Who knoweth if He will return and repent, and leave a blessing behind Him" (Joel ii. 12–14).

"For word came unto the King of Nineveh. . . . "And he caused it to be proclaimed and published through Nineveh. Let neither man nor beast, herd nor flock, taste anything : let them not feed, nor drink water.

"But let man and beast be covered with sackcloth, and cry mightily unto God : yea, let them turn every one from his evil way, and from the violence that is in their hands. Who can tell if God will turn and repent, and turn away from His fierce anger, that we perish not?

"And God saw their works, that they turned from their evil way ; and God repented of the evil, that He had said that He would do unto them ; and He did it not" (Jonah iii. 6–10).

The Fathers again and again urge the need of "bringing forth fruits meet for repentance," and when the view was first maintained that communion might be given to the lapsed without some temporal penalty being previously imposed, censured it as a dangerous innovation (St. Cyprian, "De Lapsis"). But they held, on the other hand, that when full proof of repentance had been given by the penitent, and absolution had been received, the sin and its consequences, temporal and eternal, were blotted out by God's merciful forgiveness.[1]

The Roman Church now, habitually giving absolution *before* any kind of penance or satisfaction has been really performed, and on a mere understanding that something will be performed by the penitents, and nevertheless holding, as the Council of Trent lays down (sess. xiv. c. 8), that satisfaction *must* be done, in order to a full remission of sins, practically disbelieves in the efficacy of her own absolutions, and teaches that penalties still await absolved sin ; but that people have a choice whether they will have their purgatory, in part at least, in this world by self-torture, or await the penal sufferings beyond the grave. Hence the penances come

---

[1] Morinus, "De Pœnitent." III. xi.

after absolution. If Roman penances were like those of the Eastern Church, mere *remedial advice*, and not in any sense *satisfaction* for sin,[1] it would not matter when they were performed; but as the received teaching is that they are part of the penal satisfaction, they ought to precede, not follow, the pardon. With this error of practice, a very ancient error of doctrine, surviving from a heresy which crept early into the Church, is closely bound up, that of regarding the Christian's body, not as a sacred thing, hallowed in baptism, and so to be treated with reverence in the midst of self-denial, but as a wholly evil thing, to be crushed utterly as the soul's bitterest foe; which is rank Manichæism.

Contradictions of Ancient Theory and Practice.

LXVI. Consequently, two contradictory things are seen together, which would have altogether astonished a Christian of primitive times; absolutions lavished freely by the ten thousand without any previous tokens of real penitence being exacted; and severe penances being practised, not merely by such as are in full communion with the Church, but by such as are regarded, in virtue of their penances, as exceptionally holy persons, likely candidates for the honours of saintship. Thus it is the *sinner* for whom Rome makes things easy; while the *saint*, instead of rejoicing in the liberty and joy which Christ has bought, must lead a life of incessant torture, and is held up to admiration for it; albeit what it really means is that he is unsound in the Faith on three important particulars: (*a*) practically disbelieving in the forgiveness of sins; (*b*) accounting the Blood of Christ insufficient to obtain redemption for him without his own works of penance being added to earn heaven; and (*c*) holding that God delights in the

---

[1] Blackmore, "Doctrine of the Russian Church," p. 228.

sight of man's bodily sufferings, receiving them as an acceptable offering. And so not only does his body, thus maltreated, revenge itself on the soul by disturbing its balance, but he himself comes round to a superstition in no practical, and in scarcely any theoretical, respect, differing from that of the Indian fakir, namely, that God is to be feared incomparably more than loved; and that His ill-will to man is such as can only be appeased by tortures here and hereafter; whereas the Christian doctrine is, that "the fear of the Lord is" only "the *beginning* of wisdom" (Ps. cxi. 10), but that "perfect love casteth out fear, because fear hath torment. He that feareth is not made perfect in love" (1 St. John iv. 18). So that the Church of Rome is guilty of promoting unbelief in the love of God.

Moral Failure of Roman Catholicism.

LXVII. The last of all of the broad practical reasons which dissuade from Romanism is its conspicuous failure as a guide in faith and morals. That is, while it has undoubtedly produced, and continues to produce, a very small minority of highly devout persons, whose lives are more conspicuously remote from worldliness of all kinds, and partake more of the heroic character, than that of pious members of other religious bodies, yet its influence on a larger scale is little short of disastrous. It is seen at its very best in England and other places where it is comparatively weak in numbers and influence, where it is dominated by a hostile and watchfully suspicious majority of another communion. It is at its worst where it has had entire liberty and long monopoly. In every such country, the educated classes are, as a rule, alienated from the Church; unbelief is widespread, rancorous, and increasing; and even amongst the lower classes, though the clergy are resorted to as the custodians of certain supernatural agencies, without which life here and hereafter is unsafe, yet there is little respect for them as a class, and less deference to them as teachers of conduct. Nor is this to be wondered at: for as a body, the bulk of the Roman Catholic priesthood everywhere are much below the level of Anglican clergymen in social standing, in culture, and in intelligence; being recruited almost always from the lower grades of society, and not so trained in their seminaries as to counteract the drawbacks of their origin. They descend to the lowest level of their flocks, instead of endeavouring to raise them to a higher one; and the result is, that instead of preaching the Catholic faith in its purest form, they readily fall in with, and actively encourage, the vulgarest and grossest materialism and superstition, in which the few who desire better things are forced to acquiesce,[1] because, since the educated classes have been lost, there are only the ignorant to fall back on; and it is dreaded that if they were to learn how much falsehood is mixed up in the religious system set before them, they would lose faith entirely, and reject the true along with the false, as the upper ranks have done already. And while the weapon of excommunication, with all the awful penalties attached to it, is freely employed to punish anything which seems to involve lack of submission to the hierarchy, it is scarcely ever wielded against adultery, brigandage, murder, or other great crimes against God

[1] And, in fact, instead of the Roman See teaching the Latin Church, it is precisely the ignorant and superstitious clergy who force on their immediate superiors first, and then on the Papacy, their new cults and doctrines, so that they, and not the Popes, really make the Roman creed. Thus it has been with the cult of the Sacred Heart, at first rejected at Rome under Innocent XII., then under Benedict XIII., next partly allowed under Clement XIII., Pius VI. and Pius VII., and at last fully ceded by Pius IX. (Nilles, "De Rat. Fest. SS. Cord.") So too with the Immaculate Conception, after five centuries of debate; and so with the vision of La Salette, against which the Bishop of Grenoble held out five years, while Pius IX. scoffed at the secret message sent thence to himself. "Affaire de La Salette," p. 182, Paris, 1857.

and society; such, for example, as agrarian conspiracy in Ireland, which has often found sympathizers among the Roman Catholic clergy. And so the evil goes on spreading, while Rome's determination never to admit herself in the wrong, whatever may be the evidence or the consequence, bars all hope of practical amendment.

Roman Arguments in Defence.

LXVIII. What, then, is the defence set up on the Roman Catholic side for all this startling departure and revolt from God's revealed Will, and from the teaching of ancient Christendom?

It is briefly this :—

a. God has committed all power and teaching on earth to the Holy Catholic Church, which He has endowed with the gift of infallibility, so that what it enjoins or even permits must be true.

b. The Roman Church *is* this one Holy Catholic Church, not a mere part of it, however vast, ancient, powerful, and august, but the *whole* Church; so that whatever is said of that Church in Scripture applies to the Roman Church only, and to no other.

c. The Church's gift of infallibility is divinely concentrated in the hands of the Pope, as Head of the Church and Vicar of Christ on earth, in right of his heirship to St. Peter, on whom this privilege was conferred by Christ; and all resistance to his decrees is thus resistance to Christ Himself.

d. Where there seems any discrepancy between ancient and modern Christian teaching, it is either only a mistake made by the critic, who does not understand what he is talking about; or the matter is due to the natural development and growth of what was always held and believed in germ, though not worked out in full till its appointed time had come.

Replies: The Church subordinate to Christ's written Word.

LXIX. The first answer to make to this collection of guesses—not to give them any harsher name—is, that the very highest titles of dignity given by Holy Writ to the Church are: "The Body of Christ" (Eph. iv. 12), and "The Bride, the Lamb's wife" (Rev. xxi. 9). But the Body is subordinated to the Head (1 Cor. xi. 3; Coloss. ii. 19); and a wife is not recognized in God's Word as having any independent authority. She must "submit herself" to her husband (Eph. v. 22; Col. iii. 18; 1 Pet. iii. 1); and "reverence" him (Eph. v. 33); while by both divine and human law she cannot on her own responsibility set aside any will, contract, or covenant which he has made. So, as Christians allow that Christ has declared His will and made His covenant known in the New Testament, the Church, however vast her privileges and authority, has not the right to set aside one tittle of its plain letter, or any reasonable inference from its letter and spirit. And with this agrees the saying of the Apostle, "For we can do nothing against the truth, but for the truth" (2 Cor. xiii. 8).

No Promise of Ecclesiastical Infallibility.

LXX. Next, *there is in Scripture no promise of infallibility to the Church* at any given time. What *is* promised is, that the Holy Spirit will guide us into all truth (St. John xvi. 13); and that the gates of hell shall not prevail against the Church (St. Matt. xvi. 18). But the Apostle has said: "There must also be heresies among you, that they which are approved may be made manifest among you" (1 Cor. xi. 19); and Christ Himself has implied a very general falling-away, in His words: "When the Son of Man cometh, shall He find the faith (τὴν πίστιν) upon the earth?" (St. Luke xviii. 8). The Church of one generation may err, and that grievously, but there will be always enough truth mixed with the error to bring things right again. That is to say, the Church is *indefectible* in the long run, though the teaching voice may be fallible at any given time. No claim to infallibility for the Church was ever synodically made before 1870, except in a petty synod of eight French Bishops at Paris in 1528.[1] General Councils are adjustments only, and valid just as they discharge honestly the office of attesting the continuous historical belief and practice of the Church, checked by incessant appeal to Holy Writ: whence the usage of placing a copy of the Gospels in the midst of the assembly. And the proof that they are not infallible in themselves lies in the legal fact that they are not accounted General till they have been accepted by the main body of Christendom, no matter how many Bishops may have sat in them. The Roman argument, that if God have given a revelation at all to men, He must also have provided an authority on earth which shall infallibly interpret its meaning so as to avoid all error, is one of those examples of man's attempting to dictate what God *ought to do;* not an account of what God actually *has done.*

It is just as reasonable to argue thus :—If God have given a revelation at all, He must have meant all men to know it, and therefore He must have revealed it everywhere in the world Himself, by miracle (as by letters of fire in the sky), instead of leaving it in a book, and to the slow and uncertain work of missionaries; so that even

[1] Cardinal Newman has treated this subject ably in the *Rambler* for July 1859, in an article "On Consulting the Faithful in Matters of Doctrine," wherein he shows that the laity have sometimes saved the Faith betrayed by Popes or Bishops, when, in St. Hilary's words : "the ears of the people are holier than the hearts of the priests ;" so that, the Cardinal observes, "the *Ecclesia Docens* is not at every time the active instrument of the Church's infallibility." And it is very noticeable that the strongest warning in the New Testament of a possible fall *is addressed to the Roman Church* by St. Paul, bidding it "boast not against the branches. But if thou boast, *thou bearest not the root, but the root thee.* . . . Be not high-minded, but fear . . . lest He spare not thee. . . . otherwise thou also shalt be cut off" (Rom. xi. 18–22).

now, after nearly two thousand years since Christ came, there are hundreds of millions more heathens than Christians on the earth. Or, if He pleased to spread it by missionary labour, that He must have made the power of speaking foreign tongues a permanent gift of the Church, instead of taking it away almost at once. Or, again, that as it is certainly God's will that all men should do right, He must either have prevented evil from being in the world at all, or have made every man's conscience unerring. Or, yet again, that He must have inspired the Apostles to draw up some simple primer or catechism to give authoritative shape to Christian teaching to all time. But He has not been pleased to do any of these things, choosing rather to discipline and prove us through conflict and struggle.

Disproof from the Jewish Church.

LXXI. One very plain disproof of the Roman *à priori* argument is, that God gave a revelation to the Jews fifteen hundred years before Christ, but no one pretends that they ever had an infallible living voice to keep them from all error regarding the law of Moses. And yet, as they had not Christ's example and teaching, nor the indwelling of the Holy Spirit in the Jewish Church, they needed such an infallible guide more than Christians do.[1]

The Roman Church not the whole Church.

LXXII. In the third place: it is very easy to show that the Roman Church is not the *whole* Church. It is not the whole Church *in fact*, because Romans themselves allow that Baptism is the one only way of entrance into the Church, and that every duly baptized person (even if a heretic ministered the sacrament) is a member of the Church" ("Conc. Trid." sess. VII. can. iv. viii.); but Roman Catholics are less than half the whole number

---

[1] Whatever the nature and effect of the Urim and Thummim may have been, there is no record of their use after the time of Saul (1 Sam. xxviii. 6).

of baptized Christians.[1] The Roman Church is not the whole Church *by right*, because, though it is the largest and most powerful Church in the world, it is not the *oldest*. It lays claim, in the Creed of Pius VI., to be "Mother and Mistress of all Churches." But that boast itself disproves the claim; for the mother cannot be the same as her own daughters. If there be other Churches to which Rome has given birth, she cannot be the only Church. And as she is not the oldest Church, the claim to be *Mother* of *all* Churches is not true.[2] It is plainly to be read in the New Testament that the Church at Jerusalem was the first Church set up and organised on earth (Acts i. 4; ii. 41–47) the second Church of which we read was set up in Samaria (Acts viii. 14); and the first Gentile one was at Antioch (Acts xi. 20). It was from Jerusalem and Antioch that the Gospel first reached Rome, a good while later; and as the Churches of Jerusalem and Antioch are still in existence, ruled by the successors of the Apostles in unbroken line,[3] it is plain that if Rome cannot be the same as her own daughters, still less can she be her own mother and grandmother; for the Roman tradition is, that St. Peter came to Rome himself from Antioch, while Antioch was undoubtedly evangelized

---

[1] The *Weekly Register* of Aug. 14, 1875, accepts these statistics of Dr. Hurst: Christians, 407,000,000, distributed thus,—131,007,449 Protestants, 200,339,390 Roman Catholics, 75,390,040 Orientals.

[2] Indeed, till the Jesuit missions (1542), or, more strictly, till the foundation of the Propaganda (1622-27), the See of Rome was scarcely a missionary centre. The only *ancient* Churches she is certainly known to have planted out of Italy are those North African ones which died out in the seventh century (the assertions as to Churches in Gaul are not supported by proof); the only *mediæval* mission she started was St. Augustine's to England; for the evangelizers of Holland, Friesland, Swabia, Hesse, Bavaria, Thuringia, and Pomerania, though they sought recognition and aid from Rome, began as volunteers, and were never Italians; while the *modern* Churches planted directly from Rome are only those of Central and South America, with some converts in the East Indies, China, Japan, and the Pacific Islands.

[3] See Le Quien, "Oriens Christianus," for the succession.

straight from Jerusalem (Brev. Rom. Jan. 18 and Feb. 22). But Jerusalem and Antioch have not *died out*, so that Rome can claim to be their surviving heir and representative; nor have they *abdicated* in her favour, so as to let her swallow them up. On the contrary, they, with Alexandria and Constantinople, the two others out of the five great Patriarchates into which Christendom was anciently divided, are in communion with eighty millions of Christians constituting the Eastern Church, who have always repudiated the claims of Rome, though being willing to allow the Pope, as first in rank of the five Patriarchs, an honorary precedency, such as the Duke of Norfolk enjoys amongst English peers, over whom, nevertheless, he has no real authority. A mere accident has proved of immense value to the Roman pretensions. All through early Church history, and even in the early Middle Ages, when the "Church of Rome" is spoken of, only the *local see* is meant. But after the schism of East and West, the Greeks began to use the phrase "Church of Rome" to denote *all the Western Churches* which submitted to the Pope; and this ambiguity has enabled Rome to pose as not merely *ruling*, but as *being*, the whole of the Western Catholic Church, and so at last to allege herself to be the *whole* Church. (Dupin, "Traité de la Puissance Eccl. et Temp.," p. 551 ff.). There is a most explicit admission of the separation and division of the Church into East and West in the letter of Pope Gregory IX. to the Emperor Michael Palæologus, notifying to him the intention of holding a General Council. He speaks in it of observing the "rending of the Church Universal," and prays that the Giver of all good things "may restoratively unite His Holy Catholic Church."—(Labbe, "Concil."). And as Rome is thus not the *whole* Church, she cannot speak with the authority of the whole Church, though she be the largest part; just as in English law a mere majority of a jury, however large, cannot bring in a legal verdict,

It is only when and while she teaches what the Undivided Church agreed on, that she speaks authoritatively.

Present Weakness of the Eastern Church no Disproof.

LXXIII. It is true that Rome has become powerful, while the Eastern Churches have become weak; but that can no more alter the earlier facts than the greater size and population of the United States as compared with England can ever in the lapse of ages make America the "mother" of all the English-speaking races, or make her the whole Anglo-Saxon race itself, no matter how England may dwindle. And even in its weakness the Eastern Church has made one missionary conquest, since its quarrel with Rome, greater than all Roman missionary efforts put together, namely, the conversion of the Russian Empire. Rome is evidently not the mother of the Churches of Russia.

The "Privilege of Peter" in the New Testament.

LXXIV. As to the Papal claim, in right of St. Peter, to supreme authority in ruling and teaching the whole Church, that is readily settled by an appeal to the New Testament, which practically contains all we really know about the powers conferred on St. Peter, and what he actually did in virtue of those powers. It has been already said, that the three texts in the Gospels which are alleged in proof of St. Peter's privilege, are not interpreted in the Ultramontane fashion by the majority of the Fathers; but we can go further than that, because (1), examination of the Bible shows us that the title of "Rock" is confined to God the Father in the Old Testament, and to Christ Himself in the New. One text from each must suffice here in illustration: "Who is God, save the Lord, and who is a Rock, save our God?" (2 Sam. xxii. 32). "That Rock was Christ" (1 Cor. x. 4). (2) All the Apostles were given the power of binding and loosing as well as St. Peter (St. Matt. xviii. 18; St. John xx. 21-23). (3) St. Peter is the only Apostle sternly rebuked by Christ for attempting to contradict God's will (St. Matt. xvi. 23); and that just after the blessing which had been pronounced on him. (4) He is the only Apostle, except Judas Iscariot, who actually fell away from Christ, denying Him with an oath, and that while fresh from the first Eucharist, and from Christ's prayer that his faith might not fail (St. Matt. xxvi. 69-75). (5) Though he appears in the most prominent position amongst the Apostles just after the Ascension, not one act of jurisdiction or authority on his part over any Apostle or elder is to be found; only one over two lay members of a local congregation, Ananias and Sapphira (Acts v. 1-10). (6) Any presidency in the actually organized Apostolic Church of Jerusalem seems attributed to St. James (Acts xii. 17, xv. 13-10; Gal. ii. 9-12). (7) St. Peter is sent, along with St. John, by the superior authority of the College of Apostles, on a mission to Samaria (Acts viii. 14). (8) He is the only Apostle recorded as having erred on a point of Church doctrine and order (Gal. ii. 11). (9) St. Peter is after a time divinely restricted to the Apostleship of the Circumcision, that is, the Church of Jews by birth (Gal. ii. 7, 8), and is withdrawn from any authority over the Gentiles, to whom we and the Roman Church alike belong. (10) He is entirely overshadowed, very shortly after Christ's Ascension, by St. Paul, who assumes the most active and prominent place in the Church, and also claims authority over *all* the Churches of the Gentiles (1 Cor. iv. 17, xvi. 1; 2 Cor. xi. 28), and notably over the Roman Church itself (Rom. i. 5, 6, 7). (11) There is nothing whatever in Scripture to connect St. Peter with Rome directly, except the ancient guess that "Babylon" in 1 St. Peter v. 13 may mean Rome, while, even if it does, nothing is said about any authority of St. Peter there.[1] (12) We are told that it was a mark of

---

[1] A very dangerous guess, too, in view of the Apocalyptic Babylon

schism for Christians to attach themselves specifically to St. Peter as distinct from the whole Apostolic Church (1 Cor. i. 12). (13) St. Peter never makes any claim for himself such as St. Paul does, nor asserts any primacy; for the only title he assumes, beyond that of Apostle, common to all the others, is "fellow-elder" (1 St. Peter v. 1). (14) St. Peter's own writings, in mere bulk, consist of only 8 chapters of the Bible, containing 166 verses; and the Gospel of St. Mark, his disciple, has 16 chapters, with 678 verses. But St. Paul's writings, including the Epistle to the Hebrews, amount to 100 chapters, with 2,325 verses; while St. Paul's disciple, St. Luke, gives us a Gospel of 24 chapters, with 1,151 verses, and the Acts of the Apostles, 28 chapters, with 1,007 verses, making in all 152 Pauline chapters with 4,483 verses, against 24 Petrine chapters with 844 verses. And as regards their relative importance, St. Mark's Gospel is mainly a shorter edition of St. Matthew. All that is peculiar to it is the parable of the seed in secret (iv. 26), cure of the deaf and dumb man (vii. 32), of the blind man of Bethsaida (viii. 22), the mention of the young man who fled away naked after Christ's arrest (xiv. 51, 52), and Christ's address to the Apostles before the Ascension, telling them of the necessity of faith and baptism to salvation, and promising miraculous powers (xvi. 15–20). But St. Luke alone records for us the events of St. John Baptist's birth, the Annunciation, the Nativity, the Adoration of the Shepherds, and the Presentation in the Temple, with such parables as the Prodigal Son, the Unjust Steward, Dives and Lazarus, the Unjust Judge, and the Pharisee and Publican, with much else. As regards the Epistles of Saints Peter and Paul, the only thing peculiar to the former is the glimpse we get in them as to the state of those who died before Christ's coming, and of His preaching to them in

(Rev. xvii. xviii.), and the fact that the epithet "harlot" is usually applied to an apostate *Church* (Isa. i. 21; Jer. ii. 20; iii. 1, 6, 8; Ezek. xvi. 15, 17, 20, 26; xxiii. 1—22; Hos. ii. 5; iii. 15).

Hades (1 St. Peter iii. 19, 20; iv. 6). That is all the fresh matter that the Church would have definitely lost had St. Peter's two Epistles perished. But St. Paul's Epistles are perfectly crowded with teaching on points of doctrine and discipline, and have moulded Christian teaching ever since on grace, election, free-will, on the effects of the Resurrection, on the unity of the Church, on the operations of the Holy Spirit, on the relation of the Law and the Gospel, and on the place of tradition in the Church. So thus St. Peter did not exercise the "plenitude of teaching" in Apostolic days; and consequently the Pope, even if his heir, cannot claim to exercise it now.[1] (15) It is no man whatever who was appointed by Christ as His Vicar on earth at His departure, but the Holy Spirit (St. John xiv. 16, 17, 26; xv. 26; xvi. 7, 13–15).[2]

What the "Privilege of Peter" really was.

LXXV. What then *did* St. Peter enjoy which the other Apostles did not? The answer is, that to him only were spoken the express words, "I will give unto thee the keys of the kingdom of heaven" (St. Matt. xvi. 19); and though most of the Fathers explain this as being merely the power of binding and loosing sins common to all the Apostles (so that even still that is the meaning attached to the phrase "the Power of the Keys"), yet, as Our Lord was not pleased to use these exact words to the others, the better way is to believe

---

[1] Indeed, the historian Sozomen (A.D. 439) remarks as a singular peculiarity of the Roman Church in his day, that neither the Pope nor anybody else ever gave public teaching in church to the people. ("Hist. Eccl." vii. 19.) This, coupled with the fact that Leo the Great (A.D. 440) was the first Roman theologian, shows that Rome was not a *teaching* centre in any sense whatever for the first four centuries.

[2] See the whole of this argument worked more fully out in the "Legal Evidence of Scripture on the Petrine Claims."—*Church Quarterly Review*, April, 1878.

that they have a meaning applicable to St. Peter alone. And what that meaning is declared to be by Tertullian, the most ancient Christian writer who discusses the question ("De Pudicit." xxi.), is that St. Peter was granted the incommunicable and unrepeatable privilege and glory of being the *first* to unlock the doors of the kingdom of heaven to both Jews (Acts ii. 14-41) and Gentiles (Acts x. 34-48). And as that was done once for all, it cannot be done over again by any one; so that there is nothing left for the Pope to be special heir to, any more than the heirs of Columbus, if any be alive, could enjoy a monopoly of continuing to discover America.

Civil Origin of Roman Primacy.

LXXVI. But there is no evidence whatever to prove that St. Peter's privilege, whatever it was, did not die with him, or that he ever appointed the Bishops of Rome his heirs, even if he had power to appoint any heirs at all; for the three great Petrine texts contain no clause whatever which even hints at any transmission of the privilege: unlike the grants to Abraham, Aaron, and David, where the descent of their privileges is expressly provided for. And this is an incurable defect of title according to Roman canon law, which rules that a *personal* privilege dies with the person named, and cannot be extended on any plea to persons not so named.—(Bonif. VIII. "De Reg. Jur." vii.; "Decret. Greg. IX." v. 33, ix.) Further, it is a fundamental principle of Roman canon law that whenever a claim of a right by *privilege* is made, the document attesting it must be produced in evidence by the claimant, or else his case fails.[1] Let the Church of Rome produce St. Peter's last will and testament, or even the witness of ancient writers who can say that they ever saw it, heard of it, or dreamt that it might be producible. What there is evidence of, and in plenty, is,

[1] Jenkins, "Privilege of Peter," p. 5; "Decret. Greg. IX." V. 33, vii.

that the position of Rome as the capital of a vast empire, and the seat of the most numerous and wealthy ancient Christian community, gave it great natural prominence, and obtained for its Bishop precedence everywhere, so that he exercised a very powerful influence in ancient Christendom, and much stronger in the West than in the East, because the West had no great city at all except Rome, Milan being its nearest rival, whereas the East was rich in large towns; and further, while the East had many sees of Apostolic foundation, Rome alone held that honour in the West; not to dwell on its unequalled historical prestige, which caused it to exert a powerful fascination over the minds of all, and especially of its own citizens, who, even if Christians, had a superstitious belief in and awe of "Roma Æterna," and thought that she must always rule by a Divine right, as when she was "Dea" in the pagan creed. But this is altogether different from a Divine Charter of privilege; and all the laudatory epithets regarding Rome and its Bishop which can be collected from the Acts of Councils and the writings of Fathers, go no further towards conferring, or even confirming, any such charter than a vote of thanks in Parliament, or a number of newspaper panegyrics, in our own day, bestowed on a victorious general, goes towards making him a royal duke. To establish the supremacy of Rome *two* factors are necessary; (*a*) proof of a Charter to the *person* of its Bishop; and (*b*) of another Charter to the *city*, as the immutable seat of his primacy. Whatever may be urged as to the first, there is no hint at all of the latter discoverable in Holy Writ, which is not only utterly silent as to any privileges of Rome, and names the Heavenly Jerusalem as the sole Gospel antitype of the earthly one, but tells us that "here have we no continuing city, but we seek one to come" (Heb. xiii. 14). Nor does either reason exist under the Gospel which existed under the Law for the religious primacy of Jerusalem. For Christendom is made up of many nations, and thus cannot have one political metropolis; and the highest Christian rites can be, and are, as validly performed in any village church as in St. Peter's at Rome. The special dignity of the Popes appears throughout as a matter of purely human origin and arrangement (so the General Council of Chalcedon, in its twenty-eighth Canon),[1] but as no result of a Divine Charter; for all the other great Bishops ranked in the order of the civil importance of their Sees; thus Alexandria, the second city of the Empire, was the second Patriarchate, though not an Apostolic See; Antioch, the third city, being only the third Patriarchate, though Apostolic by at least a double title, and alleged as St. Peter's first See; Constantinople going up as a new Patriarchate over the heads of both Alexandria and Antioch, when it became the capital of the Empire; and Jerusalem, the most august of all, being only a suffragan see under the Metropolitan of Cæsarea for three hundred years, not being made a Patriarchate for more than four hundred years, and even then reckoned last of all,

[1] "The Fathers with good reason bestowed precedency on the Chair of Old Rome, *because it was the Imperial City*." This canon was passed in despite of the protest of the Roman legates, who alone dissented, and was officially declared to mean that only an honorary priority belonged to the Roman See. Leo the Great always refused to acknowledge it, but on the purely technical ground that it was not competent for the Council to set aside the immutable decrees of Nicæa, and to give the second place to Constantinople, to the prejudice of Alexandria and Antioch, ranked as second and third by the Council of Nicæa (Epist. lxxix.). But there is no record of any objection having been raised by Alexandria and Antioch themselves, or that they accepted the Pope's championship; while, as regards the Council of Nicæa, it had itself provided that its decisions might be reviewed by a future council (Julius Papa, ap. St. Athanas. "Apol." 22; Tillemont, vi. 574); as, in fact, was done in the far more important matter of the Creed by that of Constantinople in 381; a change which Leo did accept. And the Synod of Constantinople in 869 (accounted as the Eighth General Council by Romans) in its most Papalizing canon (xxi) affirmed the rank of Constantinople as next to Rome, showing thereby that Leo's resistance had never taken effect.

because of its political insignificance.[1] The principle had, in fact, been laid down in Canon IX. of the Council of Antioch in 341, that the Bishop of the chief city in each province should be Primate, because the concourse of people (διὰ τὸ ἐν τῇ μητροπόλει πανταχόθεν συντρέχειν πάντας) made that the most convenient place for general superintendence. And this principle applies similarly to still larger cities, and above all to the capital of the Empire, so that it gives the simplest meaning for an obscure passage in St. Irenæus (Adv. Hær. III. iii. 3), where we have only the Latin, thus: "For it is necessary that every Church should come together to this Church [of Rome] (*ad hanc ecclesiam convenire*), because of its superior dignity (*potiorem principalitatem*)."

Disproofs of Papal Infallibility.

LXXVII. As to the infallibility of the Popes, it will be enough, out of many disproofs which are at hand, to say that,—

a. Pope Liberius subscribed an Arian creed, and anathematized St. Athanasius as a heretic.[2]

---

[1] The very fact that the Papacy is an intermittent office, becoming continually vacant, and then filled and conferred by a merely human election, proves its purely human authority and origin. Not so in the only two parallel cases. The Jewish High Priesthood, till the violent interruptions of later times, devolved at once on the hereditary representative of the House of Aaron, to which the office was divinely restricted. There was no proper vacancy, and no election. The Buddhists teach that their Pope, or Dalai Lama, never dies; for that on the death of any Lama, the Deity is at once incarnate in another person, usually a child, who is known by certain supernatural tokens, and is thus not chosen by his subjects, but received by them. These two views are logical and consistent, not so the Papal theory. The deaths of Bishops are not cases parallel with the death of a Pope; for the Episcopal order and office never dies out, lodged as it is in many hundreds of hands. But the Papal order consists of but one man; and ceases to exist every time that man dies or is deposed, being renewed through a merely human process by his *inferiors*, not even through his own nomination of his successor.

[2] "Liberius, overcome with the irksomeness of exile, subscribed

b. Pope Honorius was unanimously condemned by the Sixth General Council as a heretic, for having publicly sided with the Monothelite heresy, and officially taught it in Pontifical Letters, the legates of his own successor, Pope Agatho, taking the lead in anathematizing him; and a successor of his, Gregory II., wrote to assure the Spanish Bishops that Honorius was certainly damned; while every Pope for several centuries had to renew the anathema at his coronation.[1]

c. The Western Church alone deposed, on its own authority, Popes John XII., Benedict IX., Gregory VI., Gregory XII., and John XXIII., the last in express terms as simoniac, sorcerer, schismatic, and heretic.[2] But all these depositions have been acknowledged as perfectly *valid*, and the Popes set up in the stead of the deposed ones as lawful tenants of the Roman chair; instead of the act being regarded as a blasphemous rebellion against the Vicar of God on earth, and the new Popes as schismatic intruders. The English laws of to-day do not recognise the validity of Charles I.'s deposition and execution, nor that of any laws passed in Parliament, or decisions delivered by judges, between 1641 and 1660. That whole period of nineteen years is treated as a legal blank; and Charles II.s reign is counted in the statute-book from his father's death, no reckoning being made of Oliver Cromwell's sovereignty. That nothing like this meets us in Roman Church history shows conclusively that the Popes cannot have been viewed as infallible, but as liable to error in the discharge of their office, and to punishment from their superior, the collective Church, for any misconduct: contrary to the Vatican decrees, which allege that the Pope's decisions on faith and

to heretical error, and entered Rome as a conqueror."—St. Jerome, "Chron." A.D. 357.

[1] Renouf, "Cond. of Pope Honorius;" Gratry, "Letters to Mgr. Dechamps;" Willis, "Pope Honorius and the New Roman Dogma."

[2] Fleury, "Hist. Eccl." XII. lvi. 7; lix. 49, 53; XXI. ciii. 92, 112.

morals are "irreformable on their own merits, not by reason of approval by the Church."

d. The modern Roman Church, by directly gainsaying such utterances of former Popes as that of Pope Gelasius on the sin of half-communion, already cited, and declaring the like opinion heretical; and those of Pope St. Gregory the Great on the "blasphemous" sin of ascribing either to the Roman Pope, or any other person, the title and office of Universal Bishop,[1] which thing is explicitly done in the Vatican decrees ("Const. de Eccl." c. iii.), has itself, by a patent contradiction, expressed its own disbelief in the very doctrine of Papal infallibility which it so loudly asserts: an example set it, indeed, by the Jesuits, who, in despite of their own special vow of implicit obedience to the Pope, and their magnifying that as the highest virtue, never once thought of obeying the Bull of Clement XIV. in 1773, which suppressed the Company, declaring it broken up and abolished for *ever*,

---

[1] Writing to the Patriarchs of Alexandria and Antioch, St. Gregory says: "This name *Universal* was offered during the Council of Chalcedon to the Pontiff of the Apostolic See . . . But no one of my predecessors ever consented to use so profane a title, plainly because if a single Patriarch be called universal, the name of Patriarch is taken from the rest. . . . Wherefore presume not ever to give or receive letters with this title Universal."—(Ep. v. 43.) To the Patriarch of Alexandria he writes again: "You are my brother in rank, my father in character, and I said that you were not to write any such thing to me or to any one else . . . and behold, in the very heading of your letter, directed to me, the very person who forbad it, you set that haughty title, calling me Universal Bishop, which I beg your Holiness to do no more."—(Ep. viii. 30.) To the Patriarch of Antioch he says that this title is "*profane, superstitious, haughty, and invented by the first apostate;* . . . and that if one Bishop be called universal, the whole Church falls if he fall."—(Ep. vii. 27.) To the Emperor Maurice he writes twice: "St. Peter is not called Universal Apostle . . . The whole Church falls from its place when he who is called Universal falls . . . But far from Christian hearts be that *blasphemous name* . . . I confidently affirm that whoso calls himself, or desires to be called, Universal Priest, in his pride *goes before Antichrist*."—(Ep. v. 20, vii. 33.)

but withdrew into the non-Roman dominions of Prussia and Russia, where the Pope's writ did not run, emerging thence in full marching order and considerable numbers when Pius VII. issued his contradictory Bull of reinstatement in 1814.

Papal Infallibility useless in the Past.

LXXVIII. Further, Papal infallibility, even if it were conceded that it is true in theory, has been entirely useless in the past, and must of necessity be useless in time to come, as a safeguard against error.

a. As regards the past, we may fairly say this much in the first instance, that if there have been a line of specially and divinely inspired Heads of the Church, endowed with the fulness of *teaching* as well as of ruling power, the proof ought to lie in a succession at Rome of great Fathers and Doctors of the Church, answering to the line of Jewish Prophets. We should have a Samuel, a David, a Solomon, an Isaiah, Jeremiah, Ezekiel, Daniel, Zechariah, Malachi, &c., in the chair of Peter; only as much greater than the Hebrew seers as the Gospel is higher than the Law.

But, instead of this being actually the case, the first Pope who has any reputation as a theological writer,—nay, the very first member of the local Roman Church who has attained that position, is the forty-sixth Pope after St. Linus, original occupant of the see,[1] namely, Leo the Great, who became Pope in 440.[2] After him

---

[1] So St. Irenæus, our oldest authority, who says: "The Blessed Apostles [Peter and Paul], then, having founded and built up the Church [of Rome], committed the office of the episcopate into the hands of Linus. To him succeeded Anacletus, and after him in the third place from the Apostles, Clement." ("Cont. Hær." III. 3). Cardinal Wiseman has falsified this evidence, thus: "To Peter, *as St. Irenæus observes*, succeeded Linus; to Linus, Anacletus; then, in the third place, Clement" (Lecture viii.).

[2] A mere fragment survives of Pope Dionysius (A.D. 259-269), who might, perhaps, did we know more of him, take Leo's place as first on the list.

there is no name of eminence, and only one of moderate distinction, Gelasius I., till we come to St. Gregory the Great, sixty-fifth Pope, in 590. The next, and he only by favour, not of genuine right, is Innocent III., the one hundred and seventy-fifth Pope, in 1198 (for Gerbert, or Sylvester II., is famous as a scientist, not as a divine, and Gregory VII., however eminent as a ruler, is not great as a writer); and from him there is a blank till Benedict XIV., two hundred and forty-eighth Pope, in 1740. So, as a matter of fact, the two hundred and fifty-seven Popes have contributed singularly little to the theological treasures of the Christian Church. Four theologians in eighteen hundred years are but a poor show; and only one of these four has helped in moulding the belief of the Christian Church, namely, Leo the Great, by his anti-Eutychian writings. And what is very interesting in the same connexion is, that there has never been a School of Theology in Rome itself of the least reputation or importance; nothing, for example, like the famous School of Alexandria in the ancient Church. There was a school of Canon Law there (and even it inferior to Bologna), but students who wanted to read theology went to Paris, Oxford, &c.[1]

b. Next, there is not one solitary example to be found in the whole of Church history of any great struggle or difficult question being decided by the Pope's interference. Not one of the great heresies was put down in this way, but always by a Council or by some private theologian. Thus the Council of Nice settled the question of Arianism; and that of Ephesus the question of Nestorianism; it was St. Epiphanius who practically routed the Gnostics, and St. Augustine who refuted the Pelagians. No Church has been the parent of so many sects as the Roman, which has never been able to prevent them from forming within her bosom, and issuing thence. No Pope has ever settled the Canon of Scrip-

[1] Janus, "Pope and Council," pp. 199-204.

ture, deciding what books are to be received or what rejected; none, down to our own day, has ever undertaken to say what is the true text in the thousands of various readings found in the Greek New Testament. When Luther asked his famous question : " What is Justification ?" no Pope was ready with a reply ; and though a reply was given at last by the Roman Church, it came in the shape of a decree of the Council of Trent in 1547, more than a quarter of a century after the question had been put, when Luther himself had been about a twelvemonth dead, and when half Europe was irrecoverably lost to the Papacy. And what is very noteworthy is, that even the Council of Trent never took the slightest notice of Leo X.'s Bull against Luther, but reopened the whole question from the beginning, and decided it on quite other grounds. Contrariwise, it proceeded on its own mere motion, and without awaiting special permission, to repeal or modify a great number of Pontifical Bulls and Constitutions. Of course, there was Papal confirmation obtained at last ; but the point here is that the Council never seems to have dreamt that such decisions were irreformable.

Breaks-down of Infallibility.

LXXIX. When the Pope has practically interfered to settle a question, the result has not been altogether encouraging. Here is a leading case in point : On March 5, 1616, the Congregation of the Index published a decree condemning as " false, unscriptural, and destructive of Catholic truth," the opinion that the earth moves round the sun. It is disputed amongst Roman theologians whether Paul V., who undoubtedly set the Index at work, and entirely agreed with its finding, was personally responsible for this decree, but the balance of evidence shows that he was so, even if nothing else were forthcoming. And it is known that this Pope himself presided in a Congregation of the Inquisition on

February 25, 1616, in which, after this same opinion, that the sun is the centre of our universe, had been described as "absurd, philosophically false, and formally heretical, because expressly contrary to Holy Scripture;" and the opinion that the earth is not the centre of the universe, but moves, and that daily, "absurd, philosophically false, and, theologically considered, at least erroneous in faith;" Cardinal Bellarmine was appointed to visit Galileo the astronomer, and order him to give up these false opinions, under pain of imprisonment for refusal. It was hence that the Congregation of the Index took action, and published its decree a week later. In 1633, Galileo, having continued to propagate his views, was called on by the Inquisition to retract and abjure; and the formal notice to him to do so states expressly that the declaration of 1616 was made by the Pope himself, and that resistance to it was therefore heresy, contrary to the doctrine of the Catholic and Apostolic Church. On being brought to trial, Galileo made a formal abjuration, and on June 30, Pope Urban VIII. ordered the publication of the sentence, thereby, according to Roman ecclesiastical law, making Galileo's compulsory denial of the earth's motion—as a *theological* doctrine—binding on all Christians everywhere; although now there is no educated Roman Catholic in the world who does not agree with Galileo, and reject the judgment of Popes Paul V. and Urban VIII. as "absurd and philosophically false," and, therefore, as no binding theological utterance.[1]

---

[1] See the whole question discussed in a pamphlet, known to be from the pen of a Roman Catholic priest : "The Pontifical Decrees against the Motion of the Earth," 2nd edition; London: Longmans, 1870. There is one point, however, not clearly named in it, that Pius VI., in a Brief addressed to Bishop Pannilini of Chiusi, in 1786, declares that decrees of the Roman Congregations of the Inquisition and the Index are *ex cathedrâ* judgments of the Holy See, and must be implicitly obeyed, as *dogmatica judicia quæ Petri Cathedra tulit.* See the Acts of the Synod of Florence in 1787, vol. iv. p. 74.

Another example, somewhat earlier, is the Bull of Sixtus V., 1590, declaring, by a *perpetual* decree, an edition of the Vulgate, then just issued, the sole authentic and standard text, and that any departure from it should incur excommunication, while future editions not conformed to it should have no credit nor authority. But it so swarmed with errors, that it was called in almost immediately, and Clement VIII. published a new Vulgate in 1592, differing from that of 1590 in several thousand places, and likewise issued under penalty of excommunication for any deviation from it.[1] Such is infallibility when it commits itself to pronouncements on questions where its value can be tested by proof. Accordingly, the safer course is generally pursued of dealing with speculative matters only, outside the range of human knowledge, and thus incapable of disproof as of proof. In fact, it is maintained by some Roman theologians, at the present day, that the Popes have up to the present only *once* spoken with the formalities necessary to make their utterances *ex cathedrâ* and infallibly binding, and that was when Pius IX., on December 8, 1854, decreed the Immaculate Conception of the Blessed Virgin Mary ; a tenet which, even if true in itself, belongs to the domain of entirely unpractical speculation, was denied as heresy by orthodox Catholics, including *fourteen Popes*, for a thousand years, and is contrary to the well-nigh " unanimous consent of the Fathers."[2] At any rate, to use such a formidable engine

[1] James, " Bellum Papale."
[2] Cardinal Turrecremata, " Tract. de Concept. B. V. M." See Dr. Pusey, "Letter I. to Newman," pp. 72-286. The fourteen Popes were, Innocent I. (" St. August. contra Julian." i. and ii.), Zosimus ("St. August. Ep. ad Optatum "), Boniface I., Leo I., Gelasius I., Gregory I., Boniface III., John IV., Innocent II. and III., Honorius III., Innocent V., Clement VI., Eugenius IV. ; to whom may be added Leo X., Julius III., and Marcellus II. For such of these fourteen as are not cited by Dr. Pusey, see Bandelli, General of the Dominicans, " De Veritate Conceptionis B. Mariæ,"

but once in all the ages, and then for such an infinitesimally small result, is like building a ship of ten thousand tons burden to convey one passenger from Portsmouth to the Isle of Wight.

Papal Infallibility no help in the Future.

LXXX. It will now be shown that, even if true, Papal infallibility provides no security whatever against future theological error amongst Roman Catholics. What the doctrine really comes to is this : that all decisions of the Pope on faith and morals, being divinely inspired and infallible, become, when committed to writing, so much more Holy Scripture. It does not mean less than this ; and it cannot mean *more*. But as the infallibility of Holy Scripture has not prevented the widest diversity of interpreting its meaning, so it would be with the ever-accumulating mass of Papal decrees. Every sentence and every word would be fought over just as St. Paul's or St. John's words are fought over. And besides, as the Pope is not omnipresent nor omniscient—though he is both, quite as much as he is infallible—the ordinary Roman Catholic cannot turn to him at once for the solution of any doubt ; but has practically to go to his own confessor, who is admittedly fallible. If he do not like what he hears there, or if the confessor himself be puzzled, the next resort is to the bishop, again a fallible person. The layman who did not stop here would probably earn for himself the reputation of a troublesome and unstable Catholic ; but suppose he or the priest push further, and apply to Rome—a thing which would not in practice be done once in a thousand times—the question would in most cases not come before the Pope himself, but some lower authority, perhaps one of the Congregations—still a fallible tribunal.

Milan, 1475, and Petrus de Vincentia, Catalogue of 216 Witnesses against the Immaculate Conception, Venice, 1494.

And assuming that the Pope himself is at last reached, and does give a final answer,[1] two difficulties at once arise. First, he may have replied in his quality as a private Doctor, and not as Pope, in which case it is agreed that he is not infallible ; and next, even if he answer as Pope, yet his questioner is certainly fallible, and may *misunderstand and mis-report* the decision. Since even the Apostles persistently misunderstood Our Lord's teaching about His kingdom, until just before the Day of Pentecost (Acts i. 6), we have no reason to conclude that ordinary Christians now-a-days will prove wiser than they. And so it is plain that there is no real safeguard against error in having an infallible *teacher*, unless his disciples be also infallible *hearers*, certain not to mistake his meaning. If you ask your way in a strange place, and get a perfectly correct answer, it does not follow that you will go right, if by reason of dull hearing or insufficient knowledge of the language used, you have but very imperfectly apprehended the meaning of the words.

Questions raised by the Infallibility Dogma itself.

LXXXI. And this is not a mere fancy picture of what *might* happen ; it is what actually *has* happened with that very decree of his own infallibility which Pius IX. published in the Vatican Council—for it is not to be forgotten that it is none of the Council's own making,

[1] This cannot always be counted on. Not very long before the death of Pius IX., a deputation from the "Catholic Societies" of Italy applied to him for guidance on a question of faith and morals ; namely, whether Catholics, especially in the former States of the Church, should vote or not vote at Parliamentary elections. To vote was to acknowledge the legitimacy of the Italian kingdom at Rome ; to abstain was to throw every seat in Parliament into the hands of the anti-clerical party. Here was the great convenience of having "the living voice of authority" to appeal to. The "living voice" replied that no answer could be given, as there was a conflict of opinion amongst the ecclesiastical authorities on the subject, and no conclusion had yet been arrived at.

nor even so passed by it as to be valid and binding in Canon law.

Here it is: " *We* [*i. e.* Pius IX.], the Sacred Council approving, teach and define that it is a dogma divinely revealed: that the Roman Pontiff, when he speaks *ex cathedrâ*, that is, when in discharge of his supreme Apostolic authority he defines a doctrine to be held by the universal Church, by the divine assistance promised him in blessed Peter, is possessed of that infallibility with which the Divine Redeemer willed that His Church should be endowed for defining doctrine regarding faith or morals; and that, therefore, such definitions of the Roman Pontiff are irreformable[1] of themselves, and not by reason of the consent of the Church."

At this moment Roman theologians are at hopeless variance on three questions raised by this decree.

1. When does the Pope speak *ex cathedrâ* ?
2. How is the fact to be known publicly?
3. What *is* " that infallibility," in kind or degree, mentioned ?

And some of the difficulties which encompass the subject may be gathered from the subjoined extract from a Pastoral of the hyper-Ultramontane Cardinal Dechamps of Mechlin, dated Dec. 8, 1879, and intended to minimize the force of Leo XIII.'s disapproval of his policy :—" Infallibility is not what is alleged by the editors of certain papers, the members of certain Parliaments, the professors of certain Universities, and sometimes also by lawyers and soldiers. No; for the Pope is not infallible *when he expresses only his own ideas*, but he is infallible when, as head of the Church, he defines truths contained in the depository of revelation, the Scriptures and tradition. The Pope is not infallible *when he judges purely personal questions;* but he is so when he judges doctrinal questions affecting faith or

---

[1] That is, we may not revise any such definition, nor sit in judgment on what it has judged.

morals; that is to say, revealed truth or revealed law, the Pope being infallible *only when he rests on the testimony of God or revelation*. The Pope is not infallible when he treats as a private doctor questions even of doctrine, but when he judges by virtue of his apostolic authority that a doctrine affecting revealed truth and revealed law ought to be held by the universal Church."

Dilemma of the Dogma.

LXXXII. It is not unworthy of remark, moreover, that if the infallibility of the Pope be held to rest, as a binding dogma, on the Vatican decree, there is a very awkward dilemma. Either the Pope assumed the title of Infallible of his own mere motion, or it was conferred on him by the Council.

If he took it himself, there is no evidence in its favour, because no man may be judge in his own cause, nor decide to his own advantage on a mere ex-parte statement.[1]

If the Council gave it to him, then the Council, by declaring him alone infallible, and that without the consent of the Church, confessed its own fallibility and liability to error; and therefore its entire incompetence to decide on such a stupendous doctrine at all, involving, as it does, a complete revolution in the constitution of the Church, and reducing it to nothing.

Development.

LXXXIII. As to Development, there are two or three things to be said. First, it is only a modern excuse put forward by private persons in the attempt to get out of a difficulty and a contradiction. But the authoritative assertion of the Roman Church itself is that its teaching now is exactly what it has been from the beginning, and

---

[1] "Nemo esse queat Judex in causâ propriâ:" Benedict XIV. "De Synodo Diœc." vii. 14.

is attested by the unanimous consent of the Fathers. So speak both Trent and the Vatican Council. The latter is very precise on this head. It says: "The Holy Spirit was not promised to the successors of St. Peter, that by His revelation they might make known new doctrines; but that by His assistance they might inviolably keep and faithfully expound the deposit of faith handed down by the Apostles" ("De Eccl." iv.); and again: "The doctrine of faith which God hath revealed has not been proposed like a philosophical invention, to be perfected by human ingenuity, but has been delivered as a divine deposit to the Bride of Christ, to be faithfully kept and infallibly declared. Hence, also, that meaning of the sacred dogmas is perpetually to be retained which our Holy mother the Church hath *once for all* declared; nor is that meaning ever to be departed from, under the pretext of a deeper comprehension of them."—("De Fide," iv.) Next, there may be unwholesome developments of things that were right at first, which ought to be discarded. So wine will develope under unfavourable circumstances into vinegar; but the Roman Church will not allow vinegar to be used for the Eucharist. Thirdly, there are usages and doctrines now current which are not developments at all, but blank contradictions of the ancient faith and practice. The Nicene Creed differs from the Apostles' Creed only as a man differs from a growing lad; but the worship of St. Joseph differs from the doctrine of the Church as a huge tumour does from the ordinary condition of the body. It is a growth, no doubt, but denotes disease, not progress.

The Notes of the Church. Is the Roman Church One?

LXXXIV. By identifying the local Church of Rome with the whole Church, however, and making them mean the same thing, and still more by concentrating the Church in the Pope singly, thus making him the heart, life, and head of all, Roman controversialists have committed the proverbial folly of "putting all their eggs in one basket." They are here, as usual, in opposition to the spirit of the Gospel; for Jesus Christ said, "I am the Vine, ye are the branches" (St. John xv. 5): but the Church of Rome, by their mouth, says, "*I* am the Vine, and there are *no* branches." It is worth while showing what it comes to, when we test Rome for the Notes of the Church, to find whether it be indeed One, Holy, Catholic, and Apostolic.

The Roman Church is not, and has not been for many centuries, *One* in any clear, spiritual sense.

a. It is well to open this inquiry by citing a few of those passages of Scripture which define or describe the nature and tokens of Church Unity.

"Neither pray I for these alone, but for them also which shall believe on Me through their word; that they all may be one; as Thou, Father, art in Me, and I in Thee, that they also may be one in Us: that the world may believe that Thou hast sent Me. And the glory which Thou gavest Me I have given them; that they may be one, even as We are one: I in them, and Thou in Me, that they may be made perfect in one" (St. John xvii. 20–23).

"And they continued steadfastly in the apostles' doctrine and fellowship, and in breaking of bread, and in prayers" (Acts ii. 42).

"And the multitude of them that believed were of one heart and of one soul: neither said any of them that ought of the things which he possessed was his own: but they had all things common" (Acts iv. 32).

"Now I beseech you, brethren, by the name of our Lord Jesus Christ, that ye all speak the same thing, and that there be no divisions among you; but that ye be perfectly joined together in the same mind and in the same judgment" (1 Cor. i. 10).

"I, therefore, the prisoner of the Lord, beseech you that ye walk worthy of the vocation wherewith ye are called, with all lowliness and meekness, with long-suffering, forbearing one another in love; endeavouring to keep the unity of the Spirit in the bond of peace. There is one body, and one Spirit, even as ye are called in one hope of your calling; One Lord, one faith, one baptism, One God and Father of all, who is above all, and through all, and in you all" (Eph. iv. 1–6).

"Let all bitterness, and wrath, and anger, and clamour, and evil-speaking, be put away from you, with all malice: and be ye kind one to another, tender-hearted, forgiving one another, even as God for Christ's sake hath forgiven you" (Eph. iv. 32, 33).

There is a great deal more implied in all these and other like passages than mere agreement in Church government, ordinances, or even doctrines, though they have their place clearly defined too. A perfect harmony of will, spirit, and love, such as exists between the Persons of the Most Holy Trinity; nothing less is tendered as a pattern; and the Prayer of Our Lord, as well as the teaching of His Apostles, extends to all Christians, not to the ecclesiastical hierarchy alone.

On this broad issue, then, there is no sign visible in the whole of past history that Roman Catholic nations have been less apt to go to war with one another,[1] Roman Catholic families less apt to be divided, that litigation and other marks of division are less generally to be found in Roman Catholic communities than elsewhere. They are certainly not one as Christ and the Father are one.

---

[1] On the contrary, it is in the Roman Church alone that Popes have incited and waged wars for purely selfish and temporal interests, not counting wars of fanaticism. Thus, Sixtus IV. went to war with the princes of Italy solely to conquer dominions for his nephews, and gained Imola and Forli in this wise. So Alexander VI. did also, for Cæsar Borgia's ends, taking Rimini, Faënza, and Urbino. Julius II. went to war to recover various cities in the Romagna, for which he had some excuse; but he also seized Parma and Piacenza, where he had no claim.

b. If we narrow the inquiry to the visible organization of the Church, there is no question at all that at the present day the apparently solid massiveness of the Roman Church, its perfect drill, and the seemingly united front it presents to the numerous and conflicting sects, produce a strong impression of real unity on untrained minds, which are dazzled by the surface, and do not think of looking below. But even if that unity were a real spiritual force, and not only too notoriously due to relentless pressure, to a state of siege, and continual stamping out of all variety and independence (so that no just estimate of its genuineness can be made, nor a guess of what would happen if the screw were relaxed), it would not help the Ultramontane argument, *unless it have been found to hold good all along from the beginning.* A costly vase which is offered to our admiration, not purely for its size and beauty, but for its freedom from even the smallest flaw, must fail to produce the desired effect, if the marks of cement and riveting be clearly visible all over it, showing that, however skilfully pieced and mended *now*, it was once shattered to fragments.

This is the case to so great a degree in the Church of Rome, that *there is actually no Church in the whole world which has been so conspicuously, so frequently, and so fatally divided and rent by schisms.* It is the very worst example producible in the whole of ecclesiastical history.

Even before what is known as the "Great Schism," there were no fewer than *thirty-nine* Anti-popes, from Novatian in 251 till the titular Nicolas V. in 1328, who contested the Papacy and drew considerable followings after them. Of course, if it were certain that the successful claimant was always in fact the Pope whose election was most probably valid, this circumstance, startling as it is in any case, would be much less serious than it actually is. But in a large number of instances all we know is that the Pope who was ultimately recognized had stronger friends, larger armies, or a longer purse, than the unsuccessful claimant. Take one of the earliest and worst instances. Pope Liberius had been driven into exile by the Arian Emperor Constantius, and Felix, an Anti-pope, set up in his stead. The Roman clergy and faithful laity refused to attend the churches or to communicate with Felix, who was taking part with the Arians. Liberius, having weakly signed an Arian creed,[1] and consented to anathematize St. Athanasius, was recalled. For a while, under an imperial edict, the Pope and the Anti-pope occupied Rome at the same time, each having his own body of followers. At last Felix withdrew and left Liberius in sole possession. But when Liberius died, in A.D. 366, the factions broke out afresh, and a double election took place, Ursicinus being chosen Pope, by one party, and Damasus by the other. There are contradictory accounts, both contemporary, as to which was the prior and valid election. That question cannot now be settled; but what does appear is, that the faction which elected Damasus consisted of the Arian supporters of the schismatic intruder Felix; that which chose Ursicinus, of the Catholics who had been faithful to Liberius; and that the method which Damasus adopted to settle the competing claims was to put himself at the head of an armed rabble, and attack the supporters of his rival. He twice in person assaulted and took by storm the churches where they were collected (one of them being the well-known St. Maria Maggiore), and committed frightful slaughter. The party of Ursicinus withdrew for a time, vainly asking for a synod of bishops to inquire into the validity of the two elections, but returned twice, on each occasion for fresh riots and bloodshed; and once another horrible massacre took place. But Damasus had the Emperor and the ladies on his side, and ultimately triumphed by Erastian

---

[1] "Hæc est perfidia Ariana. This is the Arian heresy," says St. Hilary, "Fragm. Hist." vii. ; thereby excluding the plea that the creed was, at worst, ambiguous.

means, though not for some years.¹ Here is another case. When Pope Honorius II. died, in 1130, two rival parties in the conclave of Cardinals set up competitors. Sixteen of them chose, in an uncanonical fashion, the Cardinal Gregory, who took the title of Innocent II. Thirty-two Cardinals, in a more orderly and canonical manner, chose Cardinal Peter Leonis, who styled himself Anacletus II., and had all Rome on his side. But the unlawful claimant contrived to get the help of the most powerful man in Europe, St. Bernard, who persuaded one monarch after another to support Innocent, and at last replaced him in Rome by means of an invading army under the Emperor Lothair, though Anacletus held out till his death in the Castle of St. Angelo. There can be no moral or legal doubt that Innocent was the Antipope, but it is Anacletus who is so branded in ecclesiastical annals.² These two examples represent several others, less typical, but essentially of the same kind, and open a huge abyss of doubt as to the legitimacy of the Roman succession, for Bellarmine lays down that "a doubtful Pope is no Pope." (*Papa dubius, Papa nullus.*)³

The Great Schism.

LXXXV. But, at any rate, this much can be said in palliation, that all these disputes were settled somehow; and, right or wrong, one Pope always obtained final recognition. Not so when we come to the "Great Schism," which broke out in 1378, after the death of Gregory XI., and lasted till 1409, or rather till 1417. It is needless to go into the details of this prolonged strife, and it will be enough to say that during its continuance there were two (and sometimes three) rival lines of Pontiffs kept up, severally followed by whole nations on entirely political, not theological, grounds, and that no one can say now which claimant at any time was the true Pope; while canonized

---

[1] Nat. Alex. "H.E." iv. 3; Milman, "Latin Christianity," i. 2.
[2] Milman, "Lat. Chris., viii. 4.
[3] Bossuet, "Def. Cler. Gall." II. ix. 11.

saints were found on opposite sides of the question, St Catharine of Siena, for instance, holding to the Italian succession, and St. Vincent Ferrer to the competing line; so that St. Antoninus of Florence has remarked that persons illustrious for miracles took opposite sides in the controversy, and that the question cannot be settled now. Since this "Great Schism," whose lessons were severe, only one Anti-pope, Felix V., is on record.

Further Disunion in the Roman Church.

LXXXVI. But this often repeated struggle for the Papacy (with its tens of thousands of embittered partisans on both sides, each testifying its hatred for its rival by sacking churches, rifling tabernacles, and profaning the Sacrament, alleged to be consecrated schismatically) is very far from exhausting the tale of Roman dissension. The jealousies of the rival religious Orders, and notably that which raged for centuries between the Franciscans and Dominicans, extending far into the domain of theology, has much exceeded in rancour all the hostility of contending schools in the Church of England. In the missionary fields of the far East, it was the quarrellings of the Jesuits with their colleagues of the Franciscan, Capuchin, and Dominican Orders which hindered the spread of Christianity in China, and wrecked its hopeful beginnings in Japan.[1] It must not be forgotten, that to

[1] There is a most remarkable Report on the state of the Roman Catholic religion, which was drawn up for Innocent XI. in 1677, by Urbano Cerri, Secretary of the Propaganda, and translated into English by Sir Richard Steele, in 1715. Cerri says that Alexander VII. sent out three Frenchmen as Bishops *in partibus*, with authority as Apostolic Vicars, to the East Indies, and that the Jesuits immediately denounced them as intruders and heretics, declaring all their sacraments null and void, and even hurtful to souls, themselves iterating such as the Vicars or their clergy administered. They put some of the missionaries into the Inquisition at Goa, and drove out others. The Papal Briefs they declared to be forged, or illegally obtained, and though, on appeal to Rome, Clement X. sided with the Vicars and granted them fresh Briefs, the Jesuits went on just as before, disregarding even a letter from

a very large extent indeed, the numerous Orders which arose within the Latin Church, answer precisely to the sects of Protestantism in their origin, rise, decay, and denominational rivalry, as also in taking the names of human founders as more honourable or distinctive than that of Christian or Catholic, though coming short of claiming absolutely independent rights and powers for themselves. And while the bitter hostility and active competition between the Regulars and the parochial clergy are familiar in the pre-Reformation history of England, and between the Jesuits and seculars under Elizabeth and James I., they are living and disastrous facts in France to-day.

Two Distinct Religions in the Roman Church.

LXXXVII. Nor is there union in other respects even now. In the first place, two distinct and incompatible religions are contending for mastery within the Roman obedience, namely, the creed officially imposed on the clergy, embodied in the Missal and Breviary, which is— allowing for the presence of certain corruptions, chiefly in the more recent Breviary commemorations—in the main the old belief of Christendom; and that popularly urged on the laity, consisting of the idolatrous, superstitious, grossly material, and openly pagan cults, of which some account has been given above.[1] But the

their own General, which the Pope had made him send. Cerri adds, that by the King of Portugal's aid they had prevented the Propaganda from interfering effectually, so that this "damnable schism" was still raging when he wrote.

[1] There are, however, some on a still lower level, when religious homage in hymns, litanies, and processions, is paid to inanimate objects, invoked just as Saints are. The most besotted instance, perhaps, is the cultus of the "Holy Candle of Arras," a stump of wax taper declared, on very inadequate proof, to be the same with a pretended relic, alleged to have been brought from Heaven by the Blessed Virgin in the twelfth century, and long used as a charm against pestilence. After being lost and forgotten, it was professedly found again, and its cult revived a few years ago.

monuments of one of these two creeds are in a dead language, restricted to a single class; while those of the other are in the vernacular of each country, and altogether exceed in circulation and popularity the calmer and more spiritual devotions of the ancient formularies. No contrast which can be drawn between the tenets and practices of the most opposed schools within the Church of England can compare, for a moment, with the startling nature of this contradiction. Clergy and laity, High, Low, and Broad, amongst Anglicans, have the same religion tendered to them, embodied in the same book, which is used, with whatever diversity of outward ceremonial, in every one of the many thousands of their churches in Europe, Asia, Africa, America, and Australasia. But in Rome—it must be repeated—there is one religion for the clergy, and another for the laity; while, of the two books which contain the clerical religion, one is not to be had at all by the laity in their own language,[1] and the other only in an imperfect abridgment, so that they are thrown back on quite another and inferior class of publications for devotional purposes.

No Identity of Belief in Rome.

LXXXVIII. Nor is it true, as often alleged, that a complete identity of belief exists on all points of religious opinion amongst the Roman Catholic clergy, and that the same answer will be substantially given by every one of them to the same question whenever, wherever, or by whomsoever put. No doubt enormous pains have been taken of late years to create this uniformity by assimilating the text-books used in all clerical seminaries, and by ruthlessly crushing out any expression of opinion disapproved by the " insolent and aggressive faction," to quote Cardinal Newman's words, which has now the

[1] An unofficial English version of the Breviary has been lately issued by a private translator, but it is the only complete one extant.

mastery over the Latin Church. But even so, it is a
new thing, still very incompletely achieved, and not even
beginning to be successful in some respects. All through
the Middle Ages, when the Roman Church was at its
greatest height of prosperity and reputation, there were
markedly dissimilar schools of theology within its pale;
and though this variety was much diminished by the screw
applied at the Counter-Reformation, when the Jesuits
became the guiding power, yet it did exist very definitely
still. It is only in this century, since the shock of the
French Revolution, that the Roman authorities, believing
that nothing but the most compact order could hope to
resist the forces of modern Liberalism, have striven hard
to suppress all types of opinion save one; but it required
the long Pontificate of Pius IX. and the gradual filling of
almost every See in Latin Christendom with his dutiful
nominees, to achieve this result, which itself involves
such a complete breach with the ancient Church, that
Rome is no longer *one* with it: and the "Bark of Peter"
has come to resemble that galley of the legendary hero
Theseus, which the Athenians professed to show even
after the time of Alexander the Great, but which, whatever its real date and origin may have been, had been so
pieced and renewed by successive patchings, that not one
ancient plank or spar remained in it, although it claimed
to be the same old ship. There is now uniformity in Rome,
indeed, but it is compulsory uniformity in serious error,
an incomparably worse evil than such divergence on
minor points, not ruled by General Councils, as is ob-
servable in the Church of England. The old names of
"Ultramontane," and "Gallican," not invented by Protestants, but watchwords of contending parties in the
Roman Church, have almost dropped out of use, because
the Gallican party has been crushed into insignificance
and silence, while Ultramontanism, swarming over the
Alpine barriers which long shut it into Italy, has con-
quered the whole Latin obedience for a time.

Maximizers and Minimizers.

LXXXIX. Yet even the uniformity which has been achieved exists only in name. The two parties are as distinct as ever, save that they are now called *Maximizers* and *Minimizers;* the Maximizers pushing the dogma of Infallibility to its furthest possible extent, and claiming divine authority for every casual utterance of a Pope on any religious or moral question; the Minimizers endeavouring to reduce within the narrowest limits so dangerous a proposition, and inclining to hold that a Pope is infallible only when, as President of a General Council, he proclaims the decisions at which the assembly has arrived. Thus, Cardinal Manning ("Petri Privilegium," pp. 34-39) declares that the Syllabus of 1864 is "an act of doctrinal authority," and "part of the supreme and infallible teaching of the Church," therein agreeing with Pius IX., who styles it "the one anchor of safety" ("Discorsi di Pio IX." vol. i. p. 59), whereas Cardinal Newman ("Letter to Duke of Norfolk") says that it "has no dogmatic force," and "makes no claim to be acknowledged as the word of the Pope." The interval between these extremes is occupied by two intermediate sections, at variance with both and with one another on what is now a fundamental question in the Roman Church.[1] It may serve to show what divergence there was quite lately on this head from the now current teaching, to cite a question and answer from an anti-Protestant work, Keenan's "Controversial Catechism." This book received the approval and licence of Archbishop Hughes of New York, and the editions published here bear the formal approbations of the four Roman Catholic Bishops in Scotland, dated in 1846 and 1853.

Q. "Must not Catholics believe the Pope himself to be infallible?"

[1] "Results of Mr. Gladstone's Expostulation," by Umbra Oxoniensis.

A. " This is a Protestant invention ; it is no article of the Catholic Faith ; no decision of his can bind, on pain of heresy, unless it be received and enforced by the teaching body, that is, by the Bishops of the Church."
Since the Vatican decrees, this question and answer have been quietly dropped out of the volume by a clever re-arrangement of the type, but pains have been taken to make it seem the *very same edition*, nay, the very same thousand of that edition, and no hint of any change is given.[1]

Other Points of Disagreement.

XC. Once more, Cardinal Newman has denounced as a "bad dream,"[2] that very language respecting the Blessed Virgin of which specimens have been given above, and has recorded his dissent from Liguori's "Moral Theology,"[3] albeit that book is now authoritatively sanctioned in every Roman confessional. And it is only a few years since a well-known English Roman Catholic priest and controversialist extracted a series of more than *eighty* heretical propositions from the works of the late Father Faber, and endeavoured to get them censured at Rome, on the ground that they were doing serious mischief here to orthodoxy. The answer he got practically amounted to this : that his charges were perfectly true in themselves, but that it would never do to condemn so useful and thorough-going a partisan of the extremest Ultramontanism. And so the matter dropped.

There are many other subjects on which there is great division of opinion amongst the Roman clergy, such as grace and free-will, purgatory, and even the Holy Eucharist itself, and it is only the intellectual apathy and ignorance of the great bulk of the priesthood, with the

[1] For similar tampering with French theological works, see Michaud, "De la Falsification des Catéchismes Français et des Manuels de Théologie par le Parti Romaniste."—(Paris, 1872.)
[2] "Letter to Dr. Pusey," 1866.
[3] "Apologia," pp. 417, 418, 424. Ed. 1864.

sedulous exclusion of the laity from ecclesiastical topics, which prevent these facts from being as notorious as the like facts are in the Church of England, and make possible such a thoroughly false boast as that of perfect doctrine and harmony within the Latin obedience, which cannot for an instant prevail with the simplest and most credulous hearer who has any real knowledge of the truth.

Is the Roman Church Holy?

XCI. Next, is the Church of Rome *Holy?*

There have been, thank God, and are, many devout and holy souls within the Roman Church; there have been not a few, even since the great division of Western Christendom, whose saintliness has been frankly acknowledged by those who were not in communion with them; and a Carlo Borromeo, a Francis Xavier, and a Vincent de Paul, are as heartily admired outside the Roman Church as within it. Indeed, it would be passing strange if so vast a Christian body, retaining, amidst much error, the great doctrines of the Gospel, should fail to include many thousands of men and women living pure, pious, and devoted lives. But that, true in itself, is not the question now, which is, whether the mark of Sanctity be (*a*) evident in Roman teaching; (*b*) bound up with the fact of communion with Rome; and (*c*) whether the local Roman Church and See itself, as the head and heart of Latin Christendom at least, if not of all Christendom, have at all times conspicuously possessed this mark.

Nature of Proofs tendered.

XCII. The usual method adopted by Roman controversialists to prove these three points, is first to count up all the names of great canonized Saints, and to tender them as proofs. But a very large proportion of these Saints belonged to the Eastern Church, and had no more direct personal relation with Rome than with any other great see of Christendom. They prove nothing either way, for or against. Others, contrariwise, were in direct collision with Rome, as St. Augustine, when he signed the letter of the Council of Carthage, repudiating the Pope's jurisdiction; others again, such as St. Cyprian,[1] St. Firmilian, and St. Meletius, died actually out of communion with Rome, and thus make against the claim.

The Catalogue of Canonized Popes.

XCIII. The next process is to produce the catalogue of Popes, and to show how many of them have the title of Saint or Martyr. Several of these will not stand inquiry. The weak and vacillating Liberius, who betrayed the Faith, is one of these saints; the next to him on the list is St. Felix II., the very Arian schismatical intruder mentioned above (LXXXIV. *b.*), to whose character St. Athanasius, who had dealings with him, bears the subjoined unequivocal testimony: that he was elected by three eunuchs [*i.e.* to represent the Roman laity], and consecrated by three "spies" of the Emperor; that he was just fit for such electors; that his heresy was notorious, so that the faithful would not enter any church whither he came, and that his whole conduct was worthy of Antichrist.[2] A convenient miracle under Gregory XIII. discovered his body with an ancient inscription: "Pope and Martyr"[3]—it is quite certain he never was martyred— and so he figures on the roll of saintly Popes, just above the name of the murderous rioter Damasus, also sainted. Here then are three names close together, not one of which is entitled to the laudatory prefix, and hence it may be conjectured how heavily the whole list needs to be discounted.

---

[1] If St. Cyprian was reconciled to Rome before his death (A.D. 258), it was without yielding the point in dispute, to which the African Church held till after the Council of Arles in 314.
[2] St. Athanas. "Ad Monachos," Opp. i. 861 (Paris, 1627).
[3] Milman, "Latin Christianity," i. 2.

The Roman Theory of Holiness.

XCIV. As regards the practical notion about holiness in the modern Roman Church, it may be fairly said that it is regarded, like the priesthood and the monastic life, as something official and apart from the great bulk of Christians. The Roman Church does undoubtedly spend more time and pains than any other Christian body in striving to rear and train a small number of persons who shall exhibit exceptional sanctity, and has even methodized the whole system, as a florist might the process of cultivating certain rare and beautiful plants. But the general mass of the people receives extremely little training even in the rudiments of morality. And consequently the standard of life and conduct is, to say the very least, no higher in Roman Catholic populations than elsewhere. In England, on the contrary, whereas Roman Catholics are less than *five* per cent. of the population,[1] they contribute wherever they are collected—for of course there are many parts of England and Wales where there are few or none—from *sixteen* to *sixty-seven* per cent. of the criminals to our prisons; that is to say, from three to thirteen times their fair share of crime.[2] The Roman theory may be thus not unfairly compared with that of the master of a great school who neglects the great

---

[1] Ravenstein, "Denominational Statistics."

[2] On Dec. 31, 1877, there were 4,289 criminal Protestant children detained in English reformatories, and 1,346 Roman Catholic ones, more than 24 per cent. In Clerkenwell prison, during 1877-8, there were 1,395 Roman Catholics out of 8,930, more than 16 per cent.; in Wandsworth, 1,006 Roman Catholics out of 6,472, nearly 16 per cent.; in Coldbath Fields, during 1877, 23¼ per cent. The ratio in Manchester for 1877-8-9 has been 43 per cent.; in one of the Liverpool gaols 50 per cent. and upwards; and in the other, for 1871-79, 67 per cent. of Roman Catholic prisoners, *more than double* all others together. In Scotland, Roman Catholics are about 8½ per cent. of the population, chiefly collected in Dundee and Glasgow. Their ratio of criminals in the gaol of Dundee was 38 per cent., and in Glasgow 44½ per cent. in 1879.

majority of the pupils in order to cram two or three of the most promising ones for prizes; that of the Church of England, with that where the very best boys are left pretty much to themselves, with no special encouragement, but where honest pains are taken with the general body of the pupils. Clearly, though each method has its faults, the second is more for the public advantage.

Liguorianism fatal to Holiness of Teaching.

XCV. The Church of Rome has ceased to be holy in its teaching ever since the elevation of Liguori to be a Doctor of the Church, when his views were authorized in the confessional, even if we go back no further; and even as regards the modern saints it rears (such, for instance, as Benedict Joseph Labre, beatified in 1851), the gravest exceptions may be taken to its theory of saintliness. Liguori himself, as has been shown above, is liable to the charge of idolatry, blasphemy, and mendacity, and of having taught others to do the like. He was personally a man of pure and self-denying life, of amiable disposition, and has written various works with much devout matter in them; but these good points, however they may warrant us in entertaining a hope that he may yet be forgiven, are altogether insufficient to raise him to the spiritual peerage of heaven, in the face of Christ's decree: "Whosoever therefore shall break one of these least commandments, and shall teach men so, he shall be called the least in the kingdom of heaven: but whosoever shall do and teach them, the same shall be called great in the kingdom of heaven" (St. Matt. v. 19). And the three commandments broken in the "Glories of Mary" and "Moral Theology" are amongst the very greatest.

The question raised here and in section IX. is not as to Casuistry in general, or the practical need of some application of moral theology to discriminate between the degrees of guilt, according to motive and circumstances, attaching to the same kind of act; but a narrower one:

namely, whether Liguori's standard be not in itself a low and shifting one ; whether Rome can be justified in still maintaining Probabilism, after its dangers and excesses were exposed by Pascal as far back as 1656, and denounced afresh as unscriptural and immoral by the Dominicans Richard and Giraud, in their great "Bibliothèque Sacrée" in 1765; and whether, in fact, the rules have not got into popular teaching, instead of being strictly confined, as sometimes alleged, to the clergy for their guidance. Thus, in Furniss's Catechism, "What every Christian ought to know," approved by Cardinal Cullen (one of those, by-the-by, which cuts out the Second Commandment entirely), it is laid down that irreverent use of God's name, curses, if no great harm be intended by them, and small thefts, are *venial* sins; while non-fasting communion, or selling the relic of a saint, are *mortal* sins ; though it is lawful to sell the *case* of a relic—with the relic in it.

Wickedness of the Local Church of Rome.

XCVI. All these considerations, however, sink into entire insignificance when we come face to face with the question as to the sanctity of the Roman See and its occupants. As in the case of Unity, so in that of Holiness, *it is precisely Rome which has sunk lowest, longest, and oftenest;* which has been the foulest cesspool of wickedness, profligacy, depravity of all kinds ; which has had the greatest number of abandoned criminals amongst its Bishops. These are strong words. Now to justify them. Here is what Cardinal Baronius, the Ultramontane annalist, says of the Roman Church in the tenth century: "What was then the semblance of the Holy Roman Church ? As foul as it could be : when harlots, superior in power as in profligacy, governed at Rome, at whose will sees were transferred, bishops were appointed, and, what is horrible and awful to say, their paramours were intruded into the see of Peter; false pontiffs who are set down in the catalogue of Roman pontiffs merely for chronological purposes; for who can venture to say that persons thus basely intruded by such courtezans were legitimate Roman pontiffs? No mention can be found of election or subsequent consent on the part of the clergy, all the Canons were buried in oblivion, the decrees of the Popes stifled, the ancient traditions put under ban, and the old customs, sacred rites, and former usages in the election of the Chief Pontiff were quite abolished. Mad lust, relying on worldly power, thus claimed all as its own, goaded on by the sting of ambition. Christ was then in a deep sleep in the ship, when the ship itself was covered by the waves and these great tempests were blowing. . . . And what seemed worse, there were no disciples to wake Him with their cries as He slept, for all were snoring. You can imagine as you please what sort of presbyters and deacons were chosen as cardinals by these monsters."[1] This period covered a space of more than thirty years, and the reigns of nine Popes. But Gilbert Genebrard, Archbishop of Aix (1537–1597), writing of the same era, makes the duration of Papal profligacy much longer : " This age has been unfortunate, in so far that during nearly a hundred and fifty years about *fifty Popes* have fallen away from the virtues of their predecessors, being apostates, or apostatical, rather than apostolical."[2] That is to say, about *one-fifth* of all the Popes who have ever sat at Rome are hereby charged with grievous criminality. In the eleventh century, the writings of St. Peter Damiani, Cardinal Bishop of Ostia, paint the morals and lives of the bishops and clergy in the most revolting colours; in the fourteenth, the great Catholic poet Petrarch, describing the Papal Court, then at Avignon, speaks of it as the Babylon of the Apocalypse, " which had filled the sack of God's anger with impious vices, following as its own

[1] Baron. " Ann." 912, viii.
[2] Genebrard, " Chron. Sac.," iv. ann. 901 (Cologne, 1571).

gods not even Jupiter or Pallas, but Bacchus and Venus." Again, he calls it "fountain of grief, river of wrath, school of errors, temple of heresy, formerly Rome, now false and guilty Babylon, forge of lies, horrible prison, hell upon earth."[1] And Boccaccio's story in the same century is well known, how a Parisian Christian endeavoured to convert Abraham, a Jew, who proposed making a journey to Rome to see for himself if the morals of the clergy there proved the superiority of their creed over his own. His friend, knowing too well the real state of things, endeavoured to dissuade him, but in vain. On reaching Rome, Abraham found the Pope, cardinals, and clergy immersed in all kinds of vice; and returning to Paris, became a Christian, and was baptized, on the ground that no religion which was not divine could survive such enormities on the part of its ministers.[2] But what is not so familiar to the ordinary reader is, that this story is no malicious invention of Boccaccio's, as others similar in his collection may probably be, for it is recorded as a literal historical fact by Benvenuto da Imola, in his Commentary on Dante, written in 1376. About the same time were issued the Revelations of St. Bridget (1302–1373), which are allowed as authentic by Pope Benedict XIV. She says, "The Pope is a murderer of souls, he destroys and flays the flock of Christ, he is more cruel than Judas, more unjust than Pilate. All the Ten Commandments he has changed into this one, Money, Money. . . . The Pope and his clergy are rather the forerunners of Antichrist than the servants of Christ; the Pope's worldly court plunders the heavenly court of Christ; the clergy read no more in the Book of God, but in the book of the world; the reason of God is foolishness to them; the care for souls a fable."[3]

[1] Petrarch, "Sonette e Canzone," parte iv. 15, 16.
[2] "Decameron," i. 2.
[3] There is no more shocking fact than the well-attested poisonings in the Holy Eucharist, of which a memorial survives in the

Close of the Fifteenth Century.

XCVII. In the fifteenth century, despite a loud call for "Reform of the Church in head and members," and some feeble efforts made at the Councils of Pisa, Constance, and Basle, things were getting worse, while at the end of the century came a group of pontiffs as bad as in the darkest time of the harlot reign, Sixtus IV., Innocent VIII., and worst of all, Alexander VI., the Nero of the Papacy, one of the vilest criminals on record. Julius II. and Leo X., his near successors,[1] though men of ungodly lives, almost rise into decorousness beside him, and it is no wonder that under such rulers every kind of wickedness throve and flourished.

Documents of the Reformation Era.

XCVIII. What things were when the Reformation, always postponed or refused by Rome, had become inevitable and imminent, the "Hundred Grievances" may tell us on the one hand, while for the time after the revolt had broken out we have the "Report of the Committee of Cardinals" (namely, Sadolet, Contarini, Reginald Pole, Giberti, Fregoso, Aleander, Badia, and Caraffa, afterwards Paul IV.) to Paul III. in 1538. A couple of citations from these two documents, followed by the confession of a pious and reforming Pope, Hadrian VI., will suffice in illustration.

a. The German princes complain that, by the exemption of ecclesiastics from jurisdiction of temporal courts, they were enabled to commit all kinds of crimes with impunity. Amongst the specified crimes, alleged as widely common, are coining, theft, abduction, adultery, rape, arson, and murder; while, even when Bishops were

---

Rubrics of the Pontifical Mass, obliging the sub-deacon or the sacrist to swallow one of the wafers provided.—("Pontific. Roman." Ed. Giunta, Venice, 1520.)

[1] Pius III., his immediate successor, sat only twenty-six days.

willing to bring such offenders to justice, their Chapters hampered them, so that they could not.¹

b. The Cardinals report that the root of all the evils of the Church was in the Roman Curia itself, because former Popes, having itching ears, had heaped to themselves teachers for their lusts, not to learn their duty, but that by their craft and cunning some reason might be found for their doing just as they pleased; that one such artifice was to declare that as the Pope is lord of all benefices, and a lord may sell his own property, therefore a Pope cannot be guilty of simony; and accordingly that and countless other abuses had come from the Curia, as from the Trojan horse, into the Church, brought it to the brink of ruin, and scandalized the very heathen themselves. And they say that if the Pope wants to reform things, he must begin at home, by renouncing his vast gains and ceasing to issue dispensations for money. They add that the simony of the Roman Church was intolerable; that men of the most abandoned character were freely ordained; that depraved priests and Bishops were too commonly found; that the sacraments were openly sold for money; that the conventual Orders had become such a pestiferous example to the world, and so grievous a scandal, that the whole of them, without exception, ought to be summarily abolished; that the theological seminaries were at once schools of immorality and scepticism; while in Rome itself Divine service was celebrated in a sordid and irreverent fashion by ignorant priests, and notorious courtezans rode about in the streets openly squired by cardinals and other ecclesiastics.²

c. The Pope, in his instructions to Francesco Chiere-

---

¹ "Centum Gravamina," xxxi.
² Conc. Delect. Cardinal. in Natal. Alexand. "Hist. Eccl." (Paris, 1744, vol. xviii. pp. 87–94). This, a perfectly genuine document, is not to be confounded with a mere squib of the same period, in the works of Vergerio, professing to be the report of a committee of bishops at Bologna.

gato, the Apostolic Legate sent to the Diet of Nuremberg, says : " You will likewise say that we frankly confess that God has suffered this persecution [the Lutheran revolt] to befall His Church, because of the sins of men, and chiefly of the priests and Bishops of the Church. . . . . Nor is it wonderful that sickness should have descended from the head to the members, *from the Chief Pontiffs to the other inferior prelates*. All we (that is, the prelates of the Church) have gone astray, every one to his own ways, nor has there been now, for a long time, so much as one who did good. . . . On this subject you will promise that, as far as concerns us, we will use every effort *that first this Court,—whence, perhaps, all this evil has proceeded,—may be reformed*, that as corruption has streamed thence over all the lower orders, so the health and reformation of all may flow from the same source."[1] Another statement of this Pope is of importance. In his "Dictates on the Fourth Book of Sentences," written when he was a Professor at Louvain, but which he formally republished after he was Pope, he says : " It is certain that the Pope can err even in matters of faith, asserting heresy in his determination or decree ; *for many of the Roman Pontiffs were heretics.*"

Present Condition of the Roman Clergy.

XCIX. In our own day, despite much visible improvement, the moral standard of the Roman Catholic clergy is very unsatisfactory in many places, reaching its lowest point in Spanish and Portuguese America, but far from what it should be in Austria, Spain, Portugal, Italy, and even France ; while the customary usage of hushing up scandals, and merely transferring clerical offenders to other spheres, without bringing them to trial, is so far from producing belief in the impeccability of the clergy, that it brings innocent members

[1] Le Plat. " Monum. Conc. Trid." ii. 147. Cf. Ranke, " Hist. of Popes," i. 3.

under suspicion, just because immunity from official censure is no proof of good character. And whereas the Court of Rome claims to be the visible embodiment of the Kingdom of God on earth, so that the Pope is King as well as Priest, nevertheless the second post in that Kingdom under Pius IX. was held for more than a quarter of a century by Cardinal Antonelli, a man of notoriously irregular life. Thus, holiness is certainly not a mark of the Church of Rome.[1]

Is the Church of Rome Catholic?

C. By her own admission she is not Catholic simply. Her official title, as fixed by herself at Trent, and retained, in spite of a protest, by the Vatican Council, is "*Roman* Catholic," or sometimes "Roman" alone, as may be seen in the Creed of Pius IV. Now, as "Roman" is a *local* adjective, while "Catholic" is a delocalized one, the former *limits and restricts* the meaning of the latter when they are conjoined, so as to make it refer in strictness to the narrow Roman *Patriarchate* alone (see CVIII.) Next, although the Roman Church is very widely diffused, it is not so much so as to be plainly and unmistakably *the* Church in all places where it is to be found. It is in a conspicuous minority, for example, in all Eastern Christendom, especially in Russia, and also in England, in neither of those countries being clearly the true embodiment of Christianity, as distinguished from rival claimants. Its organization in a very large number of its sees is purely a paper one, and does not denote any real Roman Catholic population under the Bishops of those sees, who, without our taking account of mere titular Bishops *in partibus*—of whom there are about one hundred and eighty—often have no flocks to speak of; and a delusive effect is produced by the thick setting of dioceses even when this is not the case; as, for example, there are *sixty-five*

[1] For much information on this head see Liverani (Domestic Prelate and Protonotary of the Holy See), "Il Papato, L'Impero, e il Regno d'Italia," Florence, 1861.

in the former States of the Church, with a population about a third of that in the one diocese of London. That Rome is a part of the Catholic Church is true, no doubt, but only a part, albeit the largest. But, instead of making way, she is losing it, not only conquering no fresh territory, but without keeping up to the mere ratio of natural increase by births. Thus, in the "Almanach des Fidèles Amis de Pie IX.," 1875, there was a calculation from the Almanach de Gotha that, in 1874, there were 204,386,148 Roman Catholics in the world, being an increase of 15,000,000 since 1840. If they had increased even at the low rate of one-half per cent. per annum (which is less than half the rate of increase in England), there ought to have been a gain of 32,300,000 in this period, so that there has been in truth a loss of 17,000,000. In America, despite the Celtic element, constituting thirty per cent. of the whole population, and the conquest of a large part of Mexico, the Roman Catholics, instead of being at least fifteen millions, are estimated at no more than nine or ten millions. And Pius IX. dwelt often on the necessity of excluding all Liberals, indifferents, and non-practising members, from the roll of Catholics; alleging that when they were withdrawn, the true Catholic Church is but a "little flock." This mode of reckoning would reduce the Roman obedience within very narrow limits indeed. For, if the persons who come under the anathemas of the Bull "In Cœnâ Domini," or who are in open conflict with the Syllabus, be struck off the list of true Catholics, there will be none left save the clergy, the religious Orders, and a mere handful of laity, in any Roman Catholic country.[1]

[1] For proofs, see P. Curci, "Il Dissidio tra la Chiesa e lo Stato," cap. vi., and Cardinal Manning, "The Catholic Church and Modern Society" ("North American Review," Feb. 1880), wherein he confesses that the most Christian civil society now extant is that of non-Papal England, contrasted with the condition of France, Italy, and other Roman Catholic countries.

Uncatholicity of the Roman Spirit.

CI. But if a higher test than that of mere numbers and diffusion, which modern Rome chiefly relies on —though St. Augustine has said: "They who dissent concerning the Head Himself and *from the Holy Scriptures*, though they be found everywhere that the Church is, are not in the Church" ("De Unit. Eccl." iv.),—the test of tone and spirit, be applied, then the Roman Church is very far indeed from being Catholic. Whereas, on the Day of Pentecost, Parthians, and Medes, and Elamites, Jews, Cappadocians, Phrygians, Egyptians, Romans, and all the rest of the catalogue, each heard the Gospel preached in their own special dialects (Acts ii. 6-11); now, contrariwise, in every country where Rome plants her foot, the Divine mysteries are hidden from the people in a dead language. Whereas, formerly, the Divinely caused and permitted peculiarities of each nation were allowed for, recognized, and adopted into God's service; now every country must have the iron ploughshare of human uniformity passed over it, obliterating the ancient landmarks. Whereas competing schools of theology enabled the one Truth to be seen from many sides, and thus its wonderful harmony in complexity to become plain; now, one narrow, shallow, and modern type of religious teaching is alone permitted. Whereas the Church once strove to meet the needs of all classes of men and all varieties of mind; now only one, and that a very unlovely one, is recognized as being that of a true Catholic; and so the once mighty Church is being transformed before our very eyes into a mere Italian sect,—largest of sects, it is true, but with the whole spirit of Catholicity driven out of its borders; especially if we insist on the full import of two ancient definitions: "That may not be considered Catholic which appears contrary to the statements of Scripture" (St.

Chrysost. " Hom. de Adam et Eva "); [1] " Faith in Scripture is the most Catholic of all " (St. August. " Serm. XIV. De Verb. Apost."). And, indeed, not even one of the specially Roman doctrines or usages can stand the tests of Catholicity laid down by the learned Jesuit Véron in his " Rule of the Catholic Faith " (Paris, 1645), published in English by Waterworth, another learned Roman priest (Birmingham, 1833), as a work of standard and universally acknowledged authority on its subject. To make any doctrine Catholic or binding on the conscience of Christians, Véron tells us, it must be (*a*) *revealed in the Word of God*, and (*b*) *proposed to the faithful by the whole Church.* From this general maxim Véron draws the following conclusions:—

1. No doctrine delivered since the time of the Apostles can be an article of the Faith, even if confirmed by miracles ; nor is it an article of the Faith that any of those miracles is genuine.

2. Nothing can be an article of the Faith which is grounded on texts that have been diversely interpreted by the Fathers or by approved theologians of later date.

3. No deduction, however strictly logical, from premises, one only of which is of faith, and the other of human reason [*e.g.*, concomitance], can be an article of the Faith.

4. No Bull of a Pope is of authority sufficient to prove any doctrine part of the Catholic Faith ; and it is not of faith that the decisions of Sovereign Pontiffs, even *ex cathedrâ*, if unsupported by a General Council, are articles of the Catholic Faith, "and this is the unanimous opinion of all Catholic divines." Those who teach that " new and unheard-of dogma," that decisions of Sovereign Pontiffs, *ex cathedrâ*, unsupported by a General Council, are articles of Catholic Faith, " are under a hallucination, and must have fallen into error through wilful blindness."

[1] This homily is not certainly St. Chrysostom's.

5. No decision of a Provincial Council, presided over by the Pope or his legates, is of faith.

6. The prevalence of any usages or practices throughout the Church Universal is not sufficient ground to make them articles of faith, for to justify the Church in adopting any of them, it must be shown that such practice or usage is clearly good and commendable.

Is the Church of Rome now Apostolic?

CII. If Apostolic mean agreement with the *doctrine* of the Apostles, as divinely recorded for us in Holy Scripture, the Church of Rome is most certainly, clearly, and undeniably, *not* so. It is scarcely going too far to say that no Protestant sect which in any way at all acknowledges the Trinity and the Incarnation has departed so far and so manifestly from the doctrinal and moral teaching of Peter and Paul, of John and James, as the modern Church of Rome. Proof has been given of this already, and there is no need to repeat it.

But if Apostolicity mean the grace of duly transmitted Orders, with their accompanying privilege of valid sacraments, then the Roman doctrine of Intention makes it absolutely impossible for any Roman Catholic even to *guess* whether true and valid Holy Orders have been preserved in his Church at all. It has already been pointed out that the once wide prevalence of infidelity amongst the higher Italian[1] and French clergy, and of secret Judaism among the Spanish and Portuguese—historical facts which are not to be shaken by denial—makes the former existence of sincere Intention a matter of the gravest doubt in those countries, and throws the darkest

[1] "It was the tone of good society at Rome to question the evidences of Christianity. 'No one passed,' says P. Antonio Bandino, 'for an accomplished man who did not entertain heretical opinions about Christianity. At the court [of the Pope] the ordinances of the Catholic Church and passages of Holy Writ were spoken of only in a jesting manner, the mysteries of the Faith were despised.'" (Ranke's "Hist. of Popes," I. 2).

suspicion on their Orders; while in more recent times the frequent consecrations of bishops by a single prelate—in Italy with perhaps two mitred abbots, in Ireland with two priests (Burke, " Hibernia Dominicana," pp. 503–509), as assistants—has imported a fresh doubt into the matter. This does not affect the Church of England, which received its Orders before the doctrine of Intention was introduced in the Roman Church, and which does not recognize that doctrine.

The Succession in the Roman See long broken.

CIII. What is more, the condition of the Church of Rome in the tenth century, as described by Baronius, (see above, pp. 188, 189) destroys the last shred of possibility that the Roman Church of to-day inherits the original jurisdiction and mission of the Roman see, though Ultramontanes declare that all jurisdiction flows from the Pope. Here is the reason. The unlawfully intruded Popes, having no right to the see, could not give true jurisdiction or mission to any bishops and priests they consecrated, ordained, or instituted, nor could they create cardinals competent as electors.

But from the thirty-three years during which this process was going on,[1] thanks partly to the lapse of time and consequent deaths, and partly to the forcible expulsion of bishops and priests from their cures, which occurred as rival Popes succeeded, or desired to make simoniacal gains, there was, in all human probability, at the end of this anarchic period, not one ecclesiastic in Rome of any rank canonically in possession of his benefice, probably not one canonically ordained, unless some aged survivor of the earlier period. " These Popes," says Platina (" Vit. Romani I."), " thought of nothing save how to blot out the name and dignity of their predecessors." Accordingly, when the first free election took

[1] From the deposition of Leo V. in 903 to the election of Leo VII. in 936.

place, there was *no one competent to elect;* and by all canon law the election was void. This breach never was healed, and never can now be healed; so, consequently, even if St. Peter was ever Bishop of Rome, no Pope for nearly a thousand years has had canonical election to the see on Roman principles, and the claim of Apostolicity and heirship to St. Peter is voided. Even had this peril been escaped, there is a most serious doubt whether the seventy years' session at Avignon did not make a huge gap in the succession to the Roman Chair: and there was a final shipwreck of the Petrine succession and privileges made at the Council of Constance, assembled in 1414 to end the schism which broke out on the death of Gregory XI. in 1378. There were then three rival Popes: Gregory XII., John XXIII., and Benedict XIII. If any Papal election after 1378 had been valid, of course that one of the three claimants who belonged to the same line of succession must have been the true and lawful Pope; but the Council, by setting all three aside, and by disregarding all the acts of the Council of Pisa in 1409, pronounced them equally illegitimate, and thereby annulled all quasi-Papal acts, including the creation of cardinals, done between 1378 and 1414. But the election of the Popes had been transferred from the clergy and people of the city of Rome (the original constituency) and restricted to the College of Cardinals by a Bull of Nicolas II., in 1059, amplified and confirmed by Alexander III. in the Third Council of Lateran in 1179. Consequently the only person living in 1415 who by Roman canon law had any right to vote at the election of a Pope, was one of these very three claimants of the Papacy, Benedict XIII. (Cardinal Peter de Luna), who had been created cardinal by Gregory XI., and who expressly claimed, therefore, to be the only legitimate surviving cardinal, since the only one dating from before the schism, as well as to be the true Pope, in virtue of the cession of his two rivals, Gregory XII. and John XXIII. (Maimbourg, "Hist. du

Grand Schisme d'Occident," II. 253.) Of course he took no part in the acts of a Council which denied those claims to the Papacy which he never surrendered, and, consequently, not even one of the twenty-three titular cardinals who elected Otto Colonna as Martin V. had any legitimate character, as members of the Sacred College, entitling them to vote at all. They were aided, it is true, by thirty co-electors chosen from the Council (Von der Hardt, "Conc. Const." iv. 1448, 1452), but their votes were equally invalid, since on the one hand they did not represent the old Roman constituency, and on the other were excluded by later canon law, as not belonging to the Sacred College. Thus Martin V.'s election was void; his creations of cardinals and his recognition of existing titular cardinals were void also; so there never has since 1378 been a duly qualified electoral body, nor, consequently, a canonically valid election to the Papacy. At the very best, the Papacy was resettled in 1417 on a new basis, tracing up no longer to St. Peter and the charter of St. Matthew xvi. 18, but thenceforward deriving its root, title, and authority from the Council of Constance alone; just as in England, ever since the Revolution Settlement of 1689, the monarchy derives its title from Acts of Parliament, and no longer through a claim of indefeasible and divine hereditary right. The action of the Council, in respect of the three Papal lines and claimants in 1414, may be compared to that of the Crown in Great Britain, if, having before it the claims of three coheirs to a peerage fallen into abeyance (to any one of whom it has admittedly the power to assign the title), it were to set them all aside, and to bestow the peerage on a fourth person, not akin to the original grantee. This act, if done, would be a wholly new creation, and not the adjudging of the ancient dignity to a rightful heir, nor could the peer so nominated justly describe himself as representing the old line, though enjoying its historic title.

Above all, the Vatican decree, which declares that the

Pope's decisions are "irreformable even without the consent of the Church," has destroyed the mark of Apostolicity by destroying the Church itself. For what it means, put as a piece of arithmetic, is this: Pope + Church = Pope − Church, and therefore, Church = 0. Well might Bishop Maret, one of the most learned of recent French theologians, say, "In changing the Constitution, you are obliged to change the doctrine also; and from henceforth it will be necessary to chant at the Holy Sacrifice, 'I believe in the Pope,' instead of 'I believe in the Church.'"[1] Well might another theologian say, "These gentlemen have simplified the Bible and the Creed. They have reduced the Bible to one text: 'Thou art Peter;' and the Creed to one article: 'I believe in the Pope.'"

The Plea of Ignorance not adducible.

CIV. And to all this indictment there is one very formidable count yet to be added, namely, that whereas many of these frightful abuses and perversions of holy things began in a rude and ignorant age, and with no thought of wrong or error at first, so that it would be unjust to censure too harshly those who originally fell into, or afterwards acquiesced in, them, "and the times of this ignorance God winked at" (Acts xvii. 30); now, contrariwise, their true character has been plainly and irrefutably exposed, with full proof that they are in open violation of God's law, as revealed in Holy Scripture, and of the law of the Catholic Church, as embodied in ancient Councils and Fathers; and yet all acknowledgment of faultiness is avoided, all reform is refused, and declared impossible, nay, even blasphemous, for Romanists have not hesitated to say that, "to reform the Church is exactly the same project as to reform God."[2] And that, albeit the Council of Trent, with all its shortcomings, did carry out a multitude of reforms on many

---

[1] "Du Concile Général," ii. 375. [2] *Tablet*, March 4, 1876.

points of Church doctrine and practice; while the Letter of Summons to the Council of Pisa in 1409 convokes it "for the due and wholesome *reformation* of the Church." The Council of Constance decreed in its fortieth session, October 30, 1417, that the Pope about to be elected "ought to *reform* the Church in head and members, and also the Roman Curia, according to equity;" and the Bull of Julius II., convoking the Council of Lateran in 1512, declares its objects to be "the praise of God, the exaltation, unity, and *reformation* of the Church, and the total extirpation of schisms and heresies." But now that is come to pass again which the Prophet spoke of the sinful Jewish Church many centuries ago: "A wonderful and horrible thing is committed in the land; the prophets prophesy falsely, and the priests bear rule by their means; and my people love to have it so; and what will ye do in the end thereof?" (Jer. v. 30, 31.) For the far more numerous Vatican Council, assembled in the full light of the nineteenth century, did not touch reform with so much as a little finger (though the burning question of clerical morals was debated from January 21 to 31, 1870, as needing prompt and searching measures),[1] preferring to stultify itself by permitting the publication in its midst of that which all of its members who represented really great Catholic bodies knew to be false, and said so, fully aware, as they could not but be, that we must look to the great General Councils of the undivided Church for the laws and limits of Papal as well as of episcopal authority, and that nothing in the least resembling a supremacy, to say nothing of a gift of infallibility, can be extracted from any of them. Therefore the constituted authorities of the Roman Church are now without excuse, and are in open, conscious, and wilful rebellion against Almighty God on all

[1] Friedrich, "Tagebuch," pp. 133, ff; Fromman, "Gesch. Vat. Conc.," p. 96. This fact is suppressed in the official reports.

those heads which we have seen discussed above. The guiltless flocks are not to blame, but no one reared in a purer, older, and more stable system, such as that of the Church of England, can throw in his lot with them, save at the price of assuming full accountability for every such act of disloyalty to the Divine law. And it is to be steadily remembered that the strictly enforced discipline of the Roman Church, inclusive of a rigid censorship of all theological and devotional writings before licence to print is granted, makes the authorities of the Roman Church legally as well as morally responsible, not only for all which they formally publish or do themselves, but for all which they permit others to do or publish uncensured. It is not open to them to plead the inevitable intermingling of good and evil, of truth and error, which they might urge, were it not for their own double claim of doctrinal infallibility and absolute power.

Jurisdiction and Mission.

CV. As it is impossible for Roman controversialists to defend themselves effectually on any of the points hitherto raised, they prefer, as a rule, to assail the Church of England from another side, and to declare that it lacks, by reason of its severance from the Roman see, all true Jurisdiction and Mission. Let it be assumed for a moment that this is really the case. What then? Simply this, that jurisdiction and mission, in the special Roman sense, are creations of *human ecclesiastical law*, being no more than comparatively late deductions and *inferences* from the possible, but by no means necessary, meaning of certain vague indications of Church polity in the New Testament. But the objection to joining the Church of Rome is, that to do so inevitably involves several acts of open revolt against the *divine law*, expressly and unmistakably revealed and acknowledged. Thus the Roman objections to England are chiefly on points of mere *technical detail* (as in the cavils against the

Ordinal), while those of England against Rome are chiefly on *fundamental matters of principle*. The Roman argument resembles the fraudulent repudiation of a debt admittedly incurred, on the alleged ground of an insufficient stamp on the genuine bond; the English is a plea of never indebted, and proof of the manifest forgery of the deed put in as evidence of the claim. And, further, all Church government is a *means* only, not an *end* in itself. It is designed for the safeguard of faith and morals, as civil governments are for the protection of life and property. And they both lose their rights if they fail to discharge these duties. But the Roman Church, as shown above, does not guard either faith or morals. So the Roman canon law shall itself decide the controversy by two of its maxims: " He deserves to lose his privilege altogether, who abuses the power intrusted to him" (" Decret.," II. xi. 63); and, " He is to be stripped of his privilege, who trenches on those of others" (" Decret. Greg. IX.," V. xxxiii. 3). For, as there can be no greater abuse of privilege than to employ it to compel disobedience to Almighty God, the Roman claim on us would fail at once upon that plea alone. The commonest of all Roman cavils is that the Church of England, by yielding too much authority in spirituals to the civil power, has disobeyed Christ's command: "Render to Cæsar the things that are Cæsar's, and to God the things that are God's" (St. Mark xii. 17). The reply is, that so far as this charge has any show of truth in it at all (on which see Article XXXVII.), it is a mere separable accident, not applying to the great majority of the Pan-Anglican Churches; and next, that the Roman Church disobeys *both* clauses of Christ's maxim, by having refused the State its just rights many times over in history, and by giving to human beings the attributes and worship which belong to God alone.[1]

[1] In any case, the Erastianism of the Church of England chiefly belongs to the reign of Elizabeth, when the political action of the

Bishops Excommunicated by Rome presided over Great Councils.

CVI. A couple of good broad facts from Church history are worth a great deal of subtle discussion. Here they are: St. Firmilian, of Cæsarea in Cappadocia, who was excommunicated by the Pope, and who died unreconciled to Rome, presided over the great Council of Antioch in 264, assembled to try Paul of Samosata, though, the Metropolitan of Cæsarea, the Bishop of Jerusalem, and St. Gregory Thaumaturgus, were all present. Not only so; but, as it was necessary to hold a second council for the same purpose, St. Firmilian a second time presided, and was asked to do so a third time, but died before the Council met in 269.[1] Still more remarkable is the fact that St. Meletius of Antioch, who was also put out of communion by the Pope,[2] was, nevertheless, chosen to preside over the Second General Council in 381, and actually did so till his death.[3] It is impossible to suppose that the Fathers of these four great synods thought communion with the Roman see the test of valid jurisdiction and episcopal character. It may be mentioned, as illustrating the same feeling, that attempts are made every now and then by Italian Catholics to procure the canonization of Savonarola, though burnt as a heretic by express orders of a Pope.

Papacy inevitably provoked the civil power. But nothing can be laid to the charge of the Anglican clergy on this head which will compare with the accusation brought by M. Charles de Mazade, an eminent French publicist, against the Neapolitan Church of a much later time. He declares that when Victor Emmanuel II. was entering Naples after its annexation to his crown, an ecclesiastical dignitary drew near and asked him in a low voice *to whom were the reports of confessions to be transmitted* thenceforward. The King could not believe his ears at first, but found that such had been the usage under his Bourbon predecessors ("Revue des Deux Mondes," Dec. 1, 1866, pp. 735-6).

[1] Hefele, "Concilien," I. ii. 9.
[2] Fleury, "H.E.," xvii. 29.   [3] Ibid. xviii. 1.

Claim as Heir to St. Peter.

CVII. If the Pope claim jurisdiction over us as heir of St. Peter, the answer is twofold: that not a single one of the steps necessary by canon law to prove such heirship has ever yet been taken, and, in so serious a matter bare assertion or guess is of no legal or evidential value; and, next, that, if such heirship *could* be proved, that very fact would at once bar the right to all and any jurisdiction over every Gentile Church, as St. Peter was after a time divinely restricted to the Circumcision or Church of the Jews (Gal. ii. 7, 8), and there is no record of any subsequent removal of this limitation; while, lastly, St. Ambrose testifies against the claim, saying: "They have not Peter's heritage, who have not Peter's faith" ("De Pœnit." 7).[1]

Claim as Patriarch of the West.

CVIII. If the claim be next made on the ground that the Pope, as Patriarch of the West, is the supreme Church ruler, to whom all Western primates and metropolitans are at least as much subject as their suffragan bishops are in turn to them, then the answer is that we know exactly from Rufinus ("Hist. Eccl." I. 6) what were the limits of the Roman Patriarchate, namely, ten provinces in Central and Southern Italy, with the islands of Sicily, Sardinia, and Corsica.[2] It did not extend

---

[1] The later editions of St. Ambrose evade this by altering *fidem* into *sedem*, which does not make sense with the context. Bossuet ("Defens. Declar. Cler. Gall. II. xv. 5") remarks that the *whole* life of St. Peter is parallel to the *whole* Papal dynasty; so that some Popes, such as Leo and Agatho, are like Peter confirming the brethren, but others, such as Liberius and Honorius, are Peter's heirs in his wavering and denial only. Here, then, is another element of uncertainty brought in.

[2] Dupin, "De Antiq. Eccl. Discip." I. xi. The fact of this narrow limitation, which has often been disputed, is settled by many proofs, of which it will suffice here to give one, namely, that it was not till A.D. 571 that the Popes were able to get any footing even in Milan,

even so far as Milan, to say nothing of Gaul or Britain, and the Pope is expressly barred by the eighth canon of the General Council of Ephesus from at any time enlarging its borders: "No bishop shall interfere in other provinces which have not been *from the very first* under himself and his predecessors. . . . But if any one have taken a province, or caused it to be subject to him through compulsion, *he must restore it.*"

And every Pope at his coronation is enjoined by the *Liber Diurnus*, quoted in the canon law ("Decret.," I., dist. xv. 2), to make the following profession, as re-enacted in the eighth Canon of the Council of Constance: "The eight Holy General Councils—that is, Nice first, Constantinople second, Ephesus third, Chalcedon fourth, Constantinople fifth and sixth, Nice seventh, and Constantinople eighth—I profess with mouth and heart, to be kept *unmutilated in a single tittle*, to account them worthy of equal honour and veneration, to follow in every respect what they promulgated or decreed, and to condemn whatsoever they condemned." Consequently, the Popes are not at liberty to claim Patriarchal rights over England, unless by perjuring themselves. And this oath covers Canon XXVIII. of Chalcedon; since it is not excepted. See § LXXVI. note.

Claim from Conversion.

CIX. It is further urged that Pope Gregory the Great, by sending St. Augustine of Canterbury to England, acquired thereby direct jurisdictional rights over the country, as the source whence it received the Gospel. There are three refutations of this argument. First, that there is no precedent in early Church history for such an argument at all. It nowhere appears that the particular Church which succeeded in any missionary effort acquired permanent jurisdiction over its converts,

and not till 593 that Gregory the Great, taking advantage of a local dispute, succeeded in extending his authority over it, and sending a legate thither. Fleury, "H. E.," xxxv. 32.

whatever claim on their gratitude it may have had.¹ Clearly, had any such rule existed, Jerusalem would be the Mistress, as well as the Mother, of all Churches. Next, only a very small part of the work of Christianizing England was really effected by St. Augustine's mission.² The British succession continued to propagate itself in Wales, which was not overrun by the Saxon heathens; and by far the larger part of the conversion of Saxon England was achieved by the non-Roman missionaries of the Scoto-Irish Church, to whom the Christianizing of all the north, west, and centre of England is due.³ And, as Rome never gave mission to these two bodies of teachers, she can claim no jurisdiction, in right of conversion, over the regions they evangelized. Nor can any claim be set up on the ground of later benefits. The attempt of Innocent III. to annul Magna Charta (which may be profitably compared with Leo the Great's attempt to annul Canon XXVIII. of Chalcedon) and to excommunicate the barons who obtained it, together with the greedy extortions of patronage and money by several other Popes, are the chief memories of our dealings with Rome in the Middle Ages. See Lingard, " Hist. of Engl." vol. II., chap. v., p. 181 ; chap. vi., pp. 205–209; edit. 1855.⁴

¹ In fact, the African Church, which was planted from Rome (Tertull., " De Præscr." 36 ; St. Cyprian, " Epist." 45), formally repudiated Papal jurisdiction, and that thrice; in two synods at Carthage in 255, of seventy-one and eighty-seven Bishops, and in a third one in 419–422, referred to above, sect. LIV.

² Bright, "Early English Church History;" Maclear, "Christian Missions in Middle Ages."

³ Almost all England beyond Kent and the South-East, indeed, save what was done in Wessex and East Anglia by Birinus and Felix. But the revival of Christianity in Essex was due to Cedd, a Saxon consecrated and given mission by Celtic Bishops.

⁴ And so Langland in the fourteenth century :—
"And God amend the Pope,
That pilleth [robbeth] Holy Kirke,
And claimeth before the King
To be keeper over Christians,

St. Gregory the Great's own Action.

CX. Thirdly, St. Gregory, in fact, did not send out St. Augustine at all in the *canonical* sense of mission. That was done by his consecrator in Gaul, Virgilius of Arles, and it would therefore be to that see that jurisdiction on that ground, if yielded at all, would attach over England. Further, St. Gregory did not reserve to himself the election and confirmation of English metropolitans and bishops, but conceded them by special grant (whereby he divested himself of any claims he might suppose himself to have) for all future time, to the local synods of the two English provinces.[1]

Claim from Subsequent Voluntary Cession.

CXI. The weakest plea of all is that the English Church did, in fact, by various acts, voluntarily accept and submit to the Papal authority. To this three replies are conclusive. First, so far as it was done at all, it was in belief of the genuineness of the False Decretals, and of the binding character of the canon law based thereon, and so was procured by fraud, and void on that ground. Next, even had this not been the case, it would have required a formal act of a whole national synod to have empowered the English bishops to convey away the liberties of their Churches to an external authority, but no acts of any such synod are producible; while, thirdly, even had there been any action of this sort, the Pope was incompetent, by reason of his coronation oath, binding him to the decrees of Ephesus, to accept such cession.

       And counteth not though Christians
       Be killed and robbed :
       And findeth folk to fight
       And Christian blood to spill."
                   "Piers Plowman."

[1] Palmer, "Episcopacy of the British Churches Vindicated."

The Anglo-Roman Hierarchy schismatic.

CXII. There are only two events which could, on Catholic principles, justify a fresh mission to a country already Christianized. One is the dying-out, through any cause, of the original episcopal and clerical body, so as to need renewal or revival, in order to restore a valid succession, as was done for Scotland in 1610. The other is actual loss of the Faith itself, so that the country has fallen back into heathenism or unbelief, and has to be evangelized afresh.

Nothing colourably suggesting either of these events has occurred to justify the presence and attitude of the Anglo-Roman hierarchy in England.

a. On the one hand, at the accession of Queen Elizabeth in 1558, when the whole main body of the English clergy consisted of those who had conformed to Latin usages under Mary I., out of about nine or ten thousand, only 189 (just two per cent.) refused to conform to the Book of Common Prayer.[1]

b. Owing to the illegality, in canon law, of the deprivations of Edwardine bishops, effected by the civil power of Queen Mary, the only bishops of her reign who were canonically in possession of their sees in December, 1559, the date of Parker's consecration,

---

[1] Camden, "Elizabeth." It is worth adding that on Nov. 30, 1562, a debate arose in the Council of Trent on the relations of the Papacy to the Episcopate. The Spanish Bishops, led by the Bishop of Cadiz, urged that Papal confirmation is unnecessary, in opposition to the view of the Italian prelates. The Irish Bishop of Aghadoe, taking the Ultramontane side, spoke thus : "In England, the sovereign calls herself the Head of the Church, and creates Bishops, who are consecrated by three Bishops, and affirm that they are true Bishops, having authority from God. But we deny this, *because they are not appointed by the Pope;* and we say rightly, and we refute them by this reason *only,* for they show that they were called, elected, consecrated, and given mission." And the statement was accepted by all the Fathers present. Le Plat, "Monument. Conc. Trid." v. 576-9.

were Bonner of London, Kitchen of Llandaff, and Stanley of Sodor and Man. Seven sees were vacant through death; while Barlow, Bishop of Bath and Wells, and Coverdale of Exeter, having been uncanonically deprived, were still the only lawful holders of those sees; and Scory, who had been intruded into Chichester, and subsequently reconciled by Bonner, and Hodgskin, suffragan Bishop of Bedford, were both acting as assistant bishops to Bonner in the diocese of London. These four were Parker's consecrators, two of them having inherited canonical right to act for the province, and the other two having been left at liberty to act by Bonner, who, though himself dissenting from Parker's appointment, made no protest whatever, and by non-interference with the action of his two suffragans, was himself committed thereby. Kitchen and Stanley both accepted the Reformation, and died in possession of their sees,[1] nor was any protest made by the eight Marian bishops who alone survived 1560. They allowed the case to go by default; and no claim of local jurisdiction for the Roman titular bishops who have ministered to their co-religionists here, from James I. to Victoria, was set up until 1850, nearly three hundred years too late. The plea of disappearance of the native clergy is therefore out of court altogether, and there is no pretence that the Church of England has apostatized from the Faith, or even embodied in her formularies any tenets adjudged heretical by the voice of the undivided Catholic Church.[2]

c. Such being the case, the intrusion of an alien hierarchy here is in violation of the following laws of the Church and statements of the Fathers:—

[1] Bailey, "Defensio Ordinum Eccl. Angl."
[2] Lord Coke, in his Charge at the Norwich assizes, August 4, 1606, stated that he had often heard from Queen Elizabeth that Pius IV. had offered to accept the Book of Common Prayer; and that he had also frequently conferred with noblemen of the highest rank in the State, who had seen and read the Pope's letter.

1. "Whereas it is against ancient usage that the Bishop of Antioch should ordain in Cyprus .... we therefore decree that the prelates of the Cypriote Churches shall be suffered, without let or hindrance, to consecrate bishops by themselves; and, moreover, *that the same rule shall be observed also in other dioceses and provinces everywhere, so that no bishop shall interfere in another province which has not from the very first been under himself and his predecessors;* and further, that if any one have so encroached or forcibly subjected one to himself, *he must restore it*, in order that the canons of the Fathers be not infringed, nor the priesthood made an occasion or pretence for the pride of worldly power, nor the least portion of that freedom be lost to us unawares, which our Lord Jesus Christ, who bought the world's freedom, vouchsafed to us when He shed His own blood. Wherefore it has seemed good to this Holy Œcumenical Council, that the rights of every province should be preserved intact and inviolate, which have ever belonged to it, according to the usage which has always obtained" (Council of Ephesus, Canon viii.).

2. St. Leo the Great lays down two propositions in the same spirit:—

(*a.*) "Let not the rights of the provincial primacies be torn up, nor the metropolitan bishops be deprived of the privileges anciently bestowed" (Epist. ad Anatol.).

(*b.*) "When the election of a bishop has to be dealt with, that man is to be set over them all for whom the harmonious consent of the clergy and people has asked; and if the votes be divided between two persons, that one is to be preferred who, by the judgment of the metropolitan, has the greater zeal and merit" (Epist. ad Anastatium).

3. "No bishop may take possession of the flock of another" (Conc. III. Carthag., Can. xx.).

4. "Let no one dare to ordain a bishop without the consent of the metropolitan" (Pope Innocent I., Ep. ad Victric.).

5. "Two bishops cannot be consecrated or recognized in the same city" (Conc. Cabillon, Can. iv.).

6. "Not even the authority of the see [of Rome] can concede or alter anything contrary to the decrees of the Fathers" (Pope Zosimus, Ep. ad Episcop. Vienn. et Narbon. ap. Labbe. Conc. iv. 1570).

All these statements disprove the alleged rights of the Anglo-Roman hierarchy, which, as an institution pretending to a provincial and diocesan character, is but of yesterday, seeing that the vicars-apostolic, down to 1850, when they were bishops at all, were merely titular bishops *in partibus*, so that it is clear that no assent of the metropolitans, suffragans, clergy, and laity of the Church of England was asked or had. The intrusion was the act of Pius IX. alone, in contravention of his own coronation oath.

Even in the past, the Popes as a rule neither consecrated nor confirmed the English prelates. Only two archbishops of Canterbury, Theodore in 668, and Plegmund in 889, were consecrated by the Popes down to 1138; no archbishop of York by the Pope or his legates, till 1119.[1] As to confirmation, here is the evidence of Thomassin, one of the greatest of Roman canonists: "The Metropolitans of Gaul, whereas they had no primate or exarch, were nevertheless not confirmed by the Pope, but by the Provincial Council. *Nor was the English custom different.*"[2]

Considering the present anomalous condition of Christendom, no charge of schism would fairly lie, if the Roman clergy did but undertake to minister to foreign Catholics domiciled here, or even to hereditary members of their own society; just as is in fact the policy of the Greek clergy in England, and of Anglican chaplains on the Continent. But they set up altar against altar, deny the rightful claims of the native Church, and

[1] Palmer, "Episcopacy of British Churches Vindicated."
[2] Thomassin, "Vet. et Nov. Eccl. Discip." II. ii. 19, ix.

endeavour to entice away its members; and that not to a purer religion and a holier standard, but to heresy in doctrine, idolatry, or at least gross superstition, in practice, and an altogether lower level of Christian ethics.

Further Proof of Uncanonical Character.

CXIII. Moreover, a considerable fraction of the Anglo-Roman clergy consists of clerical and lay seceders from the Church of England. These have been universally re-baptized; not merely one or two here and there, where perhaps some reasonable doubt might have arisen as to the valid administration of the sacrament, but in *every* case, exhibiting a wanton determination to ignore its validity always. Now, by submitting to rebaptism, the converts have not only involved themselves in the guilt of *sacrilege* (Cat. Conc. Trid. II. ii. 56), according to Roman doctrine, but have incurred, together with their rebaptizer and all assistants at the rite, the penalty of *irregularity*, and perpetual incapacity for discharging any clerical office, *even if they did not know that they had been previously baptized*, "inasmuch as by yielding to so frightful a crime (*res nefanda, immanissimum scelus*), they have crucified Christ afresh" (André, "Droit Canon.," s. v. *Irregularité*). All sacraments administered by these clerical converts are therefore, on Roman grounds, null, void, and sacrilegious. And the only defence set up is, that what they do is with Papal assent and authority, and therefore with rightful jurisdiction. It remains to be shown what the facts are on that head.

The Historical Truth as to Papal Jurisdiction.

CXIV. 1. Down to the Council of Nicæa, A.D. 325, or even to the Council of Antioch, 341, the system of jurisdiction was complete within each province under its Metropolitan, beyond whom no appeal lay. He, on his election by the comprovincial bishops, in whom collectively the power of jurisdiction was vested, became at once possessed of authority to give jurisdiction and mission to those whom he subsequently consecrated or ordained for episcopal and sacerdotal office within the province. Nor is the Pope's name in the first place in any ancient Liturgy, save that of the local Roman Church itself. And it is not till the twelfth century that the decrees of any synod are issued in the name of the president only, even if Pope, but in the name of all the bishops present, as exercising collective and co-equal authority. (Van Espen, "De Schism. Sæc. XII."). Thus, the existing English system is a reverting to the ancient custom, overthrown by Roman encroachments.

2. No act or canon of any synod whatever, till that of Lateran in 1215, bestows direct authority on the Roman See. There are compliments in plenty, and even various concessions of *rank*, but none of immediate *power*, outside the narrow Roman Patriarchate, save the one restricted right of hearing certain appeals, granted by the Council of Sardica in 347, but rejected by the Eastern and African Churches, and repealed by the ninth canon of the General Council of Chalcedon, which instituted a system of appeals in which the name of the Roman See does not so much as appear.

3. No reference to Papal authority can be found in any creed, or in any gloss on any creed, till the publication of that of Pius IV. in 1564, although Leo the Great declared that "the short and perfect confession of the Catholic creed, stamped with as many sentences as there were Apostles, is itself so furnished from the heavenly armoury, that all the opinions of heretics may be cut asunder with its single sword" ("Epist." xxi. 4).

4. No charge of heresy can be found to have been brought against any one in the ancient Church for denying or resisting the Pope's authority. Contrariwise, some of those who resisted it most steadily are amongst the most famous saints, as St. Cyprian, St. Augustine, and St. Hilary of Arles.

5. No statement of doctrine or other formal act of any Pope, brought before a General Council, was ever accepted as a thing of course, or treated as Parliament treats a Queen's Message. On the contrary, every matter of the sort was carefully sifted and judged. Thus, the Third General Council of Ephesus disregarded the synodical deposition of Nestorius by Pope Celestine, and summoned him to take his seat as Archbishop of Constantinople; the Fourth General Council of Chalcedon accepted the Tome of Pope St. Leo on the express ground that it agreed in doctrine with the Creed in the first instance, and then with the teaching of St. Cyril of Alexandria at Ephesus;[1] the Fifth General Council of Constantinople refused to permit a decree sent by Pope Vigilius to be read, decided against its ruling, and struck his name, as contumacious, out of the registers of the Church; while it was the Sixth General Council of Constantinople which condemned Pope Honorius as a heretic.

6. The first instance of direct *coercive* authority being exercised by any Pope over an orthodox bishop was by Leo the Great, in the case of St. Hilary of Arles, in the year 445. St. Hilary, having, in his character of Metropolitan, tried and sentenced one of his suffragans, the latter appealed to Rome, and got the ear of the Pope, who directed his reinstatement. St. Hilary refused, both on the merits of the particular case, and also on the general ground that the Pope had no right of actual interference whatever in another province, though he might of course use his great influence diplomatically. Leo, a man devoured with ambition, and by no means particular as to the means of acquiring power, so that he got it somehow, knowing perfectly well that as a matter of canon and ecclesiastical law St. Hilary was right, fell

---

[1] "Piously and truly hath Leo taught, hath Cyril taught. May the memory of Cyril be eternal! Leo and Cyril have taught the same. Anathema to him who believes otherwise."—"Act. Conc. Chalced." ap. Labbe.

back on brute force and sheer Erastianism, and obtained from the dissolute tyrant Valentinian III. the following decree, which, despite its affected language of mere confirmation of existing law, was a wholly new and revolutionary grant: "We ordain, by a perpetual sanction, that nothing shall be attempted by the Bishops of Gaul, or of the other provinces, against ancient custom, without the authority of the venerable Pope of the Eternal City; but that to them and to all, whatsoever the authority of the Apostolic Chair has or shall have ordained, shall be law; so that if any bishop, when summoned, should have neglected to come to the judgment-seat of the Roman prelate, he shall be compelled to present himself there by the governor of the province; the privileges which our forefathers, of happy memory, have accorded to the Roman See, being preserved inviolate."[1] It is worthy of notice, that it is not possible to appeal to this law in England as beginning a prescription, whatever may be the case in France, for the Imperial rights over Britain had been formally yielded up, and the independence of the country confirmed, in A.D. 409, by the Emperor Honorius,[2] then lawful ruler of the West.

7. Similarly, it was from another Erastian ground that the next step of the Roman Pontiffs to exalt their authority was taken. "Boniface III.," says Anastatius the Librarian, "it was who *obtained* from the Emperor Phocas [the rebel who murdered the Emperor Maurice and usurped his throne] that the Apostolical seat of the blessed Apostle Peter—that is to say, the Roman Church —*should be head of all Churches*, for the Church of Constantinople was wont to style herself first of all Churches." And, what is very remarkable, it is thenceforward only

---

[1] Mansi. "Concil.," iv. 515. It may be added that St. Hilary never yielded to either Pope or Emperor, and yet is enrolled as a Saint in the Roman Martyrology on May 5. Dupin, "Antiq. Disciplin. Eccl.," II. iii. 5.

[2] Gibbon, "Decline and Fall," chap. xxxi.

that the Popes began to use the formula. "We will and command" (*Volumus et jubemus*), in ratifying Episcopal elections.[1] But although the Eastern Cæsar had some authority in Italy then (A.D. 607), he was two centuries too late for interference in Britain.

8. "Therefore, that very late invention, that Bishops receive their jurisdiction from the Pope, and are, as it were, his Vicars, ought to be banished from Christian schools, as unheard of for twelve centuries."—Bossuet, "Defens. Declar. Cleri. Gall." viii. 14.

9. Again, three things have to be steadily borne in mind when language of very high compliment and panegyric applied to St. Peter and to the see and Bishops of Rome is produced, as it can be in abundance.

First, as the claim made is that of a *Divine* charter, not that of *human* grant or prescription, no expression of human respect can add one grain of weight or one tittle of matter to that charter. We must test the claim by that document, and that only, and it refuses to be made accessory to the Pope's demands. (See sec. XI.)

Next, language in no respect less highflown is used of other Apostles and sees, as, for example, when St. Chrysostom speaks of St. John as "the pillar of the Churches throughout the world, who hath the keys of heaven" ("Hom. I. in Joann."), and when the See of Antioch is styled by the General Councils of Constantinople and Chalcedon as "the throne of St. Peter, the eldest and genuinely Apostolical Church,"[2] and that of Jerusalem, as the "Mother of all the Churches," by the Fathers of the Second General Council, in their supplementary Synodical Epistle of A.D. 382 to the Western Bishops.[2]

Thirdly, that words have to be brought to the test of dates and acts, for it will be often found that those who were willing to go furthest in mere compliment were ex-

---

[1] Platina, "Vitæ Pontif. Bonif. III."
[2] Theodoret, "Hist." v. 9.

tremely chary of committing themselves in action, as St. Cyprian's and St. Augustine's conduct sufficiently attests, or that they altered their views. The most direct and cogent passage in favour of Papalism in the whole of the Fathers is this from St. Jerome, in an epistle to Pope Damasus, written A.D. 376—"I speak with the successor of the Fisherman and the disciple of the Cross. I, following no chief, save Christ, am counted in communion with your Blessedness, that is, with the Chair of Peter. On that rock I know the Church is built. Whoso eats the lamb outside this house is profane." But seventeen years later, St. Jerome knew better, and wrote against Jovinian in 393:—"But thou sayest the Church is founded on Peter, albeit *the same is also done on all the Apostles*, and they all receive the keys of the kingdom of heaven, and the strength of the Church is established on them all *equally;* yet one is chosen amongst the Twelve, that, by the appointment of a head, the occasion of schism might be averted." This comes back from the Papalist exaggeration of the former letter to the moderate view of St. Cyprian, who, while acknowledging some primacy in St. Peter, did not admit that it proved a supremacy in the Pope, or any need of agreeing with him. And Jerome wrote another epistle to Evangelus, or Evagrius, also much later in date than that to Damasus, in which he first uses these words—showing exactly how much he meant by the phrase as to St. Peter's headship, just cited,—"A bishop and a presbyter are the same . . . But as to the later choice of one to preside over the others, that was done as a remedy against schism, lest each, drawing a party to himself, should rend Christ's Church." And then he goes on to say : " If you look for authority, *the whole world is greater than the City* [*of Rome*]: Wherever a bishop is, whether at *Rome* or at Gubbio, at Constantinople or at Reggio, at Alexandria or at Thanis, he is of the same dignity, and of the same priesthood: the power of wealth or the lowness of poverty does not make a bishop higher or lower, but all are successors of the Apostles. . . . But you say that at Rome a priest is ordained on the testimony of a deacon. Why do you quote to me the custom of a single city? Why do you urge the small number (*paucitatem*)—*i.e.*, of the Roman deacons—as if it were amongst the laws of the Church?" Thus it is clear that St. Jerome formally denied that the Roman Church had any right to dictate to Christendom generally, and even that the local prevalence of any ecclesiastical usage there was so much as an argument in its favour. It is therefore as unfair to quote St. Jerome's earlier opinions without mentioning his later change of views, as it would be to bring up schoolboy mistakes against a man when writing in the maturity of his age and powers.

9. Lastly, in Paul IV.'s Bull "Cum ex Apostolatûs Officio" of 1559 there is a clause that if at any time whatever it appear that any Bishop, Archbishop, Patriarch, Primate, Cardinal, Legate, or even the *Roman Pontiff, before his promotion to be Cardinal or Pope*, have erred from the Catholic faith, or fallen into any heresy, his election and all his acts are to be at once null and void. And F. Ryder, in the *Contemporary Review* of February, 1879, p. 471, says: "It has always been a very common opinion held by very Roman theologians, that the Pope, by manifest heresy, *ipso facto* ceases to be Pope," and that if he could conceivably define heresy, "in so defining he would unpope himself." But the insertion of the word "manifest" in the above statement weakens seriously the force of the real fact, as given by St. Raymond of Peñafort, who lays down that "every heretic, whether *secret* or manifest, incurs the greater excommunication and also deposition, whether he be cleric or laic, *Pope* or Emperor" (Summa, Lit. de Hær. 2): a view in which he is followed by Cardinal Turrecremata and a host of other canonists. And, further, they never doubted that the

Pope *could* define heresy. The view that this is divinely made impossible was invented by Cardinal Bellarmine.[1]

This opens up another deep gulf of uncertainty as to the Papal succession and decrees in the minds of all who do not accept the axiom that there cannot be an heretical Pope. Be that as it may, Pius IX., apart from those later acts and words of his which would have been accounted heresy by the ancient Church, was admitted in his youth as a Freemason—proof of his membership of the body was published in the *Capitale* of Rome on February 18, 1876—and thereby incurred the penalty of excommunication and the anathemas of Clement XII. and Benedict XIV. If the infallibility dogma be true, Paul IV.'s Bull is binding, and consequently the erection of the Anglo-Roman hierarchy by Pius IX. is null and void, and all acts done as its result are invalid.

The Argument as to the "Safer Way."

CXV. It is urged by Roman Catholics that, at the least, their way is the safest, because, while Anglicans admit that Romanists may be saved, and that their belief is at any rate largely true, Romanists do not make the same admission as to Anglicans. This proves too much, for it is just what Jews say of Christianity: "You Christians," they observe, "allow that the Law is divinely given, and that the Old Testament is the inspired Word of God. We do not allow that to be true of the Gospel and the New Testament. We had a glorious history of fifteen hundred years before yours began as a mere petty schism from a subordinate school of our scribes—a career marked ever since with the brand of division and failure. All that is good in your doctrine, your worship, and your discipline, you have stolen from us, and spoiled in the stealing. 'Look unto the rock whence ye are hewn, and to the hole of the pit whence ye are digged.

---

[1] See the authorities quoted by Renouf, "Condemnation of Pope Honorius," pp. 30-37.

Look unto Abraham your father, and unto Sarah that bare you' (Isa. li. 1), and return to the one true Church of God, for you are safer with us." What we can reply is, that God wrought miracles to show the Jews that Christianity is the better way, and His will. He certainly works no such miracles to show Anglicans that they ought to join Rome. And, indeed, Rome's way of making people "safe" by adding on a number of doctrines and practices which are, to say the very least, unknown to Scripture and to ancient Christendom, to the faith and usage of the undivided Catholic Church, is like making a sick man " safe " by persuading him to add all the different quack nostrums of a number of old women to the prescription enjoined him by a skilful physician. The least such a policy can effect is to neutralize the real medicine ; what it is more likely to do, is to kill the patient.

Conclusion.

CXVI. Better to cling fast to that great and unique English communion, whose future opens such magnificent promise, even as its roots are struck so deeply in the remote past of Christian history; which offers her children a liturgy which is pure as well as stately, teaching the mind as well as directing the emotions ; which holds firmly to the faith of undivided Christendom, and therefore speaks with the accumulated authority of the *whole Catholic Church* on all fundamental points of doctrine—whereas Rome, having broken with the past, *can offer only the private opinion of her present generation of clergy, and speaks with no authority at all;* which holds fast to the old Creeds, instead of adding more than a dozen new articles of faith, as Rome has done since the Reformation; which does not lock up the Word of God, but reads more of it to her children than any Protestant sect does, not to speak of Rome ; which encourages her children to use their intellect as well as their faith, and thereby to win the special benediction and approval which Christ bestowed on the Centurion (St. Matt. viii. 10) and on the Syrophœnician woman (St. Matt. xv. 28) who reasoned on His sayings, and so to speak, argued with Him, instead of implicitly accepting His first answer to them; which does not mutilate the Sacrament of Christ's love, nor practically deny the efficacy of Christ's mediation and the fulness of His sympathy; which has no feigned miracles, forged relics, nor gross fetish practices to be a snare to some souls and a scandal to others; which does not juggle with the Sacraments by leaving it doubtful when she really means to administer them validly; which does not make money the price of sin and the passport to heaven; which is not ashamed to confess past error, and to set about wholesome reforms; and which God has therefore blessed with a marvellous revival, unparalleled in the world's history, save by the return of the Jews from captivity, and the restoration of their faith and worship under Ezra and Nehemiah; and, above all, which worships God in Christ alone, not giving His honour to another, nor making external union with a mere man, rather than internal union with Him, the test of obedience to His will, therein agreeing with that saying of St. Augustine, "We, who are Christians in name and deed, do not believe in Peter, but in Him on Whom Peter himself believed. . . . He, the Christ, Peter's Master in the teaching which leads to life everlasting, He is our Master too." ("De Civit. Dei," xviii. 54.)

NOTE ON SECTION LXXII.—BAPTISM AND INTENTION.

This validity of schismatical baptism, upheld by the Roman Church since the third century, contradicts the modern doctrine of Intention. For the whole ground alleged by St. Cyprian for rebaptizing heretics was that there had been no intention of admitting them into the one true Church, since all the parties were outside of it (Epp. lxix., lxx., &c.; and as such admission is a necessary part of true Baptism, the schismatical rite must be null and void. But the Popes held, contrariwise, that Christ's ordinance could not be invalidated by the erroneous intention of the minister; and this is still the received doctrine of Rome. So, too, the Council of Nicæa (Canon VIII.) recognizes as valid the ordinations of the "Cathari," a Novatian sect, which itself denied the orders of the Church.

NOTE ON SECTION C.—NAME OF CATHOLIC.

Romans argue that they only call themselves, or are called by others, *Catholics*, and that this proves their sole right to that title and all that it implies, as in St. Augustine's day ("De Vera Relig." viii.). This is easily refuted. (*a*). The official title of the Russo-Greek Church is "The Catholic Orthodox Eastern Church," surely as good a one as "The Catholic Apostolic Roman Church:" nay, less local. (*b*). Even as a mere colloquialism, it is only when contrasted with Protestants that the name "Catholic" is specially used for Romanists. Their name of distinction from Eastern Christians is *Latins*. (*c*). At best, the name "Catholic" is not of Divine or Apostolic appointment, but of post-Apostolic human introduction, and therefore not inherently sacred. (*d*). But the chief disproof lies in this: that there *is* a name of Divine appointment, to which glorious privileges are annexed in Scripture—that of *Israel*. Yet, when the kingdom was divided, it was the new Northern State, as larger in area and population, though corrupt and debased in creed, which retained the name of Israel; while the smaller kingdom in the South, where the true worship was maintained, was always known by the humbler name of Judah, to which far less is assigned in Scripture, since even the Prophets who wrote after the schism speak in preference of the glories of Israel. But that did not avert the final and total forfeiture of its privileges by Israel for its sins against God's law, while it was only Judah which was restored.

Society for Promoting Christian Knowledge.

Publications on
THE CHRISTIAN EVIDENCES.

BOOKS.	Price.
	s. d.

Natural Theology of Natural Beauty (The).
By the Rev. R. St. John Tyrwhitt, M.A. Post 8vo. ...... Cloth boards — 1 6

Steps to Faith.
Addresses on some points in the Controversy with Unbelief. By the Rev. Brownlow Maitland, M.A., Author of "Scepticism and Faith," &c. Post 8vo. ......Cloth boards — 1 6

Theism or Agnosticism.
An Essay on the grounds of Belief in God. By the Rev. Brownlow Maitland, M.A., Author of "The Argument from Prophecy," &c. Post 8vo. ......Cloth boards — 1 6

Argument from Prophecy (The).
By the Rev. Brownlow Maitland, M.A., Author of "Scepticism and Faith," &c. Post 8vo. ......Cloth boards — 1 6

Scepticism and Faith.
By the Rev. Brownlow Maitland. Post 8vo. Cloth boards — 1 4

Modern Unbelief: its Principles and Characteristics. By the Right Rev. the Lord Bishop of Gloucester and Bristol. Post 8vo. ......Cloth boards — 1 6

Some Modern Religious Difficulties.
Six Sermons preached, by the request of the Christian Evidence Society, at St. James's, Piccadilly, on Sunday Afternoons after Easter, 1876; with a Preface by his Grace the Archbishop of Canterbury. Post 8vo. ......Cloth boards — 1 6

Some Witnesses for the Faith.
Six Sermons preached, by the request of the Christian Evidence Society, at St. Stephen's Church, South Kensington, on Sunday Afternoons after Easter, 1877. Post 8vo. Cloth boards — 1 4

When was the Pentateuch Written?
By George Warington, B.A., Author of "Can we Believe in Miracles?" &c. Post 8vo. ...... Cloth boards — 1 6
1-11-82] [Sm. Post 8vo.

2 Publications on the Christian Evidences.

	Price.
	s. d.

Theism and Christianity.
Six Sermons preached, by the request of the Christian Evidence Society, at St. James's, Piccadilly, on Sunday Afternoons after Easter, 1878. Post 8vo....... *Cloth boards* 1 6

The Analogy of Religion.
Dialogues founded upon Butler's "Analogy of Religion." By the Rev. H. R. Huckin, D.D., Head Master of Repton School. Post 8vo.. *Cloth boards* 3 0

"Miracles."
By the Rev. E. A. Litton, M.A., Examining Chaplain of the Bishop of Durham. Crown 8vo. .... *Cloth boards* 1 6

Moral Difficulties connected with the Bible.
Being the Boyle Lectures for 1871. By the Ven. Archdeacon Hessey, D.C.L. Preacher to the Hon. Society of Gray's Inn, &c. FIRST SERIES. Post 8vo. ...*Cloth boards* 1 6

Moral Difficulties connected with the Bible.
Being the Boyle Lectures for 1872. By the Ven. Archdeacon Hessey, D.C.L. SECOND SERIES. Post 8vo.
Cloth boards 2 6

Prayer and recent Difficulties about it.
The Boyle Lectures for 1873, being the THIRD SERIES of "Moral Difficulties connected with the Bible." By the Ven. Archdeacon Hessey, D.C.L. Post 8vo.
Cloth boards 2 6
The above Three Series in a volume .... *Cloth boards* 6 0

Historical Illustrations of the Old Testament.
By the Rev. G. Rawlinson, M.A., Camden Professor of Ancient History, Oxford. Post 8vo ....*Cloth boards* 1 6

Can we Believe in Miracles?
By G. Warington, B.A., of Caius College, Cambridge. Post 8vo... *Cloth boards* 1 6

The Moral Teaching of the New Testament
VIEWED AS EVIDENTIAL TO ITS HISTORICAL TRUTH. By the Rev. C. A. Row, M.A. Post 8vo...................*Cloth boards* 1 6

Scripture Doctrine of Creation.
By the Rev. T. R. Birks, M.A., Professor of Moral Philosophy at Cambridge. Post 8vo.............................*Cloth boards* 1 6

	Price.
	s. d.

The Witness of the Heart to Christ.
Being the Hulsean Lectures for 1878. By the Rev. W. Boyd Carpenter, M.A. Post 8vo. ....*Cloth boards* 1 6

Thoughts on the First Principles of the Positive
PHILOSOPHY, CONSIDERED IN RELATION TO THE HUMAN MIND. By the late Benjamin Shaw, M.A., late Fellow of Trinity College, Camb. Post 8vo. ....*Limp cloth* 0 8

Thoughts on the Bible.
By the late Rev. W. Gresley, M.A., Prebendary of Lichfield. Post 8vo. .... *Cloth boards* 1 6

The Reasonableness of Prayer.
By the Rev. P. Onslow, M.A. Post 8vo. .... *Paper cover* 0 8

Paley's Evidences of Christianity.
A New Edition, with Notes, Appendix, and Preface. By the Rev. E. A. Litton, M.A. Post 8vo..........*Cloth boards* 4 0

Paley's Natural Theology.
Revised to harmonize with Modern Science. By Mr. F. le Gros Clark, F.R.S., President of the Royal College of Surgeons of England, &c. Post 8vo. ....*Cloth boards* 4 0

Paley's Horæ Paulinæ.
A new Edition, with Notes, Appendix, and Preface. By J. S. Howson, D.D., Dean of Chester. Post 8vo. *Cloth boards* 3 0

The Story of Creation as told by Theology
AND SCIENCE. By the Rev. T. S. Ackland, M.A. Post 8vo.
Cloth boards 1 6

Man's Accountableness for his Religious Belief.
A Lecture delivered at the Hall of Science, on Tuesday, April 2nd, 1872. By the Rev. Daniel Moore, M.A., Holy Trinity, Paddington. Post 8vo ....*Paper cover* 0 3

The Theory of Prayer; with Special Reference
TO MODERN THOUGHT. By the Rev. W. H. Karslake, M.A., Assistant Preacher at Lincoln's Inn, Vicar of Westcott, Dorking. Post 8vo. ....*Limp cloth* 1 0

4 Publications on the Christian Evidences.

	Price.
	s. d.

The Credibility of Mysteries.
A Lecture delivered at St. George's Hall, Langham Place. By the Rev. Daniel Moore, M.A. Post 8vo......*Paper cover* 0 3

Analogy of Religion, Natural and Revealed,
TO THE CONSTITUTION AND COURSE OF NATURE: to which are added, Two Brief Dissertations. By Bishop Butler. NEW EDITION. Post 8vo..............................*Cloth boards* 2 6

Christian Evidences:
intended chiefly for the young. By the Most Reverend Richard Whately, D.D. 12mo.. .... *Paper cover* 0 4

The Efficacy of Prayer.
By the Rev. W. H. Karslake, M.A., Assistant Preacher at Lincoln's Inn, &c. &c. Post 8vo. .... *Limp cloth* 0 6

Science and the Bible: a Lecture by the Right
Rev. Bishop Perry, D.D. 18mo. *Paper cover* 4d., or *Limp cloth* 0 6

A Lecture on the Bible. By the Very Rev.
E. M. Goulburn, D.D., Dean of Norwich. 18mo. *Paper cover* 0 2

The Bible: Its Evidences, Characteristics, and
Effects. A Lecture by the Right Rev. Bishop Perry, D.D. 18mo...*Paper cover* 0 4

The Origin of the World according to
REVELATION AND SCIENCE. A Lecture by Harvey Goodwin, M.A., Bishop of Carlisle. Post 8vo....*Cloth boards* 0 4

*** *For List of TRACTS on the Christian Evidences, see the Society's Catalogue B.*

DEPOSITORIES:
NORTHUMBERLAND AVENUE, CHARING CROSS, W.C.;
43, QUEEN VICTORIA STREET, E.C.; 48, PICCADILLY, W.,
AND 135, NORTH STREET, BRIGHTON.